TEACHING WRITING IN THE MIDDLE SCHOOL

COMMON CORE AND MORE

Anna J. Small Roseboro

ROWMAN & LITTLEFIELD EDUCATION

A division of
ROWMAN & LITTLEFIELD
Lanham • Boulder • New York • Toronto • Plymouth, UK

Published by Rowman & Littlefield Education
A division of Rowman & Littlefield
4501 Forbes Boulevard, Suite 200, Lanham, Maryland 20706
www.rowman.com

10 Thornbury Road, Plymouth PL6 7PP, United Kingdom

Copyright © 2013 by Anna J. Small Roseboro

British Library Cataloguing in Publication Information Available

Library of Congress Cataloging-in-Publication Data

Roseboro, Anna J. Small, 1945-
  Teaching writing in the middle school : common core and more / Anna J. Small Roseboro.
    pages cm
  Includes bibliographical references and index.
  ISBN 978-1-4758-0540-6 (cloth : alk. paper) — ISBN 978-1-4758-0541-3 (pbk. : alk. paper) — ISBN 978-1-4758-0542-0 (electronic) 1. Language arts (Middle school)—Curricula—United States—States. 2. Language arts (Middle school)—Standards—United States—States. I. Title.
  LB1631.R62 2013
  808'.0420712—dc23
                                                                    2013027162

∞™ The paper used in this publication meets the minimum requirements of American National Standard for Information Sciences—Permanence of Paper for Printed Library Materials, ANSI/NISO Z39.48-1992.

Printed in the United States of America.

To my husband, William Gerald Roseboro, and children, Rosalyn, William II, and Robert

To Dr. Robert Infantino for his sage advice to me and other educators eager to contribute to the profession

To Joan Breher and Alison Taylor—dear friends, respected colleagues, and loyal cheerleaders

To early-career educators who accept the challenge of a lifetime and veterans who remain and mentor them, demonstrating the wisdom of balancing personal and professional lives, showing and sharing the joys of teaching young adolescents

CONTENTS

FOREWORD

Terry Patrick Bigelow

To be nobody but yourself in a world which is doing its best night and day to make you like everybody else means to fight the hardest battle any human being can fight and never stop fighting.

—e e cummings

As a student teacher in the spring of 1992, I remember struggling to compose logical, coherent, worthwhile instruction for my students. My cooperating teacher, who was retiring after nearly forty years in the classroom, suggested I search in one of her *twelve* filing cabinets brimming with blue-line masters to find assignments to "keep students busy."

Instead, inspired by my university mentor, I tried to craft instruction that would meet the district curriculum while engaging my eighth- and ninth-grade junior high students. My cooperating teacher was rarely in the classroom, and as a young, enthusiastic, soon-to-be teacher, I couldn't live with just keeping students "busy." I constantly called on my fellow student teachers, my mentor, my university supervisor, or anyone else whom I thought could help me make learning happen. It was hard work every day, and I often felt like I was barely staying afloat. I repeatedly thought that if I caught one flu bug or if my car broke down, my life would unravel.

During that semester, I leaned heavily on Kirby and Liner's *Inside Out* and Dunning and Stafford's *Getting the Knack*. I relied on the thinking in Rief's *Seeking Diversity* and Atwell's *In the Middle* to guide me. I was often moderately successful as I learned to orchestrate the music in these texts. Occasionally, I was wildly successful, but I also experienced the sting of failure regularly. Throughout this time, I learned not only how to replicate what these master authors did so successfully with their students but also *how* they created these learning experiences and *why* these lessons worked.

Looking back, I wish I also had Anna Roseboro's *Teaching Writing in the Middle School* during this formative time of my development as a teacher. My first week of student teaching had me wrestling with a cooperating teacher who turned over all of her classes to an inexperienced (and, honestly, unprepared) twenty-two-year-old of questionable maturity. The thinking in Roseboro's comprehensive narrative would have forced me to consider all of the choices I would be required to make while working with these students. The book invites the reader to consider all of the nuances of teaching a group of students for a full semester or year. From long-range planning and dealing with all of the outside influences on students' lives, to getting to know the students who sit in your class, to managing the concepts of informal and formal instruction, this book is a valuable road map to planning a successful school year. Roseboro's suggestions for how she does this are indicative of an experienced, successful teacher, but if nothing else, they compel the reader to consider which approach will work in his classroom. Seeing how skilled practitioners work gives us a chance to emulate them or even to use their success as a springboard for our own ideas. While this book will be extremely helpful to someone entering teaching, as a veteran teacher, it makes me reexamine how I handle all of these critically important facets of teaching.

The lessons in this book are a nod to the pervasive high-stakes writing exams given by states around the nation and to the upcoming exams that will spring from the Common Core State Standards. One of the biggest fears of college students who will soon enter teaching is how they will prepare students to be successful on these exams. While reading Roseboro's detailed lessons, I could not help but think of all of the teachers wrestling with how to prepare students to write well without simply forcing students to compose formulaic writing. How does Roseboro address this concern? She suggests teaching the basics, then having students write for real purposes, and finally, trusting students to make good decisions about their writing because this is what we have taught them to do.

As I entered my first year of teaching at a district in the metropolitan Atlanta area, I continued to tap into the experiences of my peers and mentors for ideas about how to create meaningful instruction. I poured over professional texts and journals for exemplary examples. I modeled elements of the best lessons and units and mirrored them when I created my own first instructional units. With their considerable help, I slowly learned how to create engaging instruction. And I saw results.

My failures became less frequent. Student success became more common.

Now, after more than twenty years as a middle school teacher, I still grapple with how to best engage students in work that they will find meaningful. I constantly look to every resource available, from publishers of quality texts for English teachers, professional journals from NCTE and IRA, newsletters from the National Writing Project, and most importantly, by discussing teaching pedagogy with colleagues.

But today, teaching has changed. Teaching no longer lets a teacher only stay on top of trying to find just the right twist on just the right lesson for each particular group of students. Teachers are required to juggle teacher "accountability," numerous, intrusive high-stakes tests, budget cuts, virtually scripted curriculums, politics, and a host of other balls that must remain aloft, all the while making sure that instruction meets the new Common Core State Standards and engages students' interest.

I grow fatigued just thinking about it.

Anna Roseboro's *Teaching Writing in the Middle School* is packed with worthwhile exercises, activities, and units of study to help support and inspire English language arts teachers of every experience. It is an invitation by a skilled teacher to visit her classroom to see what has worked so masterfully for her and for her students.

The beauty of this text is that it provides a framework for how to emulate Roseboro's lessons in your own classroom, and better yet, it also provides a model for effective instruction and inspires experimentation. As I read through the text for the first time, I found myself daydreaming about how I could adapt elements of Anna's units to improve and refine some of my own favorites.

Consider *Teaching Writing in the Middle School: Common Core and More* a destination. It is a place for new and preservice teachers to safely wet their feet as well as a place for veteran teachers to revisit some of their own lessons to inspire new perspectives. It is an opportunity to visit a master teacher's classroom and watch what she does.

Though the spring of 1992 is long gone and my student teaching semester is a distant memory, it is my hope that in an age when so much choice is being taken out of the teachers' hands, teachers with all ranges of experience will take advantage of Anna's invitation to see what engaging instruction can do to help their students consistently succeed.

Terry Bigelow has spent the majority of his professional life teaching in the school district of Hillsborough County and currently works at the Sam Rampello Downtown Partnership School, K–8 in Tampa, Florida. He has spent over twenty years searching for ways to help students make learning happen. He is the coauthor (with Michael Vokoun) of *What Choice Do I Have? Reading, Writing, and Speaking Activities to Empower Students* (2005).

PREFACE

Getting to the Core of
Language Arts Instruction

Quentin J. Schultze

Over the past few decades, education has been moving in all kinds of curricular and pedagogical directions. Language arts, in particular, has undergone tremendous changes primarily because of new technologies, multiple-intelligence teaching and learning, and multicultural opportunities. But it's time again in the history of education to focus on the core; the core becomes our agreed-upon nonnegotiables in our field. States and provinces are rightly involved in helping educators to define what all faculty must teach and what all students must learn. National initiatives are helpful, too. But we all know that educational standards are always evolving. States not only differ; normatively speaking, some states seem to be ahead of others in establishing core curricula amid social and cultural changes.

Teaching in the Western world has always addressed agreed-upon standards. Moreover, language arts educators, from the ancient Greek and Roman rhetoricians forward, have continually tried to define such standards at the intersection of ancient and modern *literacies*—that is, at the intersection of older means and methods of gaining communicative comprehension.[1] Why? Because every educator and every school has to teach both tried-and-true and the newly emerging information and practices. I still teach basic public speaking along with PowerPoint; essay writing along with blogging; library research along with online Internet searching. Each of us instructors is a medium, a go-between, who teaches at the intersection not only of "text" (broadly speaking, the "material") and student, but also of traditional and contemporary cultures. This is why developing a common core is so critically important, especially in times of great social change. Somehow we have to define and teach both traditional and contemporary methods and content. So I use low-tech, lobby-based conversation to teach my smartphone-toting students! Most fun of all, they don't necessarily see the conversation as education. Little do they realize how much I teach while they are hanging out with me.

The traditional-contemporary intersection often leads to disagreements among educators and between educators and the communities that they serve. Who will set the standards? What do we give up when we define core competencies? Who is to say that speech communication is still as important as written communication? This tension goes back at least to Plato, for whom the word *poetry* referred to all language arts, but especially to the most popular forms of artistic expression. Plato feared that the poets promoted undesirable passions, failed to pursue truth, and wasted students' time with impractical instruction.[2] Poets were eloquent teachers, but they didn't care about truth, let alone anyone else's definition of common standards. The poets were careerists who wanted job stability.

The Common Core State Standards Initiative, which focuses primarily on using standards to help students prepare for college, included particular standards "only when the best available evidence indicated that its mastery was essential for college and career readiness in a twenty-first-century, globally competitive society. The Standards are intended to be a living work: as new and better evidence emerges, the Standards will be revised accordingly."[3] So we set standards in the midst of social, cultural, and technological shifts constantly occurring in our communities and the world. Standards are never perfect, but they help us together to define and understand the needs of our students in a changing world. When it comes to defining a common core, we educators are in a pickle; we can't entirely live with the resulting standards, but we can't live without them. So we move ahead as a community of educators, setting, assessing, and revising standards. We wish we had more time, better pedagogies, wiser mentors. Just when we seem to have figured out how to teach to the standards with flair and distinction, the curriculum has to be adjusted again. But this problem has always been true of teaching. In fact, when we don't feel the anxiety of having to change what and how we teach, we are probably losing our passion to be outstanding educators. The gift of knowing our discipline's core offers educational traction and focus. We don't have to teach all things to all students. We can say "no" to some things while affirming those in the core.

Common standards in the language arts rightly focus first on language, the most basic form of human communication. The primary and most lasting media were—and still are—mass languages. Languages were the original viral media, millennia before social media like Facebook and Twitter. After addressing language skills, standards address how to apply such skills to other disciplines. In other words, we language arts educators teach our discipline in order to help students learn in other disciplines. Of course, we expect colleagues in history or the sciences to teach things such as writing and speaking along with their core disciplines. But we also know that they tend not to be quite as good at it as we are because we teach communicative competencies all day long. Nevertheless, we and our colleagues in other subjects together have to teach the use of newer technologies—or media—such as PowerPoint, video, and audio, all of which have their own "languages" that students and teachers need to understand.

My wife says she doesn't like to watch movies with me because I'm always commenting on how and how well the movies are communicating, not just on what the movies are saying. I don't just get into the story line. I have the same problem in watching and listening to other teachers teach. And I wonder whether I should have gone into a field like chemistry so I wouldn't be so conscious about how people communicate! "Language arts" seems to be part of everything human beings do. That's the rub. Our curricular standards and core competencies are especially important because they shape how our students communicate in all of life. Our teaching is "metacommunication"—communication about communication. It's not easy. But what fun! What a joy to teach about the core of what it means for us to be human beings. We humans are creatures of language. Other creatures communicate, too, but there is no solid evidence in the research that they communicate about their communication. We do it all the time—sometimes probably too much.

The College and Career Readiness (CCR) standards highlight "Reading, Writing, and Speaking and Listening Standards" as the "backbone" for language arts. Those are worthy of being at the core of our work. But then the CCR standards statement adds, "The Standards set requirements not only for English language arts (ELA) but also for literacy in history/social studies, science, and technical subjects. Just as students must learn to read, write, speak, listen, and use language effectively in a variety of content areas, so too must the Standards specify the literacy skills and understandings required for college and career readiness in multiple disciplines."[4] There is much wisdom in that interdisciplinary conclusion. I would just hope that our colleagues in other disciplines would include some of our core competencies in their standards, too. In my school, we teach writing across the curriculum. It's not just the job of the English department.

At its best, language arts instruction invites students into rich, multimedia communion with persons and cultures, with those nearby and far away, with people who lived before us and now live among us on earth. We learn with students and colleagues what others have thought, believed, and done; how others have told and still tell us about themselves through various art forms; how we can identify with their life stories; and ultimately how we can share our own stories with others. The language arts are also the cultural and social arts.

Some of this sociocultural communication is highly practical, such as writing a complex sentence, reading poetic alliteration, establishing a speech thesis, or memorizing vocabulary. Other aspects of language arts focus both explicitly and implicitly on character-building, heart-opening, mind-sharpening practices. These are among the many deeply human literacies that have existed across time and through geographic space. Good standards help us to focus on such fundamental aspects of what it means to be virtuous as well as skilled communicators. I know that when I am hanging out with my flocking students in the lobby, they are learning partly through my modeling of right, fitting, and kind communication. So I need to integrate the core of my discipline into the very core of my life. Otherwise, both I and my curriculum lack integrity.

Our professional lives are multimedia parables. We language arts educators are living texts. There is something refreshingly old and new about that vision. Thanks to Anna for inspiring us to live up to the standards of great language arts instruction. May her wisdom stir us to listen well to her words in this book, with graceful hearts and open minds.

Quentin J. Schultze, PhD, is professor of communication at Calvin College and author of many books, including *An Essential Guide to Public Speaking* and *Resume 101: A Student and Recent-Grad Guide to Crafting Resumes and Cover Letters that Land Jobs.*

NOTES

1. As Kylene Beers suggests, reading theorists and researchers generally agree that the "point of reading is comprehension." See Beers, *When Kids Can't Read: What Teachers Can Do: A Guide for Teachers 6–12* (Portsmouth, NH: Heinemann, 2002), 59. We could expand Beers's insight, considering that all human communication primarily is for the practical purpose of comprehension, not for the other purposes of personal expression—romanticism—or impact—behaviorism. If humans don't understand one another, they invariably create unhealthy conflicts.

2. Plato, *Republic*, especially books II, III, and X.

3. "The Standards—English Language Arts Standards," Common Core State Standards Initiative, http://www.corestandards.org/ELA-Literacy.

4. "The Standards—English Language Arts Standards."

ACKNOWLEDGMENTS

Colleagues who have collaborated with me and the students who inspired me when I taught in Michigan, Missouri, New York, Massachusetts, and California, especially those from The Bishop's School.

Critical readers: Sheila Bartle, Christina Berry, Shayna S. Costello, Delores Geter, Marilyn Gross, Nancy Perkins, Verneal Mitchell, Alan L. Sitomer, Brooke Suiter, and Joan Williams, whose feedback heartened me to revise and massage the manuscript with confidence.

Teachers of middle school students Lindsey Lautenbach and Michelle Shepherdson and their students from the Excel Academy in Kentwood, Michigan.

Contributions to annotated book lists by Bethany J. Kim and by the Kent District Library Teen Services staff, Comstock Park, Michigan.

Donna Lynn Russ and Tamara Swafford for their assistance.

Poetry TIME cartoon used by permission of the artist, Linda Hargrove.

Student writing used by permission of students named.

Colleagues from the California Association of Teachers of English, the Greater San Diego Council of Teachers of English, the San Diego Area Writing Project, the Michigan Council of Teachers of English, and

Conference of English Leadership of the National Council of Teachers of English and members of the online social networks for educators such as the English Companion Ning, Making Curriculum Pop Ning, and the National Council of Teachers of English Connected Community.

INTRODUCTION

If a child can't learn the way we teach, maybe we should teach the
way they learn.

—Ignacio "Nacho" Estrada[1]

Few careers in education are more exciting and rewarding than teaching middle school English and language arts. Sure, some of your friends shake their heads and maybe even feel sorry for you when they hear about your work with young adolescents. Unless they have worked with this age group, however, they won't understand your enthusiasm. You and I get to spend our days helping young adults develop the reading, writing, viewing, speaking, listening, and study skills they will need for success wherever their career path takes them. Our work is challenging but also a lot of fun; we get to share our respect for language—written and read, spoken and viewed—and to cultivate such respect in our students. Not only must we know, understand, and love the language arts content, but we must also know, understand, and love our learners in all of their remarkable diversity.

TEACHING AND WRITING ABOUT TEACHING

When a candidate for National Board Certification for Early Adolescent/ English Language Arts, I reflected seriously about what, why, and how I teach. When others heard talk about that certification experience, they enthusiastically asked for more explanation. From those conversations and from feedback to workshops presented at local, state, and national conferences and conventions, it became clear that I have valuable experience to share with my colleagues. So began the writing, putting into words some of my rationales, lessons, and practices.

In other settings, during receptions for new teachers held as part of the annual meetings of the California Association of Teachers of English and Michigan Council of Teachers of English, I recognized how thirsty novice teachers are to learn about the solid, structured lessons that successful, experienced teachers use. Concern that those starting out in the profession without the benefit of local mentors, that many states offer emergency credentialing to satisfy the rising demand for new teachers, especially in growing ethnic communities, and because most states can ill afford special courses for such new teachers, I felt compelled to record and share my experience. Many such novice teachers begin enthusiastically but soon face tough standards and accountability; while eager to do a good job, they are not sure how to serve their early adolescent students well in an increasingly multicultural, assessment-driven, technological environment that has specific long-range goals for middle school students to prepare them for college or career similar to the Common Core State Standards for English Language Arts.

GROWING PROFESSIONALLY

None of us can become an effective middle school teacher on our own. We need active mentors. We need professional colleagues and wise administrators. We all must continue to grow professionally throughout our years of service. Why? Pedagogies change. So do students. Of course, so do standards of and standards for assessment. When it comes to middle school, the technological environments that our students live in shift continually. So we must constantly learn from one another how to tap into these cultural and technological dynamics. We have to admit that the differences in our ages, even generations, factor into making such adaptations successfully. As Quentin J. Schultze reminds in the preface, we teach at the constantly changing intersection of old and new.

I have benefitted for decades from formal study, involvement in professional conferences and workshops, journal articles, advice from generous colleagues, and years of teaching that ground my lesson planning. Consequently, ones in this book are informed by the philosophies and theories from a variety of sources as well as my four decades of experience as an English and language arts teacher and college instructor. Publications by the National Middle School Association and the National Research Council have proved invaluable. Chris Stevenson asserts that middle school curricula must be challenging, integrated, and exploratory.[2]

His perspective along with Howard Gardner's, who "proposed the existence of seven relatively autonomous intelligences: linguistic, logical, musical, spatial, bodily kinesthetic, interpersonal, and intrapersonal,[3] are both reflected here.

SERVING STUDENTS ARTFULLY

These and many other currents in educational research shaped my daily pedagogy. The writings of Louise Rosenblatt and Fran Claggett inspired me to incorporate assignments to accommodate Gardner's multiple intelligences. Rosenblatt encourages educators to allow students to respond to the reading in their own ways—that students should rely on their prior knowledge to help them make sense of the literature.[4]

This approach to reading and interpretation of literature frees us from the burden of focusing with students only on what the book means. It gives us permission to let the literature speak to the students and to trust the students' own responses about what it says to them in their own cultural contexts and developmental stages. Nevertheless, the "literature" does have to be taught, standards must be met, and students must demonstrate academic proficiency, so you need to plan lessons that require students to ground their responses in the texts to show their grasp of the knowledge, understanding of the concepts, and acquisition of the skills. Otherwise, they can stray too far afield in class discussions and writing about the texts.

Here are theory-based lessons to help you plan units for the range of students you teach. Specific assignments for the course of a school year take into account myriad ways that adolescents can be taught and assessed based on their specific age and maturation as well as their individual learning styles. Keeping in mind the grade-level standards and incorporating technology helps, too. I readily admit that developing such a variety of lessons helps maintain my interest because I thoroughly enjoy learning from my students.

You, too, can find that each time you offer to your students the option to demonstrate their understanding of literature and life, you gain greater insight into the fiction and nonfiction works you are studying together. You also form a deeper understanding of the students and their ways of looking at text and at the world around them. At the same time, you have confidence that you are on the road to fulfilling the charge of preparing students for success in the years to come.

LOOKING FOR THE CURRICULUM?

Unless you have taken a college course in or are a devotee of young adult literature, chances are you are not familiar with much of the literature you are being asked to teach. Furthermore, most middle school curricula require students to learn about different kinds of writing, how to read it, how to recognize its structure, how to identify the function and understand purpose of literary structure and devices, and, of course, how to talk and write about it intelligently. But relax. The schools often are less concerned about the specific titles used in a class than they are about students' ability to read and understand any kind of writing—fiction and nonfiction, in print or digital formats. Therefore, it is more important to develop a range of strategies for teaching any kind of literature so that you can adapt to whatever the curriculum is in schools or districts that employ you.

CHOOSING ALTERNATIVE WAYS TO TEACH AND ASSESS

Reading is not the same as comprehension. Once the students have read the assigned texts, you have to determine how well the students understand them. Fran Claggett, a pioneer in the use of graphics in teaching literature, recommends that teachers employ art—either via graphics to help plot out the structure before or after the students read, or assignments for which students use art to show what they know.[5] Today the word *graphics* seems anachronistic. So do the terms *visuals* and *media*, let alone *audiovisual*. In this, the twenty-first century, students are more versed in digital, computerized media. Yet the basics of literature as art and story have not changed. There still is skillful use of language and imaginative use of arrangement. Therefore, lessons in this book incorporate old and new media to show students a work's traditional devices, such as structure and plot lines, images, and symbols. With proper guidance, students can use their artistic interests and digital talents to demonstrate their comprehension of specific works of even the most traditional literature.

What I also like personally about using art and digital media is the fact that I am neither an artist nor a techie, so my students get to see me at my mediocre best. They seem more inclined to risk being vulnerable when they see me somewhat inartfully expressing what literature means to me. My students often are better artists and technicians, adroit with PowerPoint and Prezi designing and current digital media from podcasts to movie making.

Artistic diversity goes beyond linguistic modes of reading, writing, and speaking. You can discover in this book that such diversity can help a wider range of students to shine before their peers, building self-esteem among some of those who need it most. Yet, at the same time, such variety saves you time. Generally speaking, written assignments take more time to grade even when they may not be as accurate at assessing particular types of learning. You soon realize that incorporating art and technology enhance your instruction, improve student engagement, and increase learning.

In other words, seek to reduce your students' insecurities, and strive to design lessons that build their confidence and develop their strengths. Let students use music or dance to express the mood of a literary work or characters in those works. Invite your students to act out scenes, partly to assist kinetic learners and partly to give all your energetic adolescents an opportunity to get out of their seats and move around. When auditory and visual learners hear and see the work of their peers, they, too, are learning at a deeper level.

All of this is to say that language arts learning is more than demonstrating competence in traditional linguistic modes of reading, writing, and speaking. Notice as you read that the assignments in this book invite students to apply their own multimedia abilities to show specific language arts learning and offer a variety of assessment opportunities that are equally as revealing and authentic as traditional written assignments.

TEACHING PRESERVICE TEACHERS AND GRADUATE SCHOOL STUDENTS

When I moved from California to Michigan and became an adjunct professor at a state college of education, I noticed that preservice students eagerly latched onto the study of literacy assessment. They impatiently leaned forward to hear about instructional practices useful in guiding developmentally appropriate learning. These students recognized through their internship assignments in classrooms of local schools that being able to provide instruction is only half the responsibility of teachers. The other half is choosing or developing formative assessment tools that demonstrate what students are learning and then designing subsequent lessons based on the data revealed in these assessments.

After working the year in the classroom, my graduate students found it advantageous to spend their summer examining research and theories, differentiated instruction, and assessment practices appropriate for the literacy needs of their students and then crafting curricula to meet these needs. When it comes to assessing for twenty-first-century literacies, however, few of us are well versed in the research, because it is still being done; still, we do our best based on what knowledge and skills we try to measure and what these measurements tell us about our students. Some of the lessons that follow can stretch you, maybe even pull you further along than you thought possible into the world of teaching with technology and working toward reaching Common Core State Standards without teaching solely for the tests. That is fine. We teachers have to be students ourselves, learning by doing and assessing.

UNDERSTANDING WHAT IS
APPROPRIATE FOR MIDDLE SCHOOL

Perhaps the notion that most influences effective instruction for middle school students is that they tend to work well in groups, yet you must design such group lessons to maximize individual student learning. In the early weeks of the semester, you recognize the importance of using more teacher-directed instruction, demonstrating manners, modeling lessons, and giving students opportunities to develop a set of behaviors for successful group activities throughout the year.

For this reason, a rule of thumb is student choice, teacher control. This may be another way of applying Vygotsky's notion of the zone of proximal development or what Pearson and Gallagher call the "gradual release of responsibility."[6] You are responsible for planning lessons that not only provide opportunities for students to learn in different ways from different sources, but also for designing lessons that deliberately lead to meeting the standards set forth by your respective schools, districts, and states so that students become increasingly independent learners.

Bethany J. Kim, an early career teacher who contributed the reading lists in this book, says that one of her greatest challenges as a new middle school teacher is appropriately and effectively assessing her teaching and then maintaining the right classroom atmosphere. In a sixth-grade charter school that focused on building character as well as strong academics, Bethany found it difficult to set the right tone at the beginning of the year. Student choice began to swamp teacher control. When it came time for formal assessment, she realized that it would have been better to phase in the student choice more gradually during the first semester. She loved the students and the students loved learning from her, but she had not tied the pedagogy to assessment as well as she would have liked. That need not be a problem for you.

KNOWING WHAT YOUNG ADOLESCENTS ENJOY

Young adolescents enjoy talking and often learn well from one another. As *Turning Points 2000: Educating Adolescents in the 21st Century* puts it, "Cooperative learning . . . can be a successful technique both to teach content and to raise self-esteem among all students, particularly those whose native language is not English.[7] Adolescents are very sensitive to perception of their peers. "A safe and healthy school environment"[8] requires cooperative learning and project-based learning in order to enhance relationships among different social and ethnic groups. This is why it is good to structure frequent lessons that give the students permission to do what they love to do: talk to one another. The key words here are *structure* and *talk*.

Once the students begin working together, regularly circulate among the groups, listening in, giving assistance as needed, and you begin to discover in an informal but intentional way what ideas they have grasped, what areas need further instruction, and whether or not the students are ready for more formal assessment to demonstrate individual readiness to move on to the next level of instruction. Tryon Edwards writes, "Thoroughly to teach another is the best way to learn for yourself."[9] As often as appropriate, include assessments where pairs and small groups of students can use the new technologies, even if they are more familiar to your students than to you. By teaching one another how to "do" language arts via newer as well as older media, students teach themselves and often you as well.

While students prepare together for group or student-led discussion, they are also reviewing the lessons in more depth than they might have if they were working solely on their own. Students are then able to participate in the necessary preconditions for quality: content, collaboration, and choice. When the researchers finally determine the educational value of "new" media, they might conclude that along with all of the other benefits of technology is an age-old truth: collaborating on projects can produce mutual learning.

APPLYING NATIONAL WRITING PROJECT CONCEPTS

After becoming a writing fellow of the San Diego Area Writing Project, I began incorporating the National Writing Project's strategies into my lessons. In particular, I followed the project's sequence of fluency, form, and correctness and soon noticed that both my students and I were more enthusiastic about learning. Sequencing lessons this way gives students the time to write frequently, to conduct peer editing, to revise, to edit, and to publish in a variety of ways for a variety of audiences. With more ready access to technology, it is easier to publish regularly to real audiences. They may be parents logging onto the class website, or they may be students in classes across the ocean who are participating in a collaborative reading and writing project. The lessons in this book are similarly flexible. In the chapters that follow are suggested assignments for different purposes, such as to explore, to explain, to expand, and even to entertain.

The lessons described in this book also show ways to reduce the time-consuming burden of grading each piece of writing for correctness. Following the recommendations in the lessons, you begin to see the benefits of reading some students' writing or viewing their media projects to discover whether your young students comprehend a specific text or just what they think about a particular topic. This pedagogical stance is especially apparent in the lessons in chapter 3, "Writing to Learn across the Content Areas."

These kinds of writings and media productions become no-stress assessments. As you determine what students think, know, understand, and are be able to do, you begin to adjust your instruction based on what you have observed and read. When the students realize that every word they write or image they project is to not be evaluated for correctness, your otherwise self-conscious young teens become more fluent. They are willing to write more often; and they also appreciate that you give them some choice about what writing, print, or digital media they wish to submit to peer editing, evaluation, and publication.

BALANCING STRUCTURE WITH CHOICES

While offering students lots of choice in their reading, writing, and responding is important, the key to becoming an effective teacher is to establish structures and routines on which the students can depend. These practices foster important habits: using time efficiently; maintaining useful notebooks and digital files for test and exam preparation; reading and writing efficiently; and participating cooperatively in small-group or full-class discussions, using technology with a critical eye and creative bent. The good habits help students learn the basics of language and forms of fiction and nonfiction texts. When students know the daily class requirements and routines, they have something against which to rebel without rejecting it completely. As Anne King declared in a presentation, "You Are Not Going Crazy, This Really Is Normal Behavior," once adolescents know the boundaries, they frequently challenge them, but they usually comply.[10]

Experience has shown that even though middle school students love to try the system and to test the rules—just to see how teachers respond—they also appreciate the predictability. For some of the students, a dependable pattern gives them a sense of control and power. They know what to expect and how to perform in the midst of their own physical and emotional changes.

For these reasons, the lessons for the first semester are designed like benevolent training sessions in an athletic program, providing opportunities for participants to learn the rules of the games and to develop the knowledge and skills to be successful. The effective, experienced teachers you observe seem to handle this training period effortlessly; such veterans know how to offer student choices within a fair but firm classroom structure.

REMOVING THE SCAFFOLDS

As the school year progresses, you can step aside and become more of a coach than an instructor. If all has gone well, students already know the kinds of reading, writing, media, speaking, and listening skills that they must learn. You have shown them class goals, such as the Common Core State Standards for English Language Arts. Such goals should not be a secret to the students. As with fellow travelers, if everyone knows where you are going, all can be alert and supportive along the road. Even backseat drivers come in handy sometime.

You can then increase the number of choices to practice these skills more independently and to demonstrate their growing knowledge and skills even more creatively. As you progress along the school-year journey, the students learn how to act and what to do because they develop the habits of mind and confidently and competently handle the tasks set before them. They happily rise to the challenge of future goals as they see evidence of meeting earlier ones. When adolescents feel secure, they are able to function more effectively, bringing joy to all involved.

While I tend toward student choice over teacher control, my goals are always student centered. What is it that the students want and need to know and do by the end of the school year? What kind of nurturing environment must be developed and experiences offered to ensure the students reach these goals? For a young adolescent and for a novice teacher, this may mean a little more visible structure than would be evident in the classroom of a veteran teacher. So while I recognize that many approaches can be effective, the ideas I share are those that have worked well for me and the new to midcareer teachers I have mentored.

ACKNOWLEDGING PHYSICAL AND EMOTIONAL CHALLENGES

The primary challenge in teaching middle school is that physical, emotional, and social issues often overwhelm and distract students. Both your male and female students can be manically mischievous one day and dismally depressed the next, vacillating enough to tempt the most intrepid traveler to abandon the trip and paddle back home. Lessons here can help you stay the course.

Be prepared with lessons designed to keep students excited about learning, using receptive and expressive language arts that lead to personal and academic success. You could view yourself as a ship's captain whose charge is to chart a course for safe passage through the tumultuous preteen and early teen years. As the captain, you recognize the need for balancing structure and choice. Though you already know the standards you are expected to meet, as the year goes by you develop a clearer vision of where you are going and how you may get there. You learn more specifically what this year's students need to know and be able to do. You also discover that they prefer to contribute to the journey. You may even begin to envision the curriculum as the ship, the units as the decks, and the lessons as the rooms. Within the ship, on the decks, and inside the rooms, there are choices the students can make about specific lessons.

As you become more acquainted with your traveling companions, tactfully tacking your sails, adapting and adopting strategies that best keep you all engaged, and moving progressively from port to port, eventually more and more of your students complete the journey ready to step on the firmer, more solid ground of the high school territory with self-assurance and proficiency, prepared for whatever challenges await them.

ADAPTING THE LESSONS AND IDEAS IN THIS BOOK

An equally significant teaching challenge in middle school is the fact that the literary works and required writing vary greatly from school to school. It is likely that your reading lists and specific writing assignments differ somewhat from those addressed explicitly in this book, but you can adapt the approaches because the lessons in this book are designed to

- be inviting and vigorous;
- help students connect their own lives to the readings through their speaking and writing;
- challenge students to think deeply, critically, and broadly;
- help the students write clearly, correctly, and creatively;
- encourage students to work independently, in pairs, in small groups, and as a whole class;
- expand students' understanding of themselves and their world;
- develop ways for students to express themselves in a variety of modes by reading, writing, and discussing a variety of fiction and nonfiction literature and issues in life;
- use digital technologies effectively for research, writing, and communication; and
- meet the curriculum standards of most middle school English language arts programs.

To accomplish these goals, look here for ideas to help with introductions to the various units of instruction; assignments that build on students'

BOX A: ACCORDING TO THE NATIONAL COUNCIL OF TEACHERS OF ENGLISH

Twenty-first-century readers and writers need to

- Develop proficiency with the tools of technology
- Build relationships with others to pose and solve problems collaboratively and cross-culturally
- Design and share information for global communities to meet a variety of purposes
- Manage, analyze, and synthesize multiple streams of simultaneous information
- Create, critique, analyze, and evaluate multimedia texts
- Attend to the ethical responsibilities required by these complex environments*

Source: ASCD, "21st Century Skills," http://www.ascd.org/research-a-topic/21st-century-skills-resources.aspx.

*"The NCTE Definition of 21st Century Literacies" (2008), http://ncte.org (accessed August 15, 2009); Kathleen Blake Yancey, "Writing in the 21st Century: A Report from the National Council of Teachers of English," Florida State University, Tallahassee, © February 2009, National Council of Teachers of English. Reprinted with permission.

understanding of the elements of fiction, literary terms, and poetic devices; and ideas for teaching specific communication skills, including learning vocabulary, using appropriate grammar, giving public speeches, critically viewing, and using electronic and print media. Provided are sample lessons, student study aids, rubrics, and lists of resources, along with practical ideas for engaging students in the digital world.

INTEGRATING TWENTY-FIRST-CENTURY LITERACIES AND COMMON CORE STATE STANDARDS FOR ELA

For these reasons, some chapters have suggestions for using tools of technology to help your students to develop the knowledge, skills, and understanding of these twenty-first-century literacies. These suggested applications also can serve as informal assessments to reveal how closely students have read their fiction and nonfiction texts or use the range of skills called for in the Common Core Standards for English Language Arts.[11]

To incorporate opportunities for your students to learn and hone their skills to become ready for the demands of college and the challenges of careers, choose from options to

- look for information on the Internet and learn to evaluate validity of sources
- use the digital camera to capture images for use in reports or simply to show understanding of vocabulary, literature, or life experience
- create online communities for students to post and edit their own and others' work to collaborate with peers in the class or with students across the continent
- use computer software to make word clouds or collages

These simple ideas give you jumping-off points to create assignments that interest you and your students. Other ideas are at the companion website for this book, http://teachingenglishlanguagearts.com.

Some of the chapters include examples of student-written responses to assignments and comments on what that writing reveals about student learning. They may help expand your insight and prepare you for what to expect as you accept the challenge and come to value the privilege of teaching English language arts to young teenagers.

For the veteran educators looking to revive or revise their instruction or the novice looking to rev up for the first year of teaching, here are proven ways to manage grading and assessments and strategies for students to help them reflect and assess their own work. Although specific standards change occasionally, they still address the basic goal of applying traditional literacies to new literacy contexts. At the same time, the Common Core State Standards for English Language Arts charge educators to design lessons that equip students with the knowledge and skills to be college and career ready when they complete their first twelve years of schooling. Managing both charges requires time and talent, effort and efficiency.

REACHING THE ULTIMATE GOAL—ENJOY TEACHING

To support you in your early years and sustain you along the journey, to enable you to remain an engaged, enthusiastic, and effective teacher of English and language arts in the middle school, here are ideas to develop and present lessons that meet students' emotional and intellectual needs while challenging them to complete increasingly complex tasks. When students are learning and you can document that learning through appropriate assessments, both you and your students enjoy more of your times together. It is my goal with this book to offer you practical and proven practices that bring you the kind of pleasure in teaching that I have experienced these past forty or so years.

NOTES

1. Ignacio "Nacho" Estrada, quotation from Think Exist, http://thinkexist.com/quotes/ignacio_estrada/ (accessed May 31, 2012).

2. Chris Stevenson, "Curriculum That Is Challenging, Integrative, and Exploratory," in *This We Believe . . . and Now We Must Act I*, ed. Thomas O. Erb (Westerville, OH: National Middle School Association, 2001), 63.

3. John D. Bransford, Ann L. Brown, and Rodney R. Cocking, "How Children Learn," in *How People Learn: Brain, Mind, Experience, and School—Expanded Edition* (Washington, DC: National Academy Press, 2000), 109.

4. For further information about Louise Rosenblatt's research on teaching reading, see the article Carolyn Allen, "Louise Rosenblatt and Theories of Reader-Response," *Reader* 20 (1988): 32–39, available at http://www.hu.mtu.edu/reader/online/20/allen20.html (accessed April 3, 2004).

5. Fran Claggett and Joan Brown, *Drawing Your Own Conclusions: Graphic Strategies for Reading, Writing, and Thinking* (Portsmouth, NH: Heinemann, 1992).

6.   Quoted by D. Ray Reutzel and Robert B. Cooter Jr., "Classroom Reading Assessment," in *Strategies for Reading Assessment and Instruction: Helping Every Child Succeed*, 2nd ed. (Upper Saddle River, NJ: Merrill Prentice Hall, 2003), 26.

7.   Anthony W. Jackson and Gayle A. Davis, "Curriculum and Assessment to Improve Teaching and Learning," in *Turning Points 2000: Educating Adolescents in the 21st Century* (New York: Teachers College Press, 2000), 48.

8.   Jackson and Davis, *Turning Points 2000*, 176.

9.   Quoted by Suzanne Siegel Zenkel in *For My Teacher* (White Plains, NY: Pauper Press, 1994).

10.   Anne King spoke at the Middle School Conference on "Teaching the Good Stuff in the Middle," Grand Valley State University, February 2006.

11.   "Common Core Standards for English Language Arts," Common Core State Standards Initiative, 2012, http://www.corestandards.org/ (accessed May 31, 2012).

1

SCOPING OUT THE YEAR IN PREVIEW

Plan Now to Be Effective and Efficient

The mediocre teacher tells. The good teacher explains. The superior teacher demonstrates. The great teacher inspires.

—William A. Ward[1]

Each school year is a journey, somewhat like leading an extended tour with young people you have just met. You want to be ready for the unexpected, learning and adjusting as you go but knowing you are in charge. In the era of standardization, it still is important to customize the trip and personalize instruction, keeping in mind what you are required to teach, who you will be teaching, and mainly the fact that you are a professional in the classroom. One way of making the trip an effective one for all involved is to keep in mind the features of the trip you can control and the ones you cannot.

Even with a curriculum or an itinerary handed to you, as a professional, you can incorporate personal touches that reflect the unique qualities you bring to the work based on your own interests and experiences. It may seem odd, but a good place to begin planning and personalizing instruction for a whole school year is to zone in on school holidays, breaks, and vacations. Aha! You do recall from your own days as a student how challenging it was to be attentive the few days before and the few days after any of these three!

Figure 1.1.   Plan With School Breaks in Mind

So among the ways you can assure that you stay on course for your course is to consider ways to maximize instruction time on such potentially lost days.

Take into consideration the ethnicities and cultures of the students in your classes. What holidays do they share in common? Which are unique to a few? How can you integrate into your lessons the wealth of information, experience, and passion surrounding holidays, breaks, and vacations? More subtle to think about is the emotional and physical drain, say, on your Jewish and Muslim students, who may for cultural or religious reasons be fasting on a day you may have scheduled a major test. Many Asian families observe their calendar new year with days of celebrations that may run late into the evening, making it difficult for students to attend to homework.

One way to connect with your students in a personal way is to let them know that you know, without making them the center of censure by peers who may not understand. What about rodeo and sports tryouts, dance recitals, religious confirmations, Bar and Bat Mitzvahs, and school extracurriculars? The middle school years are when students are more easily sidetracked by such out-of-school events. What kind of reading, writing, active learning, critical thinking, and even reflection can you organize to redeem the time and channel the energy of students who are sure to be distracted?

In addition to knowing the cultures and ethnicities of your students, it also is important to learn a little more about them and their families and the circumstances in which they live. How much do you know about the resources available in the community in which your school is located or from which your students come? Are there local libraries with technology available to the middle school students? Once you have your class lists, take a look at any notices regarding special physical or emotional needs. Early in the first week, you could ask students to tell you privately those special circumstances they are comfortable sharing. Some already have learned to speak up about their vision and hearing issues.

What are you learning that may impact the way you set up your classroom or design lessons? In your conversations with veterans at the school, what can you learn about the most efficient ways to initiate and maintain communication with the families regarding languages spoken at home and access to technology? What is required at your school? Do you have a choice to contact by phone or e-mail? Just as a tour company would gather such information before a trip begins, so should a teacher committed to being prepared for those inherent eventualities. As it is in Scouting, you want to be prepared.

One of the best honors you can extend to your students is to learn to pronounce and spell their names. So if you happen to be teaching in a community with a very diverse population, consider getting someone to help you with pronunciation or use online sites, such as www.pronouncenames.com, on which you can hear names from many nationalities pronounced. Can you imagine what a pleasant surprise it will be for students who seldom hear their name spoken correctly to hear it from you on the first day of school? Even if you do not say them all perfectly, the fact that you care enough about each individual student as a person will gain their respect. The students will see that you are trying, and they may be open to doing the same.

PERSONALIZING THE CLASSROOM

All right. On to personalizing instruction for the journey. Think about ways you can

- reflect you and your students;
- display a list of acceptable standards of conduct;
- shape guidelines for grading;
- devise ways to tailor lessons for the combination of students who make up the classes each particular year;
- select efficient ways to measure learning in ways that provide valid information without swamping you with minutiae; and, most important,
- preplan ways to stay healthy until journey's end.

But, even before preplanning a trip, one must know the destination. So as soon as possible, review the requirements for the course set forth by your school, district, or state. What specific ways are you expected to prepare your students for ultimate success in college or careers based on the Common Core State Standards for English Language Arts or the explicit curriculum in your school? Know these well enough to be able to state in your own words the definite portions of the school curriculum you will be required to teach in the grades assigned to you. Then work backwards as you answer questions such as

- What do students need to know and be able to do at the end of the school year?
- How will I learn what they know and are able to do by the end of our time together?
- What do they know already?
- How can I learn what they know and are able to do already?
- How can I provide opportunities for them to show me what they know already, to learn from one another, and, ultimately, to acquire the knowledge and develop the skills my students need to have by the end of the school year? In other words, how will I know we have arrived at our destination?

- What resources are available to me in my classroom and in my building or school site? To my students in the classroom, in the building, or at home?
- How can I collaborate with teachers within my department and across the content areas to design lessons that link what the students are learning in their other classes to what I am required to teach or am able to teach? Most people think of social studies and science for collaboration. Consider the arts, too, even physical education and health classes.
- What will make teaching this course fun and interesting for me?

Once you can answer these questions—in writing—you can begin to select from the resources you have on hand and then request or assemble those needed to meet the needs of the students you are assigned to teach.

The physical space in which you teach can support your instruction. Think about ways you can make your classroom an attractive and inviting place to be, knowing that one does not need to be wealthy or an artist to do so. It is possible to begin the school year with a bulletin board, covered only with an attractive neutral color and labeled "Student Work," a welcome sign, and an inspiring thought for the week, and leave the rest blank.

Then, during the first week, have lessons that call for small group or individual artwork that you can post on your bulletin boards. You will have the control of designing the lesson to show what you would like to know about the young men and women you will be teaching this school year. And the students will know from day one that the classroom is for them and reflects them. Then keep the bulletin boards up for the fall parents' night of classes, or open house, or whatever your school schedules early in the school year.

ASSEMBLING A CLASSROOM LIBRARY

Begin building your classroom library by collecting new and used books right away. Many libraries have monthly book sales, and you can find books at reasonable costs. Visit garage and yard sales as they are held in your community. Invite graduates to donate books before they move on to the next stage in their lives. Ask relatives to help. Some may be traveling and want to bring back something you can use. Contact local service organizations such as Kiwanis, Lions, and Rotary for contributions. Many such groups encourage support of educational endeavors.

See titles to consider from those recommended by Good Reads on its website's list of "Top 100 Middle School Must-Reads." Consider picture books, too. They are particularly effective for creating interest and providing background information as you start a general unit or begin teaching a specific work of fiction or nonfiction. Your school may qualify for programs such as that offered by BookMentors.org, a nonprofit, which uses micropatronage, making donations to help supply teachers, students, and librarians in high-needs schools with books.

Check offices and hair salons with waiting rooms. Managers and owners would be glad to have a dependable place to pass along old magazines when new ones arrive. (Of course, you know to add to your library only those that are appropriate for middle school students.) Invite students to bring their self-selected reading to class every day. And then encourage them to pull out the magazine or books and read silently whenever they complete assignments before the period ends.

One of your most valuable teaching tools can be a classroom library stocked with books your students can borrow and magazines they can read, scan, skim, and cut up for art projects. Do not get too attached to the books, though. Some will disappear, but they will be read by someone.

SCHMOOZING THE LIBRARIANS

Your librarians or media specialists can be your most precious human resources. These respected professional colleagues interact with teachers across the curriculum and with students from all grades; they know the school curriculum very well. Moreover, librarians know their collection of materials and can work with you to utilize them in ways that support your lessons with culturally relevant and age-appropriate selections. This means that as soon as you have an idea of what and when you plan to teach particular units of study, make an appointment to meet with your school librarian, who often will volunteer to reserve books, magazines, journals, and newspapers and identify online sites that students can use. The librarian also may be willing to prepare a talk to introduce your students to the specific media available in your school's resource center.

Equally important, librarians usually know when the science and social studies teachers assign their big projects and can help you avoid student overload by recommending alternative due dates. Of course, it is good if you work in a school setting in which those who teach the same grades work together to coordinate the scheduling of major assignments. It is better when there is interdisciplinary collaboration and common projects students do for two classes and for which the teachers from both classes share the grading. However, if that is not yet the case at the school where you teach, befriend the librarians and welcome the wealth of experience and knowledge they can add to your lesson planning and implementation.

GUIDING PRINCIPLES TO MANAGE MAYHEM

Middle school students can be marvelous and mischievous. Think about ways to maximize the former and minimize the latter. Reflect on what you can and cannot stand in terms of classroom behavior, homework deadlines, movement and noise in the classroom, and flexibility in assignments. Prepare notes on how you will outline for your students acceptable classroom behavior. Experienced teachers often have three or four general principles that can be applied in specific situations. Consider, as a start, those that refer to attendance, homework, and student behavior in class, such as:

- be present
- be prepared
- participate courteously

Once you decide your three or four guiding principles, include them on your class handouts, on your website, on the wall in your room, on all major assignments, and at the beginning of the school year in a letter to parents and guardians. It is essential for all to know the basic principles by which you plan to conduct the class. It also is good for students to be reminded throughout the course. When they understand the reason for the rules, students usually respond with compliance rather than adolescent sarcasm. Some schools have building-wide behavior statements and expect you to teach and follow them. You may find them sufficient or in need of a little tweaking.

ASSESSING PRIOR KNOWLEDGE

Your students are young adolescents, not new travelers along the road of life. They are just joining you for this portion of a lifelong journey of living and learning and therefore come to you already familiar with some experiences that can enhance their time with you. As a teacher, fellow traveler, and tour guide, you want to do all you can to prepare them for the weeks and months ahead, perhaps warn them of possible landslides that can occur and inclement weather they may experience, all the time assuring them that you all are in this together.

You are there to help them climb the rock walls of new tasks that seem unscalable; to work with them, eager to observe them open their hearts and minds to see and appreciate the beauty of reading, writing, discussing, and thinking about new kinds of writing, novel fiction and nonfiction narratives; to be ready to explore with them the natural wonders encountered along the way; and most of all, to guide their practice and use of skills as they strive to achieve their own personal goals.

You may find it helpful to use online resources to discover the range of learning styles among the students you have in each class, on sites like Edutopia.org, where you can find an online quiz called "What Is Your Learning Style?"[2] Keep in mind, however, that this information will provide just one component of the range of information you need to know about your students. You also know to pay attention to their age, readiness, and interests.

So now you need to get to know in the first couple of weeks what students know and are able to do already. This could be done by collecting reading comprehension and writing samples, conducting interest surveys, or, as described in chapter 2, observing small group activities during which students work together on a common project using the kinds of skills they should be bringing to the new class.

Begin the school year the way you would like it to continue throughout the school year. For example, consider homework deadlines. Be informative and be firm from the beginning. Of course, students understand that firm and fair do not mean inflexible. Middle school students can deal with special circumstances, so do not be afraid to be merciful. It is normal to make adjustments as the school year unfolds. However, beginning with a few general rules helps to establish the groundwork for the upcoming year. In the metaphor of the school year as a trip, you are working on the rules for the road.

DECIDING RULES FOR THE ROAD

Among the rules for the road, decide procedural matters, such as how you can organize and keep your lesson plans and master copies of handouts, as well as how you can collect and where you can store student work. Consider using color coding as often as possible. For example, you could have different colored loose-leaf binders for each grade or sturdy folders in assorted hues for each period. If you have access to colored paper for photocopying, you could use a single color for assignments in the same unit. It would be helpful to students if you were to say, "Sylvia, will you bring me the folder for your class? Yes, the purple one in the second shelf on the left corner of my desk," or to the class, "Take out the blue assignment sheet for our unit on poetry," or to Horace who's come for extra help, "Did you bring the yellow sheet with the academic vocabulary list?"

If you really are uncomfortable with lots of noise but understand the value of small group discussions, think about ways to design lessons that include specific instructions that you explain ahead of time, and then plan to circulate among the students as they work in small groups. When students know exactly what is expected and you are very present among them, they usually can discipline themselves enough to work in a focused manner and maintain a lower noise volume. It is helpful to write or project the class outline and steps for assignments right on the board.

GRADING GUIDELINES

Just as you like to know what is expected of you, the same is true for students. On a road trip, you look for signs to indicate how near or far you are from your ultimate destination. When you see familiar topography or prom-ised landmarks, you relax a bit and breathe a little easier. The same can be true about grading as it relates to you and to your students.

Grading becomes less stressful when you understand what you are looking for in each assignment and share these expectations with the students. They can review their work before turning it in, using your guidelines as a checklist. Some students, because of other commitments, may settle for a B rather than put in the time to earn the A. That's okay. It is their choice.

Fewer students challenge their grades when they have had a clearly written set of printed instructions to which they can refer before submit-ting their work. So consider a set of general grading principles that can be applied to most graded assignments. Explain these guidelines in the first couple of weeks, but not on the first day of school. Students already will be overwhelmed with the newness of everything! You can, however, have something like the following posted on your website and on any general handouts you distribute on opening day.

General Grading Guidelines

A= complete, correct, and creative

B= complete and correct

C= complete

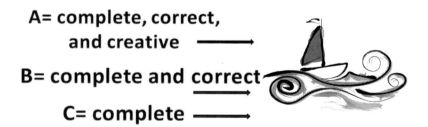

C = THE SEA - *Complete* (includes all components of the assignment)
B= THE BOAT -*Complete and Correct (rides on the sea with* minimal errors in mechanics, usage, grammar and spelling)
A= THE SAIL - *Complete, Correct, and Creative* (something above and beyond the boat ; original and fresh elements enhancing final performance/ product)

Figure 1.2.   General Grading Guidelines

C = Complete (includes all components of the assignment)

B = Complete and Correct (minimal errors in mechanics, usage, grammar, and spelling)

A = Complete, Correct, and Creative (something original, fresh, special that enhances final product or performance)

So plan to include rubrics with each graded assignment, especially those that are weighted heavily enough to have major impact on reported grades. Providing students with a list of the standards and semester goals fulfills comparable purposes. Such information provides the same comfort as a map or the voice on the GPS when you travel in unfamiliar territory.

UNDERSTANDING BRAIN DEVELOPMENT AIDS IN LESSON PLANNING

New teachers of middle school students often are surprised at how literal their students are, especially in the earlier grades and at the beginning of the school year. You may be disappointed that these young teenagers seem so very immature; few are able to see the subtleties in literature, and most seem inept at writing clever imagery. The fact is, few young adolescents are mentally ready for this kind of thinking. No need to despair.

As the year unfolds, some students may display a leap in development of the brain's frontal cortex that occurs in early teen years.[3] Others may only grow taller and wilder. Usually at the beginning of the school year, young teens still are pretty literal, thinking in concrete terms, but as the year progresses, their frontal lobes mature, and they gain practice and experience under your tutelage, these youngsters begin looking at literature and life more abstractly, recognizing and using more subtle metaphors in their speech and writing. They are growing physically, emotionally, and cerebrally. Plan with that knowledge in mind.

LEARNING THE LANGUAGE OF THE LAND

You know the value of a broad, rich vocabulary, even if you just visit a different area of the nation and not some exotic country on a different continent.

The same is true for your students. For many of them, the language of school may seem just as foreign. As you scope out the journey of the school year, you know students will need to understand some basic terms to be able to follow directions and stay on task. So you can plan from the very beginning to teach vocabulary intentionally, without having to drill students just for them to acquire the skill of recognizing and using more sophisticated language in and out of class. If they use it, they won't lose it.

Consider levels of vocabulary. As you choose and prepare lessons around specific readings, you can pull and give definitions for words that are specific to a particular book or article and also pull out some of the published academic vocabulary words students will need to know across the content areas. You may recognize these levels as tier 1, 2, and 3 words, referring to the vocabulary based on how practical the words are for everyday speaking, reading, writing, and/or academic use. In your area of the country, you may hear about the "40/40/40 rule." Decide which words students need to know for forty days, for forty weeks, and for forty years, and then allot teaching and study time accordingly.

Think about dedicating space for a "word wall" so that students see words daily during particular units and can refer to and draw from this word-wall list when they write or talk about the literature. This can be a poster to which you add words all through the school year or one that you change to coordinate with specific units of instruction. If space is available, it may be better to have one permanent poster with general words and a changing posting with specific words. Fresh lists create new interest, just as the changing road signs you notice along the highway revive interest in the trip.

Among the academic words to begin defining and using in early lessons are those having to do with instructions: explain, diagram, evaluate, describe, analyze, discuss, and so on. If your students are new to middle school, they may have different ideas about what is required when asked to do these tasks. Help your travel-mates get off to a good start by clarifying what is expected when they see or hear these terms. You can find lists of academic words on websites describing Bloom's Taxonomy verbs to help you measure students' level of knowledge, comprehension, application, analysis, synthesis, evaluation, and creativity.

TEACHING TEST-TAKING LANGUAGE

Administering standardized tests probably will be a part of your responsibility as leader of this educational expedition. Just as you find it comforting to know how to read the basic language of the land when you visit a foreign country, prepare your students to read the signs that direct their work on a test. Teach your students the language of academic assessments long before students take these tests. Use such terms on the tests you give all year long.

Once you have settled into your classes, you may want to have a lesson on the different definitions the same word may have in different content areas. Words such as *plot* that in English is an element of fiction; in history/social studies' map reading, *plot* of land or *plot* a course of action; and in science or math, *plot* a graph, and so on. *Draw*, as seen a few paragraphs earlier, is another of those multidefinition words.

REWARDING LANGUAGE LEARNING

To speed up students' acquisition of vocabulary, encourage and reward them for using words from the English vocabulary lists in the writing they do in other classes. A maximum of ten points per marking period—one point for each word in a graded assignment for other classes—should suffice. All extra-credit work should be due one week before the end of the marking period to avoid reading last-minute papers when you need time for computing grades to be turned in or posted for report cards.

Promote active learning by inviting students to bring in samples with the vocabulary words used in their reading outside of class. You could simply put up a blank poster board and ask students to bring in highlighted photocopies of passages from other published writing where students find words from the current vocabulary (no duplicates from same source). If you keep it low key, this should not escalate into a contest but remain a way to raise students' awareness of language use outside their academic setting.

You also could set aside a day in class when students are asked to include correct use of vocabulary words in their conversation in pairs, small groups, or even full class discussion. It could be great fun . . . especially if you let peers give the feedback instead of you. This is another strategy to encourage close listening. You may recall those days when you were studying a foreign language, say Spanish or French, and the teacher announced, "Hoy día, sólo se habla español aquí!" or "Aujourd'hui, seul le français est parlé ici!"

Rather than waiting for a test to measure the understanding of vocabulary, you may find it more effective to require in writing assignments the correct use of vocabulary from current lists instead of spending time making up weekly quizzes. During journal writing, students can be asked to use different words from the list in sentences that include definition, synonym or antonym, or some context clue to the meaning of the word. They can work in pairs to "check" these writings, and by the time students have an assignment that is to be graded, most students will be competent using the vocabulary words. Then, on the weekly or biweekly full-length writing assignment, students should feel confident at incorporating vocabulary from several recent lists.

KEEPING UP WITH LEARNING WITHOUT OVERTESTING

Current education theories proclaim the value of conducting both formal and informal assessments all year long. Such measuring informs both students and teachers about what is learned and taught successfully. The questions that arise for teachers new to the profession or new to teaching middle school students are when and how one should test.

Since you, the teacher, have very definite content matter that you are asked to teach and since you are expected to guide the students across tempestuous seas to learn and show what they know about good writing, efficient reading, effective speaking, courteous listening, and skillful use of technology, it may be useful to work backwards by asking yourself questions like those that follow.

- Which specific skills am I trying to develop or measure in this assignment?
  - Is it how well students understand the text we've studied together?
  - Is it how well they can show what they know about analyzing a character?

- ○ Is it how well they can write an organized response in a timed setting?
- • What will I need to see in their work to know their level of understanding or skill?
  - ○ Is it reference to the text?
  - ○ Is it correct use of literary language?
  - ○ Is it organization?
  - ○ Is it development of ideas?
  - ○ Is it correct use of vocabulary and grammar?

Some of these skills are revealed in student journal writing and in conversations during small group and full class discussion, and they may not need to be measured again on a formal test. As you become more experienced, you, too, will design more lessons to measure student learning, become a more efficient listener and close observer, and develop the habit of taking brief notes based on what you see and hear during regular class meetings. You may even find it practical to write reflective journal notes at the end of each school day. You will stay attuned, attentive to what students say and do not say and how they respond and react. In the meantime, keep reading.

You can become adept at using what you learn through formative assessments to reshape lessons, reteaching when necessary. This would be like backtracking on a trip, a time when passengers notice details they may have missed the first time they were passing by. In some situations, based primarily on informal assessments of student learning, you may choose to speed up the pace and move on to the next unit of study. You know that ahead there could be potholes that may trip them up and quagmires that may bog them down, and having extra time to negotiate them may be necessary. Still, you do not whiz on by. You take seriously your charge to teach, knowing you are more than a tour narrator who simply points out and names landmarks you pass along the way.

Making formative assessments and deciding what to do about the results take practice. You may find they are like taking a break in the trip to check the map, to assure yourself that you have not drifted off the trail and been distracted unduly by the foggy, damp weather of students complaining that the terrain is just too rough! But the more proficient you become at recognizing learning and adjusting instruction, the less overwhelmed you and your students become at summative testing time. While both may be disappointed, neither the student nor the teacher should be surprised at the results of a formal test.

It's important to do what you can to ensure that all those on the trip with you reach the destination safe, secure, confident, and competent and with the knowledge and skills they need to have continued success when you pass along this year's tour group to the next year's tour guide.

PREPARING TO ASSESS FOR UNDERSTANDING

Test-taking skills are important for students to learn, especially as they prepare for high school. You can serve your young people well by reviewing ways to take these tests and then formatting tests in a student-friendly way. Your young teens not only appreciate less-stressful testing but also perform better on tests they understand. This can be as simple as creating a "Prepare for the Test" handout that includes the test format and suggestions on how to study for each kind of question. Possessing a map that shows the topography of the hike can be comforting to a teen trekker.

For example, if you plan to test their understanding of vocabulary from the book, tell your students whether they need to know definitions, synonyms, antonyms, or how to use the words in a sentence. Or, if you have had students copy select passages from the book into their reading journals, you should be able to test successfully for quotations simply by reminding students to study the text material in their journals.

If you have test questions that require answers in a complete paragraph or short essay, remind students in advance to review the structure of each one. A test prep handout can also include the number of points allotted for each section of the test. Such information saves time and angst. Students do not have to use valuable test time trying to figure out the format of the exam or how best to allot their time. On the test review day, remind students to spend the most time studying for the sections with the highest value. Your preparation of these handouts provides time for you to reflect on what you have taught, what you are expecting to measure, and how this test will show student learning. With such thinking before the test, grading these assessments usually takes less time.

KEEPING RECORDS OF INFORMAL ASSESSMENTS

Do you know any regular travelers who do not keep some kind of written, photo, or video record of their trip? Many of the more intrepid ones do all three. The same is true for you as a teacher-tour guide. As you work with the young people, offer different ways for them to show what they are learning, assessing sometimes with quizzes, essays, art, music, drama, or video and, as often as appropriate, inviting students to choose. Then, include in what they submit for evaluation a written page to explain how their choice of product or performance will prove to anyone reading or viewing that the students really know the content and have the skills required for them to meet the standards. Keep a checklist in each of their classroom folders so that students can view them regularly.

You could schedule biweekly in-class reading days on which you meet with the individuals for three to five minutes to review their progress for the week and plan for the next. It may be useful to plan to meet with half the class one week and the other half the next week. As students learn to draw from their wealth of knowledge and apply it in new situations, they become more skilled and secure learners.

Yes, teaching this way can create a little more uncertainty on your part, but with practice on both sides, your students will be more motivated and self-assured if they know where they are supposed to be by the end of the school year and have some choices in as many ways as are appropriate in your school setting. On a tour, the guide knows the passengers need to eat and offers restaurant options within the framework of the time or budget. As you consider the year as a whole, keeping an eye on the goal, you will see there is much room for flexibility and personalization in ways that lead to effective and efficient teaching and consistent and satisfactory learning.

RETEACHING IN DIFFERENT FORMATS

A fact of teaching is that students do not always treasure the pearls of wisdom that flow from your lips. They do not always remember exactly how to do everything you present them, even things they have done well in the past. So it is imperative to solidify that knowledge and hone those skills by asking students to use knowledge and skills in different settings. You can help increase retention by designing lessons that require your students to use what they learned when reading a short story or news article when they are preparing a speech or writing an essay.

On Friday, for example, you could ask students to choose a passage they particularly enjoy in their self-selected book and pattern that passage about something the student has recently experienced or observed. Then they would quietly turn to a partner and read the original passage aloud, followed by their patterned writing. Ask the students to pay attention to the rhythm of the sentences. Each listener could be asked to listen closely to see how well his or her partner has followed the sentence syntax of the original writer. Exact duplication should not be required; coming close enough to show attentive reading and an attempt to pattern a published writer's style should suffice. Trust the students to know what works, but circulate among them to confirm their analyses.

You could have the students do scavenger hunts in their self-selected books, looking for whatever grammatical structure or reading strategy you have taught most recently. For example, ask them to find examples of complex sentences, sentences written in passive voice, subjunctive voice, use of complementary conjunctions, reflections of a text's different structures, and so on. How many different kinds of sentence starts do they notice on a single page in their book? What does this suggest about interesting and effective writing?

Grading? Just have groups check one another's work. Anything they cannot figure out together, you can discuss as a class. Teacher circulating while taking notes on level of participation; assessing informally; planning the next lessons; these help both students and their teacher continue down the road, intent on completing the trip together.

INCORPORATING MOVEMENT, COLORS, AND SHAPES TO ENHANCE LEARNING

From your own experience traveling, you know how easy it is to get bored when you have to sit a long time or you can see nothing interesting out of the windows. As the leader of the educational journey, you can keep your charges engaged if you spice things up a bit with lessons that include movement and personal decision making.

Learning Actively

Begin now thinking about ways to incorporate kinesthetic games and active learning as a regular part of your instruction. Consider lessons that invite students to get up from their seats for reasons as simple as moving into groups or as sophisticated as expressing an opinion by the corner in which each one chooses to stand. It will be like getting up and walking down the aisle while on a transatlantic airplane trip. Sometimes you just have to get up and move. In the classroom, movement can lead to learning.

Do you have access to an overhead projector and a whiteboard? If so, you can project games, puzzles, and diagrams onto the whiteboard. This way all the students can see but have to get up and write, draw, circle, or indicate a choice. Instead of worksheets students complete at their seats, you could create some on transparencies, where students have to walk up and write answers "on the board."

You can plan lessons where students have to express their opinions by getting up and going to one or another corner of the room to indicate their position on questions about literature or about life. For example, after reading about a choice the protagonist has made, you could ask students to go to the front corner or back corner, depending on their opinions or predictions about the story. "What do you think Alfonso should or will do? Four different suppositions? Okay, Sal and those who agree with him, stand over there. Those who think Hamera is right, stand with her, back there. Gerald, stand right here and Felicia, right there, and those who think their predictions are right, join them."

Ask each group to sit together and find evidence from the text to support their thinking. Choose a spokesperson to explain. Then, having heard the evidence and reasons for opposing opinion, invite students who wish to change places to do so. Thinking. Moving. Talking. Referring to texts. Speaking. Listening. Moving. Learning. Good teaching.

Using Shapes and Colors

You can plan now to increase critical thinking and to appeal to students who learn in different ways, adapting lessons for the visual and spatial learners to think about which color or shape is appropriate to add to something you have projected for all to see. For example, some students may benefit from seeing the structure of an essay and how each part of an essay has a specific function. This works when you compare an essay to a train and have different geometric shapes to represent the different kinds of train cars.

- Right-facing triangle for the introduction: the engine, moving the essay forward
- Rectangles for the body: cargo or boxcars, containers carrying the facts, explanations, and reasons
- Left-facing triangle for conclusion: caboose, looking back on what has been said
- Ovals: the couplings to represent transitions that connect the parts of the essay

Use colors to show the patterns of essay construction, with different organizational patterns for various paragraphs within the body of an essay. This visual activity can be done with photocopies of an essay, and students use colored pencils or markers to show in color the way parts of a essay should blend to explain, explore, and expand on the statement of purpose or thesis sentence. Your art students probably already know that red and blue make purple or that blue and yellow make green. They will understand the concept of blending to create something new.

- Thesis statement in purple (or green)
- Topic sentences in red (or blue)
- Supporting sentences in blue (or yellow)

Seeing colors also can help students understand both the function of parts of speech and the impact of syntax on sentence structure when you ask them to circle, underline, and draw arrows as part of a grammar lesson.

Use different colors for parts of the speech or parts of the sentence.

- green for action verbs
- brown for linking verbs
- same color for subject and predicate noun or adjective to show the relationship
- dark color for noun, with lighter version for pronoun to show agreement

Draw an arrow from the modifier (word, phrase, or clause) to the word modified. If there is a dangling modifier, students will see how out of place the dangler is.

Keep the movement in the lesson by inviting students to work on sentences written or projected onto the whiteboard or on swaths of white butcher paper. You could project a sentence with a dangling modifier and have students draw what they "see" based on the wording of the sentence. If you have space in your room, you could have groups of students working on the floor with poster board and markers. There will be giggling, but that's okay. It releases tension.

Showing Patterns in Fiction

If students are not allowed to write in their books, print out or project so that all can see a section from the exposition of a story you are teaching. Then invite one student at a time to come forward to mark on the projected passage, asking individuals to

- draw an oval around main characters when first introduced (different color for each one)
- underline in the matching color words and phrases that describe each of the main characters
  - Character A: red—words describing him or her underlined in red
  - Character B: blue—words describing him or her underlined in blue
- mark word(s) that identify the setting
  - Rectangle for place where the story or scene is set
  - Circle for time of day, year, or period in life (childhood, teen, adult) in which the story is set

Just as noise and movement outside the window of a bus or train attracts the attention of travelers who may have dozed off, these kinds of verbal and visual activities capture students' attention and reengage them in the lesson of the moment. They teach and reinforce concepts, showing students, for example, that writers of fiction usually introduce main characters early in the story and very soon afterwards and include words and phrases to help shape an image of the character and their personality in the minds of the reader.

Since the time and place of a story often are critical to the action that follows, that information is presented in the exposition as well. Seeing features together will remind your students to look for these patterns when they read themselves. Recognizing these expected patterns also will help students as they begin writing stories of their own.

SENSING SURROUNDINGS AS SOURCES FOR WRITING

How about including in your plans for this extended journey time for side trips? Consider taking the students outside to explore their environment as an alternative journal assignment. They can take along their notebooks or tablet computers, cell phones, and plastic grocery bags, and then have them write what they experience through their senses. You also carry along your kitchen timer.

Depending on your school setting, this could simply mean finding a grassy area and asking students to sit on their grocery bags and close their eyes for two minutes, alternating between sensing and writing as they listen, smell, touch, taste, and then look. If your school permits students to have cell phones in class, students who have a camera feature can take photos to add to their journal entries. First sense, then write, then photograph. (It helps to keep eyes closed as they experience the first two senses.)

- Close eyes for a couple of minutes and *listen*, and then write what they hear.
- Close eyes and for a couple of minutes and *smell*, inhaling deeply, paying attention to the different fragrances, odors, and aromas, and then describe them with vivid adjectives and figurative language.
- *Touch*, pick up a stick or a rock, touch the bark of a tree, some pebbles, a clump of soil, and describe that or just what it feels like to be sitting on the ground on top of a plastic grocery bag.
- *Taste*, if it is safe. If not, bring along hard candy in different flavors and ask students to describe the taste sensation and the feel of the candy in their mouths, on their teeth, and so on. Or bring a bag of baby carrots, radishes, or celery sticks to have something more healthy.

- *Sight*—ask students to look around, paying attention to something they may not have noticed before, and describe it. (Save sight for last. By that time, students will have calmed down a bit and are ready to look at something other than one another.)

To make excursion more active, you could have students walk around, stop, sense, write, and then walk to another spot. You also could have them do some gentle calisthenics and then sit and write as though they were a character in a story describing what that exercise felt like. The notes from this outing can be used right away in poetry or to flesh out a scene in a short narrative piece. Yes, you will have students who find it difficult to attend at each step in the lesson, so that means saving this kind of adventure until you have established rapport and can depend on students to respond promptly with appropriate classroom behavior standards. In fact, this kind of outing can be a goal for you and a reward for them.

From the very beginning of the school year, it is beneficial to create and nurture an environment in which the students feel comfortable writing personally. However, it takes time for students to trust you enough to do so. No

Figure 1.3.   Student Writing Outdoors

need to give up. Writing about something they do as a class may make them feel less vulnerable because it is a shared experience. This kind of side-trip adventure may be just one way to scaffold the writing where the students begin writing fictionally but are encouraged to use their own experiences to lend authenticity to their writing, whether poetry, short story, or narrative essay.

If it is not realistic to take a local field trip outside the school building, obtain permission from the administrator and from the person in charge of the cafeteria or library to schedule a field trip to those spaces. If you have several sections of the same class, you may end up taking different classes to different places, depending on the weather, time of day, and places available. It is surprising what students notice when they tune in to experience a place through their senses.

Even though all of the described strategies do not require all the students to be moving at the same time, what movement there is helps create and retain interest. Having to select colors and shapes gets them thinking. Sensing their space focuses their attention inward; then writing and photography move things outward into the public realm. Those sitting and watching also are checking to see whether they would have chosen the same colors or shapes had they been called to go to the front of the class. Those reading and viewing their classmates' notes and photos relive the experience from a different perspective.

Whatever you decide to do, know that it is important to create a safe and nurturing environment so that students will not be reluctant to step up and show what they think they know. If they are wrong, they should not be embarrassed by anyone in the classroom. Invite them to share their journals and pictures. Being realistic, no one attends all the time. But if lessons are varied, vigorous, and energizing, sometimes fun and consistently supportive, more student travelers remain tuned in for longer periods of time throughout the whole journey.

No matter how engaging the intellectual outings you plan or how enthusiastically they respond to the jaunts you schedule for this school-year trip, the fact of the matter is, you are a teacher responsible for seeing that the majority of your students attain the standards set for the course. Evaluation time comes, and the students must be ready.

STAYING HEALTHY ALONG THE JOURNEY

Totally exhausted after a thoroughly exasperating week, you may begin to wonder, "How do great teachers stay on top of their game and retain the energy and enthusiasm to return to the classroom year after year?"[4] Sipping a soothing cup of green tea, you ponder, "Why are so many long-term educators still healthy and happy, successful and satisfied with their career choice?" Another sip. Ah, that's better.

The knot in your lower back may loosen a bit. A little calmer, a little less stressed, you smile and envision the faces of those experienced teachers whom you would call "great," and you even try to see yourself among their ranks. However, you glance at the stack of papers still to be graded, and you sigh, "Never. Not me. Errrr. Not I!" Whatever.

Whether a novice or veteran in the field, you know that no matter how much time you give to schoolwork, there always is more to be done. "How do they do it?" stays in the front of your mind. Myriad answers swirl as you pick up your pen, readying yourself to get back to work. One reason may crystallize when you consider what you have observed over the years. Great teachers somehow manage to achieve personal and professional balance.

You probably are familiar with the idea of a Sabbath. True, Sabbath has religious connotations, but observing Sabbath also is an attitude toward work that schedules regular breaks. Plan now to rest regularly. No, rest is not necessarily sitting with one's feet up, a cold drink in one hand and the DVD remote in the other. Rest can be a brief respite from the demands of the classroom.

You may decide to set aside at least one day a week to do no schoolwork—a regular date night with a spouse or children, with a parent, friend, or significant other. If you happen to take on the extracurricular assignment as a coach or club sponsor, you still can observe Sabbath by focusing attention on the team or club and not on lesson preparation and paper grading. I coached and traveled with competitive speech teams for twelve years and resisted the temptation to take along papers to grade. It is surprising how efficiently one can prepare for Monday, rested and refreshed! Try it.

Those colleagues whom you admire for their balanced lives participate in activities completely unrelated to the specific subject of their teaching. One may cultivate roses and enter them in the state fair; another may serve at a church and others on community committees. They may serve on the board of their neighborhood library or take gourmet cooking classes. Some play in a chamber orchestra or sing in a community chorus. Like Langston Hughes, they "laugh / And eat well / and grow strong." Will you?

CONCLUSION

In other words, as the instructional tour guide in charge of the educational journey, plan now to take some time off regularly, just for yourself. When you are a little more relaxed and have reliable and healthy ways to renew yourself, you will be able to tackle these challenges with much more energy and creativity. While you cannot automatically embed what you know into the hearts and minds of your students, you can inspire them to embrace new knowledge as you model doing the same.

And you, too, can enjoy the trip.

NOTES

1. William Arthur Ward quotation from "Quotes about Teaching," National Education Association, 2012, http://www.nea.org/grants/17417.htm (accessed March 8, 2012).

2. "What Is Your Learning Style?," Edutopia, http://www.edutopia.org/multiple-intelligences-learning-styles-quiz (accessed April 17, 2012).

3. "Adolescent Brain Development," Research Facts and Findings fact sheet, May 2002, ACT for Youth Upstate Center of Excellence, http://www.actforyouth.net/resources/rf/rf_brain_0502.pdf (accessed April 6, 2012).

4. "Staying Healthy" section based on ideas from my article "Professional and Personal Lives," *California English* 16, no. 1 (September 2010): 8–9, and used here by permission.

2

NETWORKING
SOCIALLY AT
THE START OF A
SCHOOL YEAR

Getting to know you, getting to know all about you.
Getting to like you, getting to hope you like me.

—Oscar Hammerstein[1]

Even in the age of electronic social networking, in-person relationships are the most meaningful for teachers and learners. The classroom itself becomes a "site" for social networking among increasingly diverse students and teachers. Learning, as encouraged by the Common Core State Standards for English Language Arts,[2] is grounded in social connections. The best way to nurture students toward high-level thinking is to design low-tech interactions.

The following opening-of-the-school-year projects show how to get your eclectic, energetic young teens working together so that you can assess how well they are reading, writing, speaking, listening, and using technology already. Such knowledge will be useful as they begin to explore, explain, and express themselves in writing and as you and your students get to know one another in the classroom and online.

You could think of the first week of language arts classes as the staging ground for the semester, preparation for your school year journey together. As you get to know individual students, you can map out personalized approaches to student activities. In this case, "personalized" need not mean the same thing as "individualized"; here, it means drafting lessons that more closely match the personalities of the specific students assigned to you in a particular class.

The five-day collage-making activity is based on group and personal responses to a shared reading, and it works well with an older, more established class. The one- or two-day scavenger hunt using the course anthology may be more fitting for shorter class periods during the first week and works well with a younger, less-experienced group of students who are new to the school or who may be using a literature anthology for the first time.

RESPONDING TO A SHARED READING: SMALL-GROUP COLLAGE ON BOOK OR STORY

If your students have read a specified book over the summer, you are in luck. You can use a few opening days of the semester to have students work in small groups to make poster or digital collages that reflect various perspectives on the summer reading. You can even organize groups around the elements of fiction: character, setting, conflict, plot, theme, and literary devices or specific writing genres.

If your students have not already read a common book, assign them to read a short story (Gary Soto's "Seventh Grade" is a great choice), silently, aloud together in class, or for homework. You might even ask for volunteer readers so that you can begin to identify some of the eager or hesitant readers. Avoid insisting that all students read aloud. Accept a "pass." Cold reading scares and shuts down some students. You want to keep them open to learning,

A collage is created from lots of words and pictures and reveals a message about the book or story. Each group can be responsible for finding pictures and cutting out words and letters to create a collage focusing on one of the following: main characters, setting, plot, conflicts, themes, others. The collage can be hard copy on poster board or created digitally using photos, clip art, and graphics students locate online. If technology is available to do it efficiently, students could take photos, upload them, and integrate them into their collages. Survey the skills and release the students to choose as often as it seems appropriate. This assignment can be extended to include writing about the collage-building experience, too.

The idea here is to get students involved in an activity that enables them to get to know one another and enables you to get to know each one. Assemble the following:

1. poster board
2. scissors
3. glue sticks
4. magazines
5. colored markers
6. envelopes
7. access to enough computers for at least one per group
8. index cards
9. a timer (kitchen timers work well)
10. blank sheets of address labels (e.g., Avery 5160)
11. a clipboard

These lessons are designed for a fifty-minute class period, but you can adapt them as needed to fit your schedule. See "Teacher Resource A" in the appendix for a sample collage assignment based on *The Circuit* by Francisco Jimenez, a novel assigned for summer reading.

ORIENTING TO AVAILABLE TECHNOLOGY

If your students have ready access to computers in the classroom, you could assign students to create a brief movie from the still shots or slides or Prezi or PowerPoint presentations that incorporate the same elements, including the oral presentation at the end. If your students are new to the available technology, you may need to adjust the schedule of lessons to allot time to introduce them to the equipment and to get signed in with usernames, passwords, and a tutorial on the basic program you plan for them to use right away. Consider inviting the school tech aid to help you plan this orientation.

Day One: Groups Conceive their Collages

Students need instructions, especially on the first few days of class! They want to know what is expected. Therefore, project, post, or print copies of instructions somewhere in the classroom where everybody can refer to them. Inform students that while they are working together you may be

Figure 2.1. Students Working on the Floor

roaming around the room, listening in, observing, enjoying their conversations. Inform them that there are no "right" or "wrong" answers. Consider giving each group a name based on a literary term—or let them select their own names from a list. Be open and helpful. Define the literary terms as needed. Answer students' questions about the assignment.

Finally, before they begin working, distribute name tags—or tags for them to write their own names with the markers, perhaps color-coded for each group or literary term. Set the kitchen timer to ring ten minutes before the class period ends so that you have time to collect supplies, clear up the room, reflect on what they have been doing, and give the assignment for the next class meeting.

Once groups begin working, it is time for you to begin observing and listening. If you are not working with your own tablet computer, use the clipboard and mailing labels to jot down notes about individual students. If possible, write specific words that particular students say during group activities. Listen for their pithy comments, not lengthy quotations. Jot down exact words, phrases, or short sentences that can help you to structure future lessons. Note whether students understand and use literary terms or synonyms that make sense. Indicate positive/negative language toward group members. For example, "You've got that right, Lindsay," or "You dummy! Don't you know what conflict means in a story?"

Also, make short notes about student behavior. Who is talkative? Who is articulate? Involved? Pensive? Easily distracted? Who is having the most fun? Who likes asking tough questions? How are the various groups and members "doing" in their groups?[3] Most groups progress naturally from forming, to storming (arguing over roles), to norming (settling down and accepting the skills brought to the group), to performing (getting down to business.[4] Be sure to avoid looking like a severe disciplinarian. Smile.

The kitchen timer is visual as well as aural. It can help get you and the students into the rhythm of time-crunched class sessions. Students, right at the beginning of the school year, need to start thinking about completing projects by deadline. So do you. And the classroom needs to be cleaned up on time, especially if a colleague has to teach in the room shortly after your class is over. The timer also signals time for cleanup. Tell your students that when a timer goes off at the end of class, you need their help in straightening out the room so that they can mess it up the next day. They smile.

BOX 2.1: PROJECT IT! MAKING TIME FOR TIME

Language arts is all about culture and communication. Since every culture has its own sense of time, using a timer in class is an opportunity to address how meaningful time varies from place to place. Project on the screen, while the students work, an image of one of the websites around the world that count local time on a digital clock, preferably a twenty-four-hour clock situated on a website in a language other than English. Note the time you begin and the time you end the session.

At the end of the class session, ask the students to bring in pictures, from magazines or printed out from websites, that can be used to represent people, places, events, conflict, and literary devices in their particular piece of literature. Be sure that you have your own supply on hand for those unable to bring pictures or magazines to the next class meeting. For those who have access to the Internet at home, encourage them to search and save images onto a site students can access from school the next day. If the group is making a hard-copy poster, the students may decide to print out pictures and bring them to the next class meeting.

Day Two: Groups Compose Their Collages

Briefly repeat instructions for the assignment, tell students how long they have to create a layout for their collages, and set a timer to signal the last ten minutes for cleanup. Since some of the collages are not likely to be finished, provide envelopes for groups to store their unused pictures. Remind those working online to save their work on the class site you already have set up for use this school year.

Invariably, during this second class meeting, some groups wish they had the images that other groups are using or discarding. So if day one was not overly chaotic, you can encourage covetous groups to swap a few pictures. Still, be careful that cross-group racket doesn't replace intragroup collaboration. You can always institute a couple of one-minute swap sessions to limit as well as encourage picture trading—call it "Picture Jeopardy." If possible, download the TV show's theme song from the Internet and play it while students make their changes. Once the music stops, swapping ends, and groups return to work with the pictures they have on hand.

Next, begin testing the validity of your observations about students from the previous day. See whether the behavior you observed the first day continues, changes, improves, or devolves. Also start looking for additional information about your crew. Who comes prepared? Who acts like the "artistic coordinator"? Which students seem to be more concrete or philosophical in group discussions? Which classmates invite in group members who may have been on the periphery of the discussions? Do any students seem overwhelmed, suggesting that you might need to provide additional encouragement and support as they board the ship for another school year? Remember to jot down brief comments by particular students, such as "Can't you do anything right?" and "I like that picture."

Day Three: Groups Complete Their Collages

By now, students are wondering what they have gotten themselves into—through no choice of their own! They might be noting that this class is going to be a lot of fun as well as a lot of work. It is time for them and you to face the reality of school deadlines, including those for collaborative work. Students do have to demonstrate what they have learned. So keep smiling but also start acting like the benevolent taskmaster you really are.

First, refresh their memories about the assignment. Tell them that the collages have to be completed that day. Finally, joyfully deliver the news that during the next class meeting, the groups are to give oral presentations based on their collages—and that each student is expected to contribute. Even your overachieving groups with already-completed collages now have plenty to do. A few of your students might be thinking uncomplimentary thoughts about school and especially about you. As Huckleberry Finn put it, "All I say is, [teachers] is [teachers], and you got to make allowances. Take them all around; they're a mighty ornery lot. It's the way they're raised."[5]

Hand each student a three-inch by five-inch index card. Inform the class that each group should jot down a couple of comments answering questions about its collage, such as "What does a particular image or group of pictures signify to them with respect to the story?" and "What does the collage reflect about different parts of the story or book?" Again, emphasize that there are no right or wrong answers. These presentations are not graded. Stress the fact that you are looking for creative responses to the reading. After all, this is language arts.

Undoubtedly, a few students become preoccupied with the stressful fact that they have to make an oral presentation already on the fourth day of class, when they are still anxious about their relationships with their classmates and teacher. Some students are relieved to know that they get to present in groups. Remind them that they can refer in their presentations to the ideas that they have already jotted down on their index cards. Even just a few key words or phrases should help each student follow through with her or his part of the presentation.

Day Four: Students Individually Convey Their Group Thoughts

Provide ten or fifteen minutes at the beginning of the period for groups to meet briefly to determine their intragroup speaking order and to recall what each member is going to say on behalf of the group. Ask a member of each group to write the speaking order on the class board so that each one can see when to present to the rest of the class.

To aid in smooth transitions between presentations, ask students to arrange the poster boards on the chalk or marker tray in the order of the presentations, but with posters facing away from the audience. When group members rise to share their collage, one of them can turn their board to face the audience. When the group finishes, the board turner should place their board behind all the others. If you have decided to have digitized presentations, have all files open so that students only have to toggle to open their files.

Whatever their final projects look like, you will be able to determine fairly quickly where they are in terms of reading standards as occur in most curricula, such as their ability to "Analyze how and why individuals, events, and ideas develop and interact over the course of a text"[6] as well as what this group of students' ease is in using the literary terms they will be expected to know by the end of the school year.

If the room has space, invite the class members to sit on the floor close to the collages so that students can see more of the details on the collage, as individual pictures are too small for most to see clearly if they all remain in their seats. For now, smaller-than-optimal collage details are acceptable since the purpose of making these posters is primarily to provide opportunities for students to work together and for you to get to know more about them, rather than to require polished speeches with equally professional-looking visual aids.

After the presentations, you can display the poster boards for a few weeks, giving group members more opportunities to examine other groups' posters up close. If the resources are available and the classroom is equipped, digitally photograph each collage and project the resulting images on a screen on day five or to show other classes who have a similar assignment. The digital photos also could be posted on your class website for families to view at home.

Day Five: Students Individually Compose Their Reflections

At the beginning of class, with the group posters in sight or projected onto the screen, ask the students to prepare to write a short reflection piece about

Figure 2.2. Daily Journal Writing Need Not be Graded

their experience in class during the first four days. While you take attendance and review your label notes about students—associating your notes with their faces—they can be writing their first journal entries for the course. They get to practice metacognition (think about their own thinking) in their responses to the collage-creating experience. Here are sample prompts.

- What did you have to consider about your story before creating a collage?
- How did you decide which picture worked better than others for your collage?
- Why did your group organize pictures and words a particular way?
- What would you have done differently if you had been working alone?
- Why do you think this is a useful activity to start the year?
- What did you learn about yourself as you worked on this collage?
- What did you discover about your reading skills while working on this collage?

Ask students to write neatly while assuring them that their personal reflections are not to be graded like exams or evaluated as though they were formal papers. Then collect and simply read the journals, thinking about what you learned as you observed them working together and as you read what they have written about the experience. These students' journal entries

BOX 2.2: PROJECT IT! USING WORD CLOUDS

Numerous websites create a word cloud or word collage based on words entered by a user. Ask each group to enter ten to fifteen words that describe the images in its picture collage. Then project the resulting word collages and compare each image collage for the respective groups. Which collages are more meaningful to each group? Why? Students soon see that the result is more than words and that interesting and revealing results occur when students create together.*

Wordle, http://www.wordle.net/ (accessed June 3, 2013).

are now baseline writing samples—not for grading, but for future comparisons along with additional samples forthcoming in students' own journals.

SCAVENGER HUNTING IN THE COURSE ANTHOLOGY

Most middle school students are oblivious to the range of resources in language arts anthologies. Some students are unaware that an anthology is a treasured collection of words, literary passages, similar to the idea of a collection of flowers.

As you explain the concept of anthology to your students, ask them to mentally store an anthology image in their minds by picturing a bouquet of a variety of beautiful, fragrant flowers. If you have access to fresh-cut flowers, bring in a vase full of different varieties and colors and label the vase "anthology." If not, simply project a lovely bouquet of familiar intermixed with exotic flowers. Meanwhile, ask students to prepare for a scavenger hunt inside their anthology. They are likely to look at you askance. That is simply curiosity and is exactly what you want to create.

Planning the Hunt for Pairs of Students

Some publishers may include a scavenger hunt handout with their textbook resources. If yours does not, you can easily prepare fifteen to twenty questions with clues to help students know where to find various elements—using the helpful journalistic method of asking the "five Ws and an H" (who, what, when, where, why, and how). You may be surprised at how much you learn yourself if this is your first time using this particular textbook. Here are helpful categories:

General Content

1. Who is the author or publisher (explain the difference)?
2. What does the title mean or suggest about the contents?
3. When was it published—and when were various pieces written?
4. Where is the table of contents? How is it organized?
5. Where is the index? How is it organized—and why?

Graphics and Graphic Design

1. What is on the cover? Does it make the book seem interesting? Inviting?
2. Is there an introduction? If so, what is in it? Are the introductory pages in roman or arabic numbers (iii or 3)?
3. What kinds of design elements or text features are included (subheadings, captions, lines, colors, text boxes, drawings, maps, photos)?
4. Is the artwork acknowledged? Ask students to find the name of the artist of a particularly interesting piece of artwork. (This information may be found in a separate index or is simply identified in a special font within the complete index to the anthology.)

Organization

1. How is the table of contents organized? Genre (category of artistic composition, similar to types of flowers, such as roses), theme, time, nation or country? Chronologically? Other?
2. Use the table of contents to find . . . an author who has a name beginning with the letter of one of the students' names. Is it a short story, a poem, or a play?
3. Use the index to find a short-story title that includes words beginning with letters of your first name and your partner's last name.
4. How is each literary work introduced? (Devise a question that sends the students to this reader aid.) Some anthologies include background information on the author, historical period, genre, or literary device featured in the particular story, poem, essay, or play.
5. Where in the book is information about authors of individual works or the editors of the anthology? (Send the students to a particular page to learn something unique about an author whose work you may teach later in the school year.)
6. Does the anthology have questions following the text of each literary work, after several related pieces, or at the end of a unit? Send students to one such page and ask them to list the kind of questions found there—such as facts or interpretative responses, maybe even connecting the literature to their own lives.

7. Some anthologies include vocabulary and grammar and links to useful websites. Does yours?

Supplementary Resources

1. If there is a glossary of literary terms, ask students to locate and read the definition of a term that may be new to them but that you plan to teach them during the year—For example, onomatopoeia, pantoum or limerick. Middle schools students like the unusual sounds of these words.
2. Does the anthology include vocabulary definitions? If so, ask students to find the definition of an interesting new word—maybe in a story they may soon read.
3. Or is vocabulary defined in footnotes or side notes? If so, devise a question that requires students to use this text feature.
4. Does the anthology include grammar or writing resources—why or why not? (Question: Why would the publisher put such resources in a book about literature instead of in a book about writing?)
5. Are there lists of suggested readings? Website links? Other resource references?

Of course, it is best to avoid pressing students into feedback about the various social, ethnic, and national groups represented in the book. No

BOX 2.3: SURVEY IT!

If you have an online blog or school website with a "polling" feature, create a list of the readings and ask students to vote for their top choice to read first. When you present the results to the class, ask students what seemed appealing to them about the top choices. Was it the title? Familiarity with the author? Length of the piece? Peer influence? Then explain that anthology entries are not popularity contests as much as hard, imperfect decisions that publishers and educators make about the educational as well as artistic value of a work.

anthology is completely diverse or thoroughly unbiased. Focus on the resources available in your anthology rather than on its deficits.

Time to go hunting. The student pairs now can complete the hunt by exploring the book for answers to the questions and then listing three to four literary works they hope the class is to study during the year. Circulate, listen, and learn. As you hear them talking about what they notice in the book and hear the stories they mention, you begin to get a sense of what interests them. When possible, modify your lessons to include works that seem to draw their attention. Each pair of students also could be asked to come up with a couple of challenging scavenger questions to stump the panel of other classmates once the preliminary worksheet is completed.

If students take their textbooks home, assign the last question as homework. This gives individual students a reason to review the book on their own and possibly introduce the book to parents or guardians. You might even ask the students to show their book to other family members and ask them which pieces of literature they have read or would like to read.

It would be worthwhile to conclude this scavenger hunt by assigning a one-page summary or reflection. Ask students to write a letter to their parents or guardians explaining what they have learned about their textbook during this exploration. You can then save this ungraded, one-draft writing as a preliminary assessment demonstrating the writing skills the students have at the start of the school year, keeping in mind that they all probably would do better if there were time to revise. Just from reading these one-pagers you will have a sense of students' organization skills, quickly accessed vocabulary, sentence structure, and use of MUGS (mechanics, usage, grammar, and spelling).

Finally, for each of your classes, end the first week of meetings by reviewing some of your personal objectives for the school year that may include

- to increase their appreciation, understanding, and enjoyment of reading
- to improve their understanding and use of the writing process
- to help them become more at ease when speaking in front of a group
- to help them increase their knowledge and use of sophisticated vocabulary
- to review and extend their knowledge of correct grammar
- to discover more ways that technology can help them learn

CONCLUSION

Keep in mind that the first week of class needs to be both task oriented and relational. While introducing students to the work, be sure to help them get introduced to one another and to you. Middle school students are some of the most creative people on the planet. Half of your job as teacher is to keep from squelching their bubbling personalities and literary imaginations. They love using language to express themselves. They especially enjoy telling stories. They probably have been telling their families stories about you and your class. Now you get to tell them about how written language works. That is the focus of the chapters that follow.

NOTES

1. Oscar Hammerstein, "Getting to Know You," quotation from Sound Track Lyrics, http://www.stlyrics.com/lyrics/thekingandi/gettingtoknowyou.htm (accessed April 2, 2012).

2. "English Language Arts Standards » Anchor Standards » College and Career Readiness Anchor Standards for Language," Common Core State Standards Initiative, http://www.corestandards.org/the-standards/english-language-arts-standards/anchor-standards-6-12/college-and-career-readiness-anchor-standards-for-language/ (accessed March 15, 2012).

3. For more on observation strategies and record keeping, see "Royce Sadler: Conversations about the Learning Record," *Learning Record Online* March 31, 2004, http://www.learningrecord.org/sadler.html (accessed April 3, 2012).

4. Bruce W. Tuckman, "Developmental Sequence in Small Groups," *Psychological Bulletin* 63, no. 6 (1965): 384–89, available at http://aneesha.ceit.uq.edu.au/drupal/sites/default/files/Tuckman%201965.pdf (accessed March 16, 2012).

5. Mark Twain, *Huckleberry Finn*, quotation from Literature.org, http://www.literature.org/authors/twain-mark/huckleberry/chapter-23.html.

6. "English Language Arts Standards » Anchor Standards » College and Career Readiness Anchor Standards for Reading," Common Core State Standards Initiative, http://www.corestandards.org/ELA-Literacy/CCRA/R (accessed July 5, 2013).

3

WRITING TO LEARN ACROSS THE CONTENT AREAS

Writing in math gives me a window into my students' thoughts that I don't normally get when they just compute problems. It shows me their roadblocks, and it also gives me, as a teacher, a road map.

—Maggie Johnson[1]

Writing is a means of expressing, exploring, and expanding our understanding. Those who teach in content areas other than English can tap into this powerful neurological experience to enhance the learning of both the teacher about the students and the students about their subject. According to research conducted during my pursuit of a master of arts degree, I learned how important it is to have students write about their experiences learning. "Unless students write about what they are learning in their own words, they will experience 80 percent loss of retention within three weeks."[2]

This amazing research compels teachers in all content areas to consider ways to incorporate a range of writing opportunities in their lessons. As you mull over whether this practice is worthwhile, please know that writing in and of itself is a heuristic, a way of knowing. As students search for words to express themselves, they are thinking about what they know and what they are able to do. And, to be beneficial, the teacher does not have to collect, read, or grade writing assigned for this purpose. It can be used as preparation for talking about newly taught concepts and reflecting on ones being practiced. On the other hand, for quizzes and tests, when teachers substitute questions requiring students to explain how to solve problems, the writing is graded for clarity and accuracy.

The benefit of assigning writing to learn is twofold: expressive or exploratory writing activities increase the confidence and competence of students taking the course. This kind of writing also provides an ongoing evaluation tool to help the teacher assess what students are learning without having to give stressful tests or tedious grading assignments.

The second value of assigning writing to learn is to bring your teaching in line with the current curricula goals, such as the Common Core State Standards that call for literacy—both reading and writing—across the content areas. As you incorporate these strategies, you soon see how writing can help meet the standards requiring students to show they understand the various processes in solving math problems, as described in the "Standard for Mathematical Practices" section of the CCSS[3] and the standard in the CCSS that calls for students to "write routinely over extended time frames (time for research, reflection, and revision) and shorter time frames (a single sitting or a day or two) for a range of tasks, purposes, and audiences."[4]

Reading what students write can help you to diagnose more quickly specific deficiencies and to measure understanding of the various content-specific concepts and their applications. This kind of writing stimulates both metacognition and verbalization—both talking and writing—and encourages shared inquiry as your students discuss and question their peers in collaborative and cooperative learning-group activities.

SHOWING WRITING IS REVEALING

When and where should students do this kind of writing? They should write several times a week in their paper or digital journals. In addition to their traditional class notes, students can

- record specific concepts they believe they learned after a specific in-class presentation or homework assignment;

- react to what they are learning or what they are assigned but not learning;
- explain how to perform specific procedures as in math or science; and
- explain how to read graphs, charts, and maps in history and social science.

Most curricula ask teachers to assess student learning formatively and summatively. This kind of writing can validate what students know and are able to do throughout the course.

What do these kinds of assignments look like? Peruse and adapt from the student samples in my booklet, "Writing to Learn in Math: Collaboration/ Cooperation—Learning Pairs and Groups,"[5] written for teachers interested in implementing this kind of writing to learn.

Expressive writing is students putting into words what they think they are learning and is very much like speech. It is usually uncensored for grammatical correctness and is usually intended to communicate with the writer, not the teacher or other reader. The students put into their own words their understanding of what is going on in the math or science problem and how they feel about what they are learning.

10/28
Dear Journal:
My first C!! Boy did I bomb this baby! My mistakes are mostly careless and since I didn't get time to check it, they couldn't be corrected. Some of the word problems were misinterrupted and so my answers weren't checked out. The exponent mistakes were just stupid!
EM

Exploratory writing helps them figure out how to solve certain procedures.

9/28
$3(x5) = 1/5(10x25)$ You should distribute 3 and 1/5 to the numbers. Then you would get the ex's to the left and the 3's to the right. Then you should simplify and solve. Ones I can't do are $c-2y=b$. I cannot understand this! Which variable do you solve? How could you do it? I don't UNDERSTAND!!!! I was trying to solve for yb instead of just solving. I missed what the book said.
JL

Exploratory writing can be assigned in any course—science, math, history and social sciences, art, music, even physical education—to have students show they know the correct way to cite resources in the school-required format. So much better to discover this early, before that ream of research papers comes in for grading.

Discovery writing is done when students analyze and figure what they know about the various assignments they are given. In assignments that call for this kind of writing, students look carefully at the kind of errors they made on specific assignments and then write what they discovered about their own work.

10/28

Dear Journal. I could of done better on the test. I got two wrong on the exponents which I knew how to do but forgot. I made one silly error on Sci. Not (Scientific Notation) by forgetting it was a negative (insert 10 (-4 exponent). One part I did not know the difference between of % and more than % and on the chemical prop I set it up right but worked it out wrong. And I messed up on the age problems. Now I know to stick with the first answer.

BA

You probably notice that the student entries include elements of multiple kinds of writing: expressive, exploratory, and discovery. This will be true of the writing to learn that your students do, too. To be most useful, assign this kind of writing early in the course, and continue doing so on a regular basis. Part of the value of expressive/exploratory/discovery writing is the fluency that develops once students are used to it. They begin to look forward to the opportunity to unravel their thoughts and to ask focused questions of clarification of you and their peers.

CLARIFYING TEACHING AND FOCUSING STUDY

Consider adapting from this series of activities to maximize this learning experience of your students. Your writing test questions that require students to explain how to solve problems can elicit strong evidence of their understanding in more ways than simply showing work in numbers reveals. You find yourself preparing to teach each unit with more care and clarity as you think about what you will ask students to know well enough to write at the beginning, middle, and end of the unit. Both you and your young students begin approaching learning in more positive ways when writing regularly is part of the course.

Students respond to these kinds of writing-to-learn assignments by paying closer attention to their textbook reading and in-class activities because they know they will be asked to articulate their understanding in their own words. Students begin to

- focus on their assignments and performance;
- analyze reasons for their success or failure in the subject;
- reflect on what they read in their text and experience in class;
- verbalize more comfortably in written and oral form with you and their classmates; and
- collaborate more confidently because they already have begun thinking and finding words to express themselves more precisely.

Of course, none of these is isolated. A student may focus and analyze during a reflection and verbalize during a collaborative situation. Your goal as the teacher is to understand and implement writing and speaking assignments that increase learning for you all.

TALKING TEACHES

Combining writing activities with talking in collaborative pairs, triads, and small-group discussions further enhances the learning experience. Once students have written their thoughts about what they are learning or not learning, they have the words to talk about it with peer partners and in whole-class discussion. As you circulate among the pairs, observing, listening, and peeking over their shoulders at what the students have written, you can quickly determine what students know or still find confusing and then adjust the lesson to meet the current state of their learning, comfort, or discomfort.

Adding Paired Sharing

You can vary the kind of writing you assign based on the lessons you are teaching. For example, if students have had a particularly challenging home-work assignment, you may begin the next class by assigning an "admit slip" on which students write a sentence or two admitting or acknowledging what proved difficult for them to understand. Ask them to be specific and refer to the problem, the section, or the page of the document or text they found challenging. Then ask students to pull their desks or chairs together so that they can work in pairs, using their "six-inch voices" to discuss the question or problem, and try to come up with a response using class notes or their textbooks.

Another time, while presenting a particularly complex lesson, stop and ask students to write summary sentences that could be

- a definition of a concept;
- a summary of what they have learned so far; or
- a question they have about what has been presented or viewed.

Allow a couple of minutes for a few students to read aloud what they have written. These readings can reinforce the value of writing while revealing whether or not the students are grasping the ideas being presented. Frequently, students will phrase the definition in words more familiar to their classmates and more easily comprehensible than those in the formal definition with academic or content-specific vocabulary you may have used.

At another time, it may be valuable to have students practice answering classmates' questions themselves. Collect the slips and redistribute them to students on the opposite side of the room. Give the students a minute or two to read the slips to see whether they can resolve the issue themselves. It may take a few times of working this way for students to stay focused on task.

Resist the temptation to berate the students for getting off task. It may take a couple of weeks for them to be comfortable with this kind of vulnerability. As you nurture and model trust in them, the students soon will follow your lead. When they become restless with this uncertainty, gently call attention to the front and go on with the lesson of the day, using the admit or summary slips to guide your instruction for the remainder of the period.

The next day, allot just a little less time for paired talking, and then on subsequent days extend the time in half-minute increments until you reach five to six minutes. Circulating among the pairs helps maintain order and provide opportunities to listen, observe, and redirect attention as necessary. Students will come to value this time to figure out answers and clarify their thinking.

The exit slip can be used in a similar way. Five minutes before the end of the period, distribute small pieces of paper and have students write what has been taught that period and what they have learned. If they are working on computers, have them send you a message. Again, content, not form, is important in these notes. Merely collect these anonymous notes as students leave the classroom. Reading them later will give you a better idea of which concepts the students have grasped and which ones need further clarification before proceeding to new material.

All three—the admit, summary, and exit slips—are effective ways for both student and teacher to learn. If the students can find the words to write fairly clearly what they know, they know they know; if they can't, they know that, too, and can either ask for help or study themselves. They do not have to wait until a graded assignment to learn what they know. This kind of writing helps tell who knows what, now.

ANALYZING IS DIFFICULT BUT VALUABLE WRITING

After a test, you could ask students to analyze that experience by responding to such prompts as

- What question or kind of problem was most difficult for you that you are proud you could answer?
- What question or kind of problem could you not solve?
- Can you describe the errors or kind of errors you made most?

Writing the Steps

This comforting activity is a version of the summary sentence and should work well in a math, science, physical education, music, or ceramics art class. After explaining a new procedure for an important process in your class, have students write in order, in their own words, the steps for completing that task. It could be solving a math problem, setting up a lab, calling a foul, tuning an instrument, or preparing a piece of clay before throwing it on the wheel.

Ask the students to turn and talk to a partner, group, or class about the steps they wrote. As the steps are read, all can listen to these versions and all can hear various ways of stating the procedure. When necessary, clarify any cloudiness or confusion. Resist the temptation to force students to use formal language if what they have written is correct.

Somehow, this can be a reassuring exercise for the class. All can hear how classmates are not thinking and recognize that they are not alone in getting or not getting the new material. At the same time, you can monitor and adjust teaching and time as needed. By writing the steps, the students can focus and reflect, figure out, and clarify their thinking under your guidance, thus advancing the learning for more students in less time.

CONCLUSION

Combining writing-to-learn activities with collaborative talking is an efficient way to use class time. Once students have written responses in their journals and turned and talked with their partners, they often can resolve problems on their own. This concurrent learning is less time consuming than your answering each of their questions one by one. As you circulate among them, listening and observing, you learn right away what needs more instruction and time for practice or what is clearly understood and therefore can be tested with confidence.

So if you are among those who are reluctant to add writing to learn to classroom practices, you can relax. Unless the question is part of a test, this is ungraded writing. It is designed for you and your students to process what is taught and being learned. Reading what students write provides a window into their understanding, which, as a no-stress formative assessment, effectively guides you in future lesson planning. Being asked to write helps students know what they know and how to zone in on what they do not know . . . yet.

NOTES

1. Vicki Urquhart, *Using Writing in Math to Deepen Student Learning* (Denver: Mid-continent Research for Education and Learning, 2009), available at McREL. org, http://www.mcrel.org/~/media/Files/McREL/Homepage/Products/01_99/ prod19_Writing_in_math.ashx (accessed April 17, 2013).

2. Jane McGill and Toni Miller, "Using Writing to Improve Learning in the Classroom" (Chula Vista, CA: Sweetwater High School District, 1989).

3. "Standards for Mathematical Practice: Introduction," Common Core State Standards Initiative, http://www.corestandards.org/Math/Content/8/introduction (accessed April 16, 2013).

4. "English Language Arts Standards » College and Career Readiness Anchor Standards for Writing » 10," Common Core State Standards Initiative, http://www. corestandards.org/ELA-Literacy/CCRA/W/10 (accessed July 5, 2013).

5. Anna J. Small Roseboro, "Writing and Learning Groups in Math" (unpublished master's thesis for University of California, San Diego, 1989).

4

EXPLORING TRADITIONAL AND CONTEMPORARY GRAMMARS

It is no longer an advantage to speak English, but a requirement!
Just speaking English isn't so impressive anymore—unless you
speak it really well.

—Heather Hansen[1]

Language is a glorious art, a phenomenal means of communication, and linguistic diversity is a gift to humankind. At the same time, there are always more formal, mainstream versions of languages that symbolize what it means to be educated. In so many areas of life, skillful use of languages leads to success in the workplace and in society in general. This chapter explores reasons for incorporating discussions of culturally sensitive grammar and writing into the study of writing and speaking.

In a diverse world full of different idiolects and dialects, students increasingly need to know how languages work so that they can "code switch" in personal, professional, and public life.[2] Fiction is one of the best ways to introduce students to Standard English usage so that they become more fluent in "good grammar," even as they become more amenable to other grammatical styles.

So think about the ideas in the chapter as you plan lessons to help raise awareness of grammar—that set of rules that govern the structure of oral and written speech—and design activities to help your students understand and value knowing when to use Standard English grammar to achieve academic and professional success. At the same time, you will be helping them achieve one of the Common Core anchor standards for language, which state that students should be able to "adapt speech to a variety of contexts and communicative tasks, demonstrating command of formal English when indicated or appropriate."[3]

CHOOSING THE RIGHT GRAMMAR

Few students and not all teachers use perfect grammar, but both groups recognize when others use it incorrectly. Even though you and your students may come from backgrounds with linguistic variations, students generally expect learned prose to sound the same—formal and correct—and see school as a place for more elevated language, not necessarily as it is in the real world as they know it outside of the classroom.

For those students who did not grow up learning Standard English, school is a place where this different language is spoken, read, and written. This reality, then, may be a good a reason to teach English dialects in the same way language teachers teach English speakers to learn languages such as Arabic, French, or Spanish. In order to encourage speaking the specific language, some instructors tell students that once they cross the threshold of the classroom, they are to communicate only in the language they are learning. This is pretty drastic for an English language arts class but worth considering in a modified form.

Of course, when middle school students talk among themselves in small groups, there is no need to stop them from speaking their dialects, but in full class discussion, urge them to code switch or code blend and incorporate as much Standard English as possible. This practice can serve them well outside the classroom when they find themselves in situations where it is personally or professionally advantageous for them to speak Standard English.

Your young teenagers become amenable to grammar lessons when they learn that you are teaching them a form of speaking and writing that is useful to them, not only in school but also in the broader community of college, career, business, and civic life. True, Standard English is not all there is to the real world. Still, it is essential for students of all linguistic backgrounds to learn when, where, why, and how to switch among linguistic variations. The real issue is not who speaks or writes "properly," but instead how well someone can communicate effectively. Because middle school students can understand this, you do not need to avoid the issues of language, culture, power, and privilege. Use the issues as teaching topics that hit home for many students, even for those from superficially homogeneous communities.

During their study of literature, students discover that some successful authors break the rules of Standard English.

Some students are shocked that a Mark Twain or a Toni Cade Bambara, author of "Blues Ain't No Mockingbird," do not seem to write "good grammar." You can show how authors, too, employ code switching or code mixing in order to lend legitimacy to characters that would seem phony if they used only Standard English grammar.

Except perhaps in semifictional autobiography, writing fiction requires character-building code switching. Authors of young adult fiction who write well in other dialects include Rudolfo Anaya, Toni Cade Bambara, Sharon Draper, Rosalinda Hernandez, Zora Neale Hurston, Barry Milliken, Walter Dean Myers, Alberto Alvara Rios, Juanita Sanchez, Gary D. Schmidt, Amy

Figure 4.1. Middle School Students Plan to be Successful

Tan, Wing Tek, and Mark Twain. So yes, teaching fiction is a propitious time to teach about both Standard English and the use of the dialects students may speak, hear, or read in their literature.

Showing your students ways that published authors use dialect to create valid and interesting stories is another reason to end a short-fiction unit in which you can ask students to write their own stories. When they focus on their own writing while also thinking about others' prose, your normally impatient students become more conscientious about revising their own work. They realize that they have to think about their characters and readers and especially about communicating with the reader as authentically and respectfully as possible. These young writers then realize they must get it right on behalf of the people they are writing about, not just for themselves.

Some students, inspired by fiction, decide to incorporate dialect or syntax that reflects the oral language of a specific ethnic group or geographical region. If other authors can do it, they reason, why can't they? Why shouldn't they at least try? If it is appropriate for their story, by all means give them the freedom to try it. But your aspiring writers need to know that it is easy to offend those for whom a dialect is their own. The easiest place to start is writing within one's own dialect. Even then, here is the key: students need to understand that when they write in their own voice—the voice of the linguistic group with which they identify—they are making a choice with consequences for them as well as their readers.

Fortunately, many students are already learning some code switching by writing for digital media. They learn "texting" on a cell phone or tweeting online. They learn about writing blogs, somewhat similar to journaling. Some write "fan fiction" on popular websites, trying to imitate their favorite writers. In other words, middle school students tend to be published code switchers already, even if they do not think of Facebook, MySpace, or Twitter and other social networking websites as "publications" with their own styles and rules. Moreover, whether they like it or not, students realize others are interpreting and evaluating what and how they write.

PRACTICING STANDARD ENGLISH

If the students you teach speak different dialects of English, you could set up a schedule for them to practice Standard English. In the first semester of the

BOX 4.1: SEND IT! VIDEO JOURNALING

If you have access to a class-based listserv for your students, try this simple assignment about code switching and linguistic variations. Send the students a one-sentence message for translation into "phone texting" or online messaging. Select the sentence from one of the readings the class has not yet read—and don't tell the students in advance where the sentence came from.

Then copy and paste in a list the students' text "translations" on a sheet of paper or a projection slide to show to the class. Discuss two things: (1) the variations (idiolects) in students' translations, and (2) the difference in coding by the original author and the students. Why don't most novels use texting? When would it be appropriate—such as for dialogue by a specific character who texts? Finally, read to the students the full paragraph from the original author's work. Question: What does each version communicate about the writer and his or her opinion of the reader?

school year, after you have introduced the idea of dialects and reasons to be fluent in Standard English, you could set aside one day a week for speaking only in Standard English once the students cross the threshold into your classroom.

In order to avoid silencing reluctant students and discouraging shy ones from speaking at all, commend those in the class for their efforts rather than correcting each one who makes an error. The second semester, you could add a second day a week. If students are amenable, during the final quarter or marking period of the school year, add a third day. As students become more fluent in reading and writing Standard English in the classroom, they gain more competence and confidently use it when the need arises outside of the classroom.

Occasionally, for practice in journal writing, you could require them to use specific Standard English grammatical structures and more of the sophisticated vocabulary they encounter reading the fiction and nonfiction you assign. There is no need to grade these practice entries; simply read and comment on their entries. In all cases, do what you can to ensure that students' own languages and dialects are never disparaged.

SELECTING THE RIGHT TEXTBOOK

Linguistic codes get even more complicated and potentially political in education when it comes to textbooks. Who gets to dictate language, and presumably culture, by mandating textbooks? Many school districts and school sites select their own grammar books, and some even choose literary texts that include grammar sections.

Textbooks are big business, so publishers pitch their books to school boards, state associations, individual administrators, and teachers. Their marketing includes all kinds of special features and selling points, including access to multimedia resources such as password-protected websites with both downloadable resource materials and links to other publicly available, but sometimes difficult to discover, resources.

In other words, there are many different language arts texts from the major publishing houses, and experienced educators are not likely to argue adamantly for the use of one book over another. Depending on the teacher, the parents, the community, the school, the state, or Common Core State Standards for English Language Arts and the like, each textbook has its own advantages and disadvantages. If you have a choice, select a textbook with the most accessible explanations and examples so that your particular students can learn both how language works and how to use language effectively and fittingly in a diverse world.

Introducing the Grammar Text

If your textbook can help you accomplish this goal, it is a viable teaching tool. But do not assume that students understand the purpose of the text or that the text itself is adequate to engage students steeped in multimedia experience when you first distribute the book to students. Address the first issue by showing them how the book is organized, what it contains, and what it's for—a resource and a guide.

Few students appreciate or use their textbooks fully unless someone has taken time to teach them how to do so, as you probably noticed if you had your students conduct a scavenger hunt within that text as described in chapter 2 of this book. If appropriate, adapt that hunt to this grammar text. You may be surprised how much you learn as you design such an adventure for your students.

Address the second issue by considering not only the insights and activities in this book but also the digital resources provided by the publisher. You are the professional in the classroom, the one who knows the students and their specific needs. Even if some of the resources are impractical or excessively time-intensive tools, you still might find a few student-engaging gems.

Honoring "la Différence"

Inevitably the issues of dialects in reading, writing, and discussion arise when teachers require that students use Standard English texts and require Standard English–based assignments. Sometimes parents get the impression that teachers disrespect students' native tongues or linguistic variations— even students' multilinguistic competence.

Who says that Standard English is more academic, more worthy of being taught? Invite your students to ask adults they know about the experiences they have had with language. Often these stories substantiate your claims

BOX 4.2: SEARCH IT! VIDEO JOURNALING

If you have not already done so, spend some time exploring the world of online publishing. Facebook, MySpace, and Xanga include natural writing in students' own "young adult dialects." Fan fiction is a fascinating look into what young people care about and how they think good authors write. Visit fanfiction.net and its sister site, fictionpress. net (intended for pieces of writing that are about real people or original characters). You don't need to read specifically what your students are writing on these sites to discover what students are writing.

better than anything else. Consider reading and talking about the poem "The Phone Booth at the Corner" by Juan Delgado,[4] which relates such a situation. Since few students are familiar with phone booths, you may need to show them a picture of how one works.

Why speak Standard English? That is a good question. Consider what you experienced in your own college or postcollege education training. Recall your exposure to the scholarly lingo, the "educationese." The American aphorist Mason Cooley once said, "An academic dialect is perfected when its terms are hard to understand and refer only to one another."[5] That is what some parents and students think about what is being taught in the schools. The language can seem like "school lingo," especially when it comes to the study and use of grammar. But it should not be limited to in-school speaking and writing.

Proficiency in speaking and writing Standard English is the ticket to career advancement in many professions. For this reason, educators have the responsibility to help students acquire this language even while honoring students' heart or heritage languages, the language with which they are most comfortable and consider their own. By so doing, effective teachers model what it means to respect others' languages and cultures.

In the ancient world, this was the basis for hospitality—making room for the "stranger" who is different from us and our culture. You can teach and honor by respecting the students' ability to communicate effectively in their own codes. When you do this, you may realize that you also are a stranger. Why? Because one's standard grammar and mother tongue are different from the linguistic norms of others. By practicing linguistic hospitality, students and teachers learn what it is like for others to be strangers, and all come to recognize their own "strangeness."

SEEING AND HEARING THE VALUE OF STANDARD ENGLISH—A PERSONAL STORY

The occasion to demonstrate the value of speaking Standard English occurred when a friend invited me to present in classes at the Youth Tutoring Youth Program in Rochester, New York. This community project offered high school students an opportunity to learn the skills necessary to tutor elementary and middle school students in after-school programs. During the week prior to my visit, my friend, Nettie, sang my praises. She told students that I was an experienced teacher who also had had a successful sales career. Student expectations were high.

When I arrived, dressed rather casually, I quietly sidled into the classroom without saying a word until I was introduced. Then I began speaking in slang, using the street English vernacular similar to the dialect of that community. The students looked at each other askance, puzzled that my pre-established ethos (thanks to my friend!) did not match the image I conveyed in my attire, posture, and speech. As part of my monologue, I fumbled with my papers and blurted, "Oh darn it! I cain't find my notes." I fled the room as if to retrieve them from somewhere out in the hall.

The students erupted with comments to one another and with questions to my friend. "She don't sound like a teacher, do she?" "I thought you said this woman is educated!" "She don't look like it!" "Where'd you get her from?" "Teachers ain't supposed to sound like that!"

My friend let them talk for a few minutes. I stood outside the classroom door; quickly removed the vest that clashed with my blouse, straightened my skirt, and with briefcase and notes in hand, I reentered the room. This time,

Figure 4.2.   Diploma

I walked more erectly to the front of the room, addressed the class in Standard English, and then invited them to repeat their impressions of when they had first seen and heard me.

When asked why they were surprised, and even disappointed, in my appearance and speech, the students acknowledged the disconnection between their preconceptions and my presentation. They eventually admitted that, based on their teacher's description of my educational background and experience, they had expected me to speak "better" English. They realized and soon grasped the fact that just as they had made assumptions about me based on my clothing, grammar, and articulation, others could make the same assumptions about them. Point made.

The form of English that one knows and uses is important. The manner in which one speaks and writes Standard English makes a difference in the way one is perceived by others. These students had witnessed firsthand the practical value of code switching and were ready and open to practicing another way of speaking. Lesson learned.

BOX 4.3: RECORD IT! PICTURE IT! ILLUSTRATING CODE SWITCHING

Code switching is visual as well as aural and depicted as well as written and printed. One of the best ways to highlight each of the various code-switching grammars or media is to hold one medium constant while you vary the others. For instance:

1. Ask students to read silently a paragraph with vernacular dialogue from one of the text readings.
2. Play a recording of the same paragraph made by one of your friends who speaks that vernacular or dialect.
3. Show students a photo of the person who made the recording.

Along the way, stop after each step and ask the students who is "speaking"—what they think they know about the voice behind the text.

CONCLUSION

Language arts are about life and the human condition. Professionals like you in language arts education are called on to teach many grammars of code switching and code blending, using words and images in text, audio and verbal, print, and digital media. The job is not to promote particular cultures or languages over others but to make sure that students are competent in Standard English and develop the basic ability to move from nonstandard idiolect to standard and back or learning to blend the two when appropriate. You are called on to show the appreciation of your students' languages as well as the particular language arts skills you bring.

You do this because you recognize that knowing and understanding language is practical; language is an art as well as a skill, a means for all human beings to be able to understand and be understood, to serve others and be served by them. Language essentially is at the center of who we are as people, cultures, nations, ethnic groups, communities, religious groups, and the like.

Studying language as it is written and spoken helps students to understand communication and to practice it more ethically and effectively. You see, it is primarily through visual and verbal language that your students can begin to understand what separates people and what unifies them. Honoring linguistic abilities, then, is a major component of honoring those shared differences. Through the lessons you design, you show your students that all humans share this amazing ability to switch codes in the midst of the very differences that confuse and divide people.

As an educator, you can model respect, thus teaching your middle school students to honor differences. And when students question why a "great" author can break the rules while a student might be viewed as inept or is marked down for using the same nonstandard code, the answer is straightforward: students need to be able to switch from one to another linguistic variation depending on the setting. Most school writing is the setting for using Standard English.

NOTES

1. Heather Hansen, "Speak English Clearly and Grammatically, and Boost your Success!" Articles Base, http://www.articlesbase.com/communication-articles/

speak-english-clearly-and-grammatically-and-boost-your-success-195745.html (accessed 3 April 2012).

2. "Code-switching is the practice of moving between variations of languages in different contexts. Everyone who speaks has learned to code-switch depending on the situation and setting. In an educational context, code-switching is defined as the practice of switching between a primary and a secondary language or discourse." Heather Coffey, "Code-Switching," Learn NC website, UNC School of Education, http://www.learnnc.org/lp/pages/4558 (accessed April 3, 2012).

3. "English Language Arts Standards » Anchor Standards » College and Career Readiness Anchor Standards for Language," Common Core State Standards Initiative, http://www.corestandards.org/the-standards/english-language-arts-standards/anchor-standards-6-12/college-and-career-readiness-anchor-standards-for-language/ (accessed March 15, 2012).

4. Juan Delgado, "The Phone Booth at the Corner," in *Braided Lives: An Anthology of Multicultural American Writing*, ed. Minnesota Humanities Commission (Bloomington: Minnesota Council of Teachers of English, 1991).

5. Mason Cooley quotation from Brainy Quotes, http://www.brainyquote.com/quotes/quotes/m/masoncoole396165.html (accessed March 28, 2012).

5

TELLING IT LIKE IT IS

Inviting Informative Writing

People are usually more convinced by reasons they discovered themselves than by those found out by others.

—Blaise Pascal[1]

Writing is a personal way to express oneself. While purpose determines the mode one uses, the arrangement, length, style, and vocabulary one uses remain the choice of the author. This fact creates a dilemma for teachers who are charged to teach their students specific ways to write and may be obligated to test students on their ability to write in several different modes.

Unless teachers plan carefully, this predicament could reduce the time they allot for students to choose the most effective ways of communicating to achieve their personal purposes. This chapter describes ways to manage this quandary with suggestions for teaching the basics and then freeing students to write for personal purposes. As students see how effective writing can be, they are more inclined to work hard and develop their own skills.

In the classroom, it sometimes is easy to lose sight of the ultimate goal of education—to help students acquire knowledge and develop the range of skills needed to live self-sufficient, productive lives in a pluralistic society. However, as teachers work backwards, accepting that goal and working out lessons to help reach that goal, these educators learn to stay on track without becoming rigidly shortsighted.

So what does this have to do with teaching students how to write? It means remembering that our classroom is a training ground where we, like athletic coaches, introduce new information, demonstrate skills, schedule opportunities for students to learn and practice those skills, but ultimately, when the game begins, trust our young adolescents to choose what works in the heat of the game—when they want to express themselves in writing.

The Common Core English Language Arts Anchor Standards for Writing[2] as well as those used in your school setting require teachers to present a range of strategies for prewriting, revision, editing, and publishing that have proved to be effective for different kinds of writing and for different purposes. Successful educators somehow learn to do this without insisting that every student execute each step in the same way for every assignment. You know from your own schooling, college training, and work in the classroom that there probably are as many different configurations for prewriting, drafting, and revising as there are years you have been on this earth!

None works well for every writer every time. Ask the zillion published authors out there. So how does one teach in light of this reality? Make plans guided by the curriculum standards and remain flexible. Ideas here can help you plot a course for this part of your school-year voyage. No need to worry. You can navigate the tricky waters without fearing Scylla and Charybdis, those rocks and whirlpools that could distract you from teaching writing effectively.

LEARNING FROM A STUDENT—A PERSONAL STORY

After weeks of instruction, I just knew my young writers were ready to move on to the next step: applying what they'd learned about the writing process in an on-demand, timed setting. I'd taught them well. They'd responded enthusiastically. Now, I thought, is their time to shine and my time to . . . gloat! Not.

They arrive to see an engaging prompt on the board and the start and stop times written prominently as a reminder to pace themselves. Now, to commence the show. Students pull out pens, sheets of lined paper, and a piece of scratch paper on which to create their prewrites. No more questions? They get started. I stroll around the room, observing their writing, nodding as I notice that nearly every option for prewriting appears among the papers I can see. Good!

Then I spot one girl across the room gazing off into space. "Hmm. Why isn't she writing?" Carefully, so as not to alarm anyone, I quickly make my way over to her desk and peer around her shoulder. I glower in disbelief. Her paper is blank . . . nothing there . . . no list, no diagram, no drawing . . . nothing at nearly fifteen minutes into the period! How is she going to finish in time?

I lean down and whisper, "What's the holdup? When are you going to get started?"

She whispers back, "I'm thinking."

A little louder, but still keeping my voice low, I point and ask, "Can't you see the clock?"

"Yeah, I see it. I'm okay. I'm thinking."

"When are you going to start writing?"

"When I can see my paper."

"See your paper?" I quietly yell. She scowls, letting me know she has things under control and won't I just trust her and shut up and let her finish, for crying out loud, don't I see the clock?

I get the message, shrug my shoulders, purse my lips, and let it go, dooming her to her fate. She is going to be a disappointment. I certainly don't look forward to reading a paper not written the way I'd spent all this time teaching.

As you probably surmised, this student's paper was one of the better ones in the bunch. I was surprised, yes, and just a little disenchanted. I apparently hadn't been the one to teach her how to write so well in a timed setting. Who had?

Afterward, wanting to understand, I invited her in to talk about the paper. I asked how she organized her thoughts if she wasn't using any of the prewriting strategies I'd demonstrated so assiduously and seen her practice so enthusiastically. The young lady didn't appear the least bit reticent and freely acknowledged that she'd done all the exercises because they were fun, but they didn't really work that well for her. Is that so?

She explained to me that she produced better writing when she brainstormed, organized, and reorganized her thoughts in her head. She even visualized what her paper would look like. Then, she just wrote what she saw.

"Well! That's just great," I thought. "How am I going to grade a student's prewrite if I can't see it. Should I insist she do things the way I taught her, *just so I'd have something to grade? Even if what she produces is good without them?" Thanks a lot for this quandary!*

The young lady left. I sat, trying to sort out my thoughts. Then I recalled some of the research about multiple intelligences and the need for differentiating instruction. Students process information in different ways. Here was concrete evidence. While this student does not fall into the typical alternative categories that show up on the charts (auditory, kinesthetic, musical, and the like), hers definitely is a different style from those I have encountered before. I'll have to make some adjustments. What I learned from experience and reading apparently is not all there is to writing.

After that incident, I recognized the need for even more flexibility and differentiation in my teaching and in the options I offer for students to show what they know. More of my assignments began to include student choice within teacher controls guided but not constrained by curriculum demands and grade-level standards. Planning lessons, I conscientiously focused on what I have to assess and then, during instruction, striving to articulate for the students what I need to measure about their learning in order to confirm their level of understanding and degree of skill development. No, this is not the same as "teaching to the test." Instead, it simply means offering alterna-

Figure 5.1. Students Resort to Strateegies that Work Best for Them

tive assessments and letting students choose ways they can best show what they know. I urge you to do the same.

WRITING RIGHT—JUST THE RIGHT
MODE FOR THE OCCASION

The five-paragraph essay is one of many structures you may be expected to teach. It is a formula designed to encourage students to flesh out their writing by developing their position statements into meaty paragraphs. However, this prescribed mold does not work well for some students, and it is seldom seen in professional publications. So rather than adhere strictly to a formula that can stifle writing, teach it as an option, but do not require that every student write this way for every essay assigned. Assign your students to try each structure, and then let them choose which works better for them.

Alternatively, teach students the parts of an essay: introduction, body, and the conclusion, as well as the function, purpose, or responsibility of each of these parts. For some students, writing three paragraphs is sufficient for what they have to say and the way they can say it best. For others, four will suffice; other may need six or more paragraphs. In other words, be flexible about the number of paragraphs students are permitted to write. Insist, instead, that the final essay include the necessary parts.

Acting Out an Essay

How about a little kinesthetic activity to help students understand the structure of an essay? You could invite small groups of seven to ten students to demonstrate an essay that has the three requisite parts. Jock Mackenzie, author of *Essay Writing: Teaching the Basics from the Ground Up*, recommends instructing students to organize themselves into an essay with at least three groups—to represent the introduction, the body, and the conclusion.[3] This may take a little time, so help pace the steps using your timer.

For the first step, set your timer for five to seven minutes, depending on the number of students and the classroom space, and then step aside, listen, and watch how students decide who should stand where and why. When the buzzer rings, ask the students to freeze and look around. You could ask those in the introduction section to raise their hands; those in the section(s) for body paragraph(s) to raise their hands, and then those in the conclusion section to do the same.

What are you looking to see? Proportion. Are there fewer students in the introduction and conclusion sections? Next, direct the subgroups to move into separate corners of the room. Each group—introduction, body, and conclusion—is to come up with a gesture or body pose that would indicate the function of their part of the essay. Again, set the time for five to seven minutes, step aside, and observe and listen to what they do and say.

For example, the introduction group may arrange themselves into a triangle with each of the members gesturing forward with their pointer finger to indicate that the introduction shows the way the essay will go. One person may represent the thesis statement. The body group may arrange themselves into two or more smaller groups to indicate multiple paragraphs. Each subgroup may have one student representing the topic sentence. The conclusion group may stand and gesture "time-out" to indicate that the essay is coming to an end. This group may arrange itself in a triangle and point thumbs over shoulders to indicate that the conclusion may look back or point to what has already been developed in the body.

Finally, ask the students to demonstrate the need for transitions between sections and between sentences by reaching out and linking pinky fingers. Yes, they will giggle, but that's typical for middle school students. Then, call a freeze, a pause for silence. If you have a digital camera or cell phone, snap a photo before directing them to return to their seats. Close with a debriefing session reflecting on the choices they made and how their final tableau did, in fact, demonstrate the structure of an essay. In the lessons to come, remind them of this exercise and maybe point to the photo of them that you post on the bulletin board or upload into a slide you can project during class.

Choosing Topics for Writing

An effective way to get to know the travelers on a trip through the school year is to invite them to talk about themselves. This also is an efficient way to obtain baseline writing from your middle school students. You see, talking and writing about themselves removes the additional burden of showing what they know about an assigned topic, a piece of fiction or nonfiction writing they have read. Your student writers can pay attention to organization, sentence structure, and choice of language. You can wait until later in the year to see how well they can "Draw evidence from literary or informational texts to support analysis, reflection, and research," as set forth in many curriculum standards and mentioned in the Common Core State Standards for English Language Arts.[4]

Yes, some students are reluctant to write about personal matters in an unfamiliar classroom or uncomfortable setting. It may take weeks before the environment of your classroom feels safe. So consider assignments in which students can fictionalize details if they wish. One such assignment asks students to think about their futures, the value of education, and career planning. It is a human-interest story—about themselves or someone they know. While you know that the choices they make still will be revealing, the students experience the detachment that makes them feel more secure.

Consider the assignment in the box "Writing a Human-Interest Story about Yourself." It combines the two—opportunity to talk about themselves and to fictionalize a future event. It even has an option for conducting informal research as students consider the qualifications for certain awards. This

BOX 5.1: WRITING A HUMAN-INTEREST STORY ABOUT YOURSELF

With what prestigious award will you be honored in twenty-five years?

Paragraph 1—Who, what, when, where, why, and how about award ceremony

Paragraph 2—Education and career of winner (the student in twenty-five years)

Paragraph 3—Others who have won the award in the past

Paragraph 4—Ways this year's winner (the student) compares to former winners

Paragraph 5—When and where award will be given next year

After revising and editing your articles, add a recent photo of yourself.

human-interest story requires students to learn the qualifications for various awards and come to an understanding that awards are given for outstanding performance, contributions, and/or excellence in a career: community service, philanthropy, science, the arts, sports, and other areas. Your students may consider well-known Nobel Prizes in the various categories; the Oscars, Grammys, Tonys, and other awards for the arts; halls of fame for various sports, such as the Cy Young Award or MVP awards; rodeo, fishing, ballroom dancing; Miss America or Mr. Universe, or those lesser-known but coveted awards given in your hometown or state.

With minor editing, these articles will make fine additions to your class bulletin board, or class website or can be sent home in letters to families.

DISCOVERING PURPOSES AND ORGANIZATION PATTERNS

You have a required curriculum to follow, right? As general policy, introducing or reviewing specific modes of writing, letting students write about themselves, and giving students choices all sound good, but you still may not be sure where to start. Why not at the beginning with a couple of exploratory adventures?

Let your middle school students discover or review the elements found in different modes of writing to communicate. You may begin with brainstorming, asking students to list a range of reasons people would want to write in the first place. The list should include such purposes as

- to inform
- to explain
- to report
- to argue
- to persuade
- to entertain
- and more

Use the students' words at first to validate their contribution. You then can move along in a later lesson to use the more formal terms they may see later. It will be important for them to know the academic vocabulary to be successful in other educational settings, like those standardized or end-of-the-year exams many schools administer.

Setting Up the Discovery Expedition

Gather age-appropriate samples or mentor texts of different types of writing in your textbook and online. Look for writing on topics that interest the students you have or that introduces topics you plan to teach later in the school year. No need to leave out essays that are humorous. They sometimes are more accessible and memorable.

Organize the samples and subtly color code similar kinds of writing with a rainbow color to match the groups suggested below. It is okay to have duplicates as long as you have at least two of each mode you want students to consider at the time. Be prepared to distribute the papers randomly so that no two colors are at the same table or given to students seated side by side. Resist the temptation to rush the process by giving students clues ahead of time. Let them discover by talking with partners or in small groups.

Create slides with the step-by-step instructions so that those who may be not paying close attention can glance up, confirm they heard you correctly, and get back to work. Usually, one slide per step will suffice. You can advance the slides as the class completes each step. Have your timer ready.

Grouping Homogeneously and Heterogeneously

How about using a jigsaw-style grouping? In this case, students begin in homogeneous, single-topic groups—all looking at samples of the same kind of writing—and then reassemble in heterogeneous, blended groups with at least one member from each original group in the new configuration. For example, set up color-name teams: red, orange, yellow, green, blue, and purple, with each group looking at a couple of samples of a single kind of writing.

Rather than have students talking together at first, consider a version of the think, pair, share option. First, let students read the sample(s) on their own. Set the timer for about three minutes for each step. It is okay if students do not finish reading the entire essay each time. They are doing preliminary investigation. You can have the entire list of types projected.

- Hand out colored pencils and ask students to read silently the first sample they have and to mark anything they notice that may be a clue to the kind of essay they have.
- Exchange pencils for a new color. Read the same or a second sample, this time marking what they recognize in terms of text structure and organization.
- Exchange pencils, once more, getting a third color. This time, read and mark in the left margin symbols to indicate the beginning, middle, and end of one of the sample essays. Students may need four to five minutes for this task.
  - a triangle pointing down next to the beginning section
  - a rectangle where the middle or body begins
  - a triangle pointing up to mark the start of the ending section
- Finally, ask students to write what they think is the purpose of their sample essay: to inform, explain, compare, argue, persuade, entertain, or whatever.

During this initial ten to twelve minutes that students are working independently, remember to circulate among them, paying attention to which students get right to work. Who seems to be puzzled and needs you to re-explain what they should be doing? Your physical proximity helps these young investigators stay focused and to ask questions without attracting embarrassing attention from their peers. Remember to advance your slides, showing what students should be doing for each reading. As time allows, write some anecdotal notes about what you observe regarding specific students and the class as a whole.

- After ten minutes or so working independently, move them into their color teams, and let them work together for ten to fifteen minutes. Change to the slide showing the color teams and names of students in each one. Set the timer for ten minutes.
- Now, ask students in their color groups to look carefully at their samples, discuss what they have marked as they paid attention to the features: their marks identifying content and structure based on their observations, how they labeled their writing sample.

- Ask the young sleuths to list characteristics of the writing they put into each of the categories.
- Urge students to try to reach consensus about the kind of essays they have. It is not necessary that they do; the discussion is what is important during this discovery expedition. Ask them to note the dominant structure used.
- When the timer rings, move students into their heterogeneous, rainbow teams. These rainbow groups, identified as A, B, C, D, E, and F should include a member from each of these first groups. The lettered groups now should include all five or six colors. Decide, based on your understanding of the class, whether you need to set up these groups or whether students can do this voluntarily. Set the timer again for ten or fifteen minutes for this next step.
- Again, be prepared for students to notice that essays often reflect multiple structures. Few pieces of writing reflect only a single structure. Writers sometimes use narratives and tell stories as they attempt to persuade their readers. Some writers write descriptive passages when their goal is simply to report.
- During these group meetings, each representative should explain to the others how their color-group members labeled their sample(s) and which organization and text-structure clues helped them decide the purpose of their sample essay. As before, listen and observe to help decide what they already know and what still needs clarification. Thankfully, students often are good teachers and save valuable time by explaining the key points in ways their peers understand.
- Finally, call the class together to merge their findings and to reflect on what they have discovered. How consistent are the findings? What characteristics do students notice in different samples?
- Another day, you may project two or three sample essays and invite students to come forward and point to different parts, signal words, and other characteristics of the essay. Encourage them to use academic language as much as possible.

Taking Time for Discovery

These discovery expeditions may take two or three days. No need to rush. If it makes sense to send the samples home for homework review, do so, and then, at the start of the next class meeting, reassemble the adventurers into rainbow groupings. If this kind of homework is unrealistic, begin the next class meeting in the single-color groups to review what they discovered, and after ten minutes or so, move the students into the rainbow groups.

After the independent, homogeneous, and heterogeneous looks at the samples, the students are likely to have detected some of the patterns of organizing that you taught them to watch for when they are reading to learn.

- description
- sequential order
- problem and solution
- compare and contrast
- cause and effect
- directions
- narrative, telling a story

You can try to keep it simple at first, but be prepared for students to notice that a writer may use one or more of these structures to fulfill any of the purposes for writing: to inform, to argue, to persuade, or to entertain. So you really are asking students to try to identify the purpose for the writing and to notice the use of text structures as well as the patterns of organization.

It also is likely your discerning students may find it difficult to distinguish between the samples you may have included that illustrate argument and those that exemplify persuasion. You may have to point out, after such a discussion, that argumentation simply presents opposing views and maybe adds reasons for believing one side or the other, while persuasion usually has a call for action or a plea to change one's belief or behavior.

TEACHING IS MORE THAN TELLING

Yes, this kind of teaching will take more time than your giving a simple lecture, showing a set of slides with definitions, or even labeling the writing samples and highlighting the different features for them, for in that case, you will have done the thinking. More effective teaching and long-term retention occurs when students seek out and find answers for themselves. You may use alternative methods of lesson delivery until the majority of the students can demonstrate they have learned. Effective teachers teach spirally, drawing earlier lessons into current ones so that students hear, see, and do enough to develop proficiency. In the long run, this could mean less reteaching on your part or that of next year's teachers. What students discover for themselves, they remember.

Even with increased implementation of teaching strategies that appeal to the multiple intelligences, consider building in reteaching, but with a twist. Plan multisensory lessons that require students to use physical as well as mental muscles, such as the earlier activity that asked for students to "act out an essay." Lessons like that have something for students to see, to hear, and to do. Note recommendations for each of these kinds of presentations as you continue reading this book.

Will you have to remind students of what they have seen, heard, and done? Of course. You very well may have some of these same students in

Figure 5.2.   Carefully Help Build a Firm Foundation

later grades and shake your head that they will have forgotten so much of what you thought you had taught so well. That probably is the main reason students have English classes the majority of the years they are in school— not only because language arts form the basis for learning in most content areas, but also because students forget or see no immediate use for what they are taught. And if they do not use it, they lose it. Teachers, therefore, continue to provide multiple opportunities for students to exercise their skills so that their thinking muscles do not atrophy, making it difficult to use these muscles when they need them.

BUILDING THE FOUNDATION FOR CONVINCING ARGUMENTATIVE ESSAYS

An effective road to teaching students to write argumentative essays is to take time to build on skills they already have learned. Most middle school students have been writing reports since third grade. It makes sense, then, to embark on this part of the trip that includes a direct writing instruction unit by having your middle school students practice writing to inform because that simply requires students to gather, organize, and present facts in much the same way as they wrote those elementary school science reports.

So begin there. "What," you could ask them, "are some of the reasons a person would want to write an informative essay?" Their answers are likely to include such things as to report, to explain, to describe, and to just share their feelings. You probably will have taught text structures already as they relate to reading; now is the time to have students demonstrate what they understand about text structures by employing those devices in their own writing. Post on your website, include on printed assignments, and display on your word wall some of the signal words used in published informative writing and that probably are listed in the textbook you are using.

You could have students practice by reporting or explaining something they already know about. Their topics could be drawn from literature, real life, or lessons students are learning in other content areas. In fact, inviting them to do so is an excellent way to reinforce what your students are learning elsewhere and to validate the work of colleagues in other departments and the value in English class for learning to write well.

Consider inviting your young companions on the road to use what they are learning in social studies and write about a historical event; explain how to accomplish a task—build something, cook, sail, fish, rope a steer, ride a horse, pop an "Ollie" on their skateboard, or strategize in a board or computer game. To reduce student temptation to copy from published work, begin the drafting in class. If students then decide to do research before the final draft is due, remind them to cite their sources. As always on a multidraft assignment, students should date, keep, and turn in all drafts, earliest on the bottom and latest on the top. If they are working online, save all drafts so that they and you can see how their writing evolves. Varied topics students choose make for more interesting, even informative, reading for you, too.

TAKING LOGICAL STEPS TO OTHER KINDS OF WRITING

The next logical step toward more complex writing would be to move on to the compare-and-contrast essays for which students gather, organize, and write about two different people, places, things, events, or ideas. To keep this concrete, again invite students to consider something they already know about. You could have them compare/contrast short stories they have read for your class and one they read on their own; a movie version versus a printed version; movies or television programs on the same topic; kinds of music; food; different computer games; clothes; animals; cars, bicycles, boats, fishing rods, or saddles. Let students choose.

Show your teen writers two basic ways of organizing compare-and-contrast essays and invite them to use the pattern that works better for them. They could write the body of their paragraphs in blocks or stripes.

- Blocks
  - Introduction of the features to be considered
  - All comparisons or ways alike
  - All contrasts or ways different
- Stripes
  - Feature of comparison 1—A and B together
  - Feature of comparison 2—A and B together
  - Feature of comparison 3—A and B together

Their task, of course, is to decide which features or elements to compare or contrast. A Venn diagram is an effective graphic organizer for brainstorming and arranging the facts and explanations about how the two subjects of the essay are alike or different or are both alike and different. For example, the students may look at two stories and compare the different ways the author employs literary devices: What point of view? Are there flashbacks? A dominant method of characterization? Use of realistic or stilted dialogue? Or, keeping it personal, students may compare and contrast themselves and the main character in a biographical work they read. See the end of the chapter for a list of autobiographies and memoirs you may assign your students to read and use as a springboard for writing.

For this basic compare-and-contrast essay, the students are simply reporting, but you may ask them to add an element of evaluation and write about which author the students think uses the elements more effectively, which product, song, or sport is better, or why fishing with one kind of rod is safer than another. Then the writers will be moving into argumentation, making a case for one story, product, or the other. While it is okay to use "I think" and "I believe" in earlier drafts, ask the students to remove these phrases from the final draft. Just state their observations and let those statements stand firmly on the reasons the student gives for taking those positions on the topic, thus encouraging students to develop confidence in their supported assertions. In the appendix is "Teacher Resource D," a book report option for writing a comparative essay.

CONNECTING WRITING TO CURRENT EVENTS

To keep the learning relevant, you could ask students to bring in samples from their reading that exemplify the kind of writing you are teaching. Several students come from homes where magazines and newspapers are regularly read. You can direct students to the school or neighborhood libraries where they can find samples in the magazines and newspapers to which most libraries subscribe. You could offer students minimum credit for bringing in articles, but no one should be penalized for not doing so. You know your school community and know to choose assignments that affirm the households from which your students come and resources that are readily available to them. Consider loaning them magazines from the stack you keep in your room.

If you know the members of the class do not have comparable access to resources, you could schedule a library visit or make this a triad or small-group project. In that case, one student can bring in the article(s); another mount them on white sheet(s) of paper and mark the parts; and another can speak for the group, describing the article(s)' contents, kind(s) of writing, and special features the group has noticed. Then plan a gallery walk for students to see and hear what their classmates have brought.

Half of the groups sit facing one direction with seats facing them. The other half would move from left to right and explain their sample to the group opposite them. Here is another situation where a timer is useful to keep the groups on track. In this activity, the value is in the students' talking and making decisions about how to present what they are learning about published writing.

A benefit of assigning students to bring in samples is the insight you gain into what interests your students. You can use that knowledge to design subsequent assignments. Depending on your school community, students may bring in articles from *ESPN* or *Sports Illustrated*, *People* or *Time* magazines, or *Car and Driver* or *Teen Vogue*. Some of your techie teens may regularly read zines online and print something from one of those sites. Remind those students to include the citation that includes the website name, title, authors, URL address, and date they access the article. Those who bring in printed articles should label them with source and date. Regularly remind them to be honorable young men and women who consistently give credit when they use the work of others.

It would be prudent to check all the articles brought in to assure they are appropriate for in-class discussion. These are, after all, middle school students who may not yet know exactly what is off-limits in your classroom. You can conduct an inspection subtly by having students bring in the article at least a day before you plan to have the students meet in triads to talk about them. Just discretely remove questionable articles and offer that group a magazine from which to choose another. No need to create a scene. Some students have different sets of standards, and no matter how shocked you may be, you can help them develop discernment without embarrassing them.

What makes this kind of student-generated assignment so rich is that students tend to read more when they get to choose what to contribute. Students usually want to make sure they understand the selection, just in case you ask them to talk about it! Some may want to impress you and their peers and bring in articles from *Business Week* or the *Atlantic* that they or their parents regularly read. Then, too, even though this is middle school, some of the youngsters truly may be interested in the articles in what generally are considered adult journals. So act as though you expected nothing less.

DECIDING HOW LONG

So far in these writing assignments, students are not being asked to argue a position in order to bring about a change in belief or behavior. They have been gathering facts and writing about them in some logically organized fashion. Whatever the assignments though, they probably have begun to ask, "How long should this be?" You may be tempted to say, "Long enough to get the job done," which is a good answer but not very helpful to young writers. Instead, you could go on to tell them that to be complete, an essay, like a good story, should have at least three parts: a recognizable beginning, middle, and ending, and for an essay, the names of these parts are introduction, body, and conclusion.

Now would be a good time to review with your curious writers the function of each of these parts of an essay. Yes, even if you have bright, experienced eighth- or ninth-graders who have been writing very well all through middle school, you reinforce these functions in as much depth as needed with the students you currently are teaching, and then hold them accountable

- for *introducing* their essays in ways that invite, intrigue, indicate direction, and guide the reader into the body of the essay;
- for *developing the middle* part of their essays with well-built paragraphs sequenced in a logical way; and
- for *concluding* their essays in a way that summarizes or reflects on what has been written (without repeating it) or projects onto the future considerations without introducing new information.

USING GRAPHICS TO SHOW STRUCTURE

Diagrams, cartoons, and other images can show the structure of an essay and the function of each part. Using them enhances your instruction, making it easier for students to visualize different features of an effective essay. Consider the idea of a train. It is a metaphor to illustrate both purpose and order that makes sense to students living in the most geographical settings—city or country, mountain or plains. Show the engine, the cargo cars, and the caboose. They will get it. The engine is the introduction, gets the essay going, and pulls it along; the cargo cars are the body (of whatever number needed to carry the information); and the caboose is the conclusion, signaling that the essay has come to an end. The couplings are the transitions (signal words) that both hold the ideas, words, sentences, and paragraphs together and show the relationships among those components. To see a sample of this train metaphor in slides, check the companion website for this book at http://teachingenglishlanguagearts.com.

CONFERENCING TO CLARIFY STUDENT THINKING

No matter how well you have presented lessons or scheduled time for practice and review, sometimes only talking to individual students will serve to ensure learning. One-on-one conferencing during the class time is difficult to manage, but planning ahead can help you incorporate this valuable teaching strategy fairly early in the school year. Begin right away modeling ways to respond to writing; then have students work for short periods of time in pairs—reading and responding to drafts; then they can work as small groups in structured read-around groups; and finally, perhaps by the second quarter, you can begin to integrate in-class conferencing with individual students.

Figure 5.3. Train Couplings Signify Transitions

When students experience the value of having your professional responses to their drafting, they may be patient enough to work independently, reading or writing, while you meet a few students each day in one-on-one conferences. The major reason for holding off scheduling in-class one-on-one conferencing is not due to class management but to have time to build students' confidence in themselves and in one another to become reliable readers and peer writing partners rather than rely solely on you. Knowing what can be expected also prepares them to come to conferences with good questions and open minds.

In school settings with ready access to technology either at home or for all students to work on computers simultaneously in class, it is practical to teach students to do online peer responding as you work your way toward one-on-one conferencing. See "Teacher Resource F" in the appendix for optional ways to structure such an in-class activity. Until you can manage effective in-class conferencing, consider inviting students who wish to work in this way to meet with you before or after school or during their study periods. As the word gets around that getting one-on-one feedback from the teacher is helpful, students may be willing to cooperate in class so that they, too, can gain the benefits of this teaching and learning opportunity.

It will take time to teach students how to use class time efficiently, so plan carefully and keep working toward this goal. Commend them when they do well with pairs and small-group responding, and continue to model and expect their cooperation. Often they respond just as they should.

PREPPING FOR ONE-ON-ONE CONFERENCES

How do you prepare students for conferencing so that they will bring some insight to their own reading or writing process and remain open to taking something valuable from the conversation? One strategy is to have students come with specific, written questions based on the assignment guideline. It is soon enough to schedule time for in-class conferencing after students have done in-class prewriting to prime the pumps, written their first drafts to explore and organize their ideas, used the grading rubric to read and revise, participated in some form of peer feedback task, and already written a second revision.

If you get involved too soon, students may think all they have to do is follow your advice and earn an A. That erroneous idea seldom is the case when you use the general grading guidelines for which an A is awarded for the student's own creative touch. Most can accomplish a C; you can teach a B and only acknowledge the originality evident for the A. See the general grading guideline diagram in chapter 1.

Your question may be about what the rest of the class should be doing while you conduct one-on-one conferences. Depending on the makeup of the class and which other assignments students have for the course, students could be doing independent reading, could be listening to audio books, or could be working on handwriting or word-processing drafts or revisions. Early on, it would not be unusual to be able to use only a portion of the period for conferences. Once the students become accustomed to them, you may be able to use the majority of the period because the students are coming prepared to work and to wait. By then, they are less uncomfortable with quiet on their side of the room, and they are less distracted by the hushed conversation at the teacher's desk.

In your school setting, consider withholding the grade until the students meet for the conference. Then they are more likely to pay attention to those time-consuming comments you have written as you read and decided the grade. In this case, students would come to the conference with one section of the paper revised and prepared to show how their revision improves their paper. You could begin the conference asking the student, "Based on the comments on the essay I returned to you, what grade do you think you earned?" Then have the student show you the revised section, discuss the merits of that revision, and answer questions the student may have.

The grade on the original essay should not be changed unless it is clear you made an error. Instead, encourage students to use what they learn in the conference when writing the next paper. Writing conferences themselves need not be graded, simply acknowledged with a check or plus in your grade book. These meetings serve as a formative assessment, as a tool for you and your students to learn more about ways students view their own writing and ways they approach revisions. You will find that keeping some notes about these conferences provides good information for parent conferences and questions from administrators, too. Having specific information about specific students demonstrates your attention to individuals that all three value: students, parents, and administrators.

Time, patience, modeling, adapting, and adjusting by both the students and teacher ultimately lead to productive in-class conferencing.

TRAINING FOR SUCCESS

The first quarter at most schools is much like preseason training for sports teams. It is not that the athletes do not know the rules or no longer have the physical prowess to play the game; it is that they probably have not had to utilize that knowledge or those muscles during the off-season. It's much the same way with students and is the reason teachers find themselves reviewing and reteaching what they know students have been taught before: not because the students do not know, but because they have not been using what they had learned. You know that for yourself. When you are preparing to teach a lesson, you are reviewing details about general topics you know you have known for years. What's that adage? If they don't use it, they'll lose it. So go ahead and reteach, and then begin to hold the students accountable for using what they are learning . . . again.

CONCLUSION

It may take several weeks to cover the distance between reviewing informative writing to teaching persuasive writing. For some teachers, it takes the entire first three quarters. However, for you who know where you are heading, the expedition does not seem interminable, as long as you are confident that you have not gotten lost along the way. Stop occasionally to rest and enjoy the side trips that confirm the value of teaching different modes of writing. Look at ways published writers and speakers use the skills you are teaching. Invite students to bring in examples they see in other classes, in their own independent reading, or even in the fiction and nonfiction you study together in class. Craft lessons for students to model what they read and view.

This does not mean, however, that you will never have to review or remind students of what they know. Teaching and learning is a spiraling process. What they are trying themselves students are likely to notice and point out during peer editing sessions. What they are discovering with your guidance is more lasting and useful than what they are simply shown or told. As they explore with their peers, paying attention to features in the different texts, the emerging writers begin using this knowledge in their own reading and their own writing. By this time, your student traveling companions are prepared for the more sophisticated thinking required to write convincing arguments and persuasive essays and speeches as described in the next chapter, "Making the Case."

NOTES

1. Blaise Pascal, quotation from "Persuasion," Proverbia.net, http://en.proverbia. net/citastema.asp?tematica=888&page=2 (accessed July 6, 2012).

2. "English Language Arts Standards » Anchor Standards » College and Career Readiness Anchor Standards for Writing," Common Core State Standards Initiative, http://www.corestandards.org/the-standards/english-language-arts-standards/ anchor-standards-6-12/college-and-career-readiness-anchor-standards-for-writing/ (accessed May 17, 2012).

3. Jock Mackenzie, *Essay Writing: Teaching the Basics from the Ground Up* (Pembroke, NH: Pembroke Publishers, 2007).

4. "English Language Arts Standards » Anchor Standards » College and Career Readiness Anchor Standards for Language," Common Core State Standards Initiative, http://www.corestandards.org/the-standards/english-language-arts-standards/ anchor-standards-6-12/college-and-career-readiness-anchor-standards-for-writing/ (accessed March 15, 2012).

RECOMMENDED BOOKS ABOUT REAL PEOPLE

Memoirs

Hitler Youth: Growing Up in Hitler's Shadow by Susan Campbell Bartoletti

Explores the various factors that led many of Germany's young people to pledge their loyalty and support to the dictator and join the Hitler Youth during Hitler's rise to power.

Boy: Tales of Childhood by Roald Dahl
 The British writer recounts humorous and memorable events from his child-hood, including summer vacations in Norway and an English boarding school.

We Beat the Street: How a Friendship Pact Led to Success by Sampson Davis
 Making a pact to stick together through the rough times in their impoverished Newark neighborhood, three boys found the strength and determination to work through their difficulties in order to make their dreams come true by completing high school, getting through college, and attending medical school together.

Autobiographies

The Autobiography of Benjamin Franklin by Benjamin Franklin
 Originally written as a guide for his son, Benjamin Franklin discusses his life, accomplishments, and ideas.

Living Up the Street by Gary Soto
 The author describes his experiences growing up as a Mexican American in Fresno, California, in the 1950s and 1960s.

Rosa Parks: My Story by Rosa Parks
 The woman whose name is synonymous with the civil rights movement dis-cusses her role in the Montgomery NAACP, her now famous refusal to give up her bus seat to a white man, the Montgomery bus boycott, Dr. Martin Luther King Jr., and more.

Soul Surfer: A True Story of Faith, Family, and Fighting to Get Back on the Board
 by Bethany Hamilton
 The teenage surfer who lost her arm in a shark attack in 2003 describes how she has coped with this life-altering event with the help of her faith, the changes in her life, and her return to the sport she loves.

6

MAKING THE CASE

Persuasive Writing

READING TO WRITE

Reading maketh a full man, conference a ready man, and writing an exact man.

—Sir Francis Bacon[1]

Looking back at what students have read is a good way to prepare them for what they are going to write. As the Francis Bacon quotation suggests, when students have read, they are full and are ready to conference and talk with others about their thinking and eventually prepared to write with the kind of exact—precise and concise—language that leads to inviting reading for others. Oddly enough, this process seems particularly effective when teaching students how to write persuasive essays—ones that require writers to understand the audience they are intended to influence and to meet the Common Core Anchor Standards, which state that "students must take task, purpose, and audience into careful consideration, choosing words, information, structures, and formats deliberately."[2]

Before readers are convinced to respond in a particular way, they must be motivated. It is worth the time spent looking at motivation in the literature already studied this school year to help students understand what causes characters to change. Students then can use what they observe in their reading when they begin to write. Your young teens may not have the vocabulary yet but would acknowledge that change occurs when characters believe that refusing to do so will be dangerous, is illegal or immoral, or will betray someone about whom they care deeply. If your students are ready, share with them the following terms and the explanations that follow. If not, use general terms you know they will understand.

- Beliefs—what the character or audience accepts as fact. "The temperature is below freezing." "The Great Spirit created the universe."
- Attitudes—what the character or audience believes about forces outside their control that makes the proposed change favorable or unfavorable, positive or negative based on the character's beliefs. "My parents will never get me a. . . ." "I'll be grounded if I go." "That group never liked me anyway."
- Values—the principles upon which character or audience base their lives—moral codes, what is right or wrong. In many cases these relate to religion and politics. "It is dishonest to steal, even when you're hungry." "Never narc on a relative." "Our family always votes . . ."

Ask students to return to the text of the readings you have studied together. Instruct your curious young people to seek out passages showing what the authors reveal about the beliefs, attitudes, and values of the characters. Then identify who or what in the story convinces the character that making a change in behavior would be a good or right thing to do. Remember, in many stories there are at least three attempts to solve the conflict in which the protagonist is embroiled, and usually the third, most difficult attempt involves a values decision.

This same kind of looking at beliefs, attitudes, values, and behavior helps students read nonfiction, too. When they are asked to identify the author's tone in articles and essays, paying attention to words, phrases, and imagery the writers use to make their points, even the youngest middle school students discover what the writers seem to value. These close readings reveal the attitudes and behavior writers directly or indirectly invite or attempt to persuade the readers to adopt.

As you select mentor texts for your writing assignment, consider those that your students can model as they write about topics that interest them.

You could assign an independent book report requiring students to identify the beliefs, attitudes, and values of the main character and attempts made by others to persuade him or her to change those beliefs or behaviors. See a list of possible biographies listed at the end of this chapter.

PRESENTING ARGUMENTS PRECEDES PERSUADING

A writer needs to know something about the readers in order to choose facts and use reasons that will be convincing. Middle school students know this but may not realize they do. An effective way to illustrate this fact is to assign students to draft a letter to persuade their parents or guardians to let the young teens do something previously not allowed for any number of reasons. This is an audience even immature middle school students know how to approach; they understand they must come up with both facts and reasons to get permission to do that forbidden thing and they must not finagle with the facts or use faulty reasoning. Once the youngsters have giggled and guffawed about times they have gotten caught doing either of these things, go ahead and present a lesson on the ethics of argumentation. Keep it light, but keep it real. You may even share a story of your own.

Then take your students back a couple millennia and enrich your mini-lesson with the classical foundation of the art of rhetoric or honesty in arguing as attributed to Aristotle. You may find that cartoons will make it more accessible while telling the story that for eons an essential part of a classical education has been learning to argue well. Your youngsters will readily accept as true that writers and speakers who can convince the audience to change are the ones who rise to become leaders in the school, the community, the nation, and even the world. Invite them to name leaders they know about from history, movies, and current events.

UNVEILING ARISTOTLE'S ART OF RHETORIC

Go ahead and use the Greek words *ethos*, *pathos*, and *logos*. These premium roots make up many words in the academic vocabulary these middle school students encounter now and certainly will encounter in high school. Additionally, the students feel so sophisticated using them as they brag to their family and friends relating what they will have learned from you in their English class.

You probably can find PowerPoint slide presentations online to adapt for your middle school students. No need to belabor the points or require students to memorize the definitions of each Greek term. The purpose is to show that what they are studying now has been a part of education curricula since the time of . . . whatever hyperbolic term for a long, long, long time ago impresses your students: the gladiators; the Roman Empire; the ancient Chinese dynasties; when Muhammad or Siddhrtha Gautama Buddha lived.

Perhaps the most important lessons to teach about persuasive writing and speaking have to do with integrity. With your instruction, students soon realize that the effective communicators know the audience well, appeal to their feelings, and explain with reasons that benefit the individuals in that audience. Such influential writers and speakers convince, inspire, and more consistently compel their audience to think and do as they say. However, the more respected writers and orators are those who can be trusted to act with integrity. They are those men and women who resist the temptation to twist evidence and use sloppy reasoning. That is the kind of honesty you strive to instill in your students.

DETERMINING THE KIND OF AUDIENCE

Middle school is not too soon to begin teaching students to become skeptical consumers and skillful producers of arguments to bring about change. What will help them become more conscientious is to raise their awareness of kinds of audiences and the fact that they, themselves, at different times fall into each of these categories. Your students soon see that audiences generally fall into one of these types and that the kind of evidence used to bring about change is slightly different for each one.

- An audience may be hostile, totally opposed to the ideas the writer wants to get across. The people in this audience need to be appeased, to know the writer understands why they feel, believe, and act the way they do before this group decides to listen and to consider changing.

- A second kind of audience is neutral and may not have thought about the topic or problem. They primarily need to be informed of a need and the personal benefits of changing their beliefs and/or behavior.
- The third general kind of audience is positive, already on the same side as the writer, but they may not be inclined to act until they read or hear convincing reasons to do so.

Middle school students understand this right away when you ask them to consider situations in their own lives—at home, at school, or around the neighborhood, when they want to get their family members, schoolmates, or neighbors to change their minds about or support the student in doing something they were totally opposed to or neutral about at first. Remember that letter the students wrote to get their parents to change their minds?

These youngsters already know that they can tip the scales in their favor if they bring in weighty evidence that will impress their audience. In some cases, the evidence may be facts or opinions of experts that appeal to the head; the student writers may use an anecdote or passionate story that tugs the emotions and appeals to the heart; in addition, the students may bring up financial implications and point out the cost of remaining the same or changing, thus appealing to the pockets of their audience.

However, facts and stories alone will not convince. Communicators also must marshal and present reasons for change. The members of the business world know this and spend a significant portion of their budgets learning what their target audience thinks, believes, and does already. They then develop ads to convince potential customers that using their products or services will make them safer, healthier, or longer living, more attractive, popular, or influential. The reasons for using the product are what make for more convincing arguments.

Viewing Ads Adds to Understanding

Just a couple more steps before sending the students off to write effective persuasive essays of their own. Bring in print, media, and digital advertisements to show your students ways that they are, yes, even your most astute ones, persuaded to buy clothes, games, and unhealthfy food and drinks. As students view commercials that manipulate prospective customers, the students develop an understanding about ethos, pathos, and logos more quickly than simply by hearing the terms defined. If time permits, you could present a lesson about logical fallacies and faulty reasoning that include bandwagoning, hasty generalization, snob appeal, slippery slope, and appeals to authority that young teens will be able to recognize in advertisements they see online, on TV, and in magazines. See chapter 9 for specific lessons on reading media.

Sparring to Practice Listening for Sound Arguments

Practicing aloud arguments and attempts to persuade is an effective way to prepare students for writing strong, convincing essays. Consider conducting SPARs in class. They are SPontaneous ARguments based on everyday topics, such as which is better, more nutritious, more popular, more useful, more economical, more fun than something else. What should be required or banned?

Here is a simple way to demonstrate the value of listening and responding to opposing views on topics appropriate for middle school discussion. You can have two pairs of students debate each other for about ten minutes per topic. They must include facts and not just opinions in order to be convincing. The topic could be about a product, a school policy, or a social activity. The goal is not to change the mind of the opponent but to offer information for the audience to use in making a decision. On scrap-paper ballots, the student audience members indicate with a plus, check, or minus what they believe about the topic before the SPAR and then what they believe after the SPAR.

A member of the A team draws a topic and announces it to the class, which remains silent and marks the ballot. Speaker A has just two minutes to prepare and then present a case for supporting one side of the issue or for making a change in behavior regarding the issue. The first member of B, the opposing team, must listen carefully to be able to address each argument presented by the first speaker and then, within three minutes, counter each argument with her own.

The second speaker on the A team can offer rebuttal or response, and then a B team member speaks once more. That second speaker sums up the case for B's side. The audience decides who presents the more convincing case by voting anonymously on a prepared ballot. Then another set of students comes to the front, draws, and presents arguments for their topic.

Usually three rounds at a time suffice to demonstrate the value of listening and responding with logical reasons.

A structure that helps the SPARrers stay on task says

- *Name* it—What's the problem or issue?
- *Define* it—In this context, what do key terms mean? What makes it good or bad?
- *Explain* it—Show why this is a problem or issue of concern for the audience.
- *Prove* it—Use factual evidence, not just the opinion of the speaker.
- *Conclude* it—"Therefore . . ." State a good reason to consider the alternative view or to make a change or make no change.

Students are likely to notice how similar this is to the PIE structure described later in this chapter, where writers state their position, offer illustrations that exemplify the position, and then explain the link between the two. Still, it should not be surprising that it takes several days of SPARring for students to learn the structure and stay on task without erupting into side arguments. This is hard work that requires attentive listening and disciplined thinking.

The value of SPARring is that students hear how important it is to counter opposing views without insulting the intelligence of the reader or audience. If the writer or speaker does not appear to respect the fact the other side has valid reasons for holding to those beliefs or supporting those behaviors, the reader or audience is likely to close down and stop reading or listening. Be prepared. You may have to admonish your students that volume does not convince; practical solutions do.

WRITING ABOUT ISSUES THAT MATTER

> *If you would persuade, you must appeal to interest rather than intellect.*
>
> —Benjamin Franklin[3]

Students are more enticed to learn the specifics of persuasive writing when they see an immediate purpose for doing so. It therefore makes sense to assign the persuasive essays in conjunction with current events that take place on your school site or in the community, state, or world. A worthwhile reason for students to use their newly crafted skills is to write letters to persuade someone to change a policy or a law that affects them.

Members of your class can use the same strategies for writing these letters or articles as they did to write letters to their parents or guardians. You get more buy-in from the students when you resist the temptation to force the whole class to write about the same topic or on one that is important only to you. If they have no passion for the topic, students are likely to resist expending effort as they plan and are less likely to write credible essays that answer these kinds of questions:

- What is the problem?
- What does the audience believe or feel about the problem? How do you know?
- What has the audience said or done to show that is what they believe or feel?
- What should be done to solve the problem? How do you know?
- Which arguments will appeal to the head (facts), the heart (emotions), and the pocket (financial cost)?
- Why will a change in belief or action benefit the audience?
- How will life be better once the change is in place?

Now that they have a better understanding of knowing their audience, marshaling their facts, articulating reasons for change, and practicing countering arguments, they are ready to write more nuanced essays zoning in on the specific purpose that will compel their readers to take notice and maybe even take action, becoming part of the solution.

Taking Steps to Excellent Writing

Don't get it right.
Get it written,
Then get it right.

—Goran "George" Moberg[4]

Students sometimes wonder how they can make a well-written early draft even better. If you teach them specific steps they can take to improve their writing themselves, you will have taught a skill they can use for life. Consider using alliteration to help them recall the tasks that can be done in any order. During revision, encourage students to

- *Expand*—develop what is written to make ideas clearer and more interesting without being repetitive. Add more information to show rather than tell. Use carefully chosen examples from literature (any reading and viewing), life (personal experiences and observations), and lessons learned in other content-area courses. This may require research to find credible sources and experts to add weight to their arguments.
- *Explain*—clarify what is written by using various reasons based on experiences, observations, and lessons learned in other courses. "This is important because . . ."
- *Exchange and rearrange*—what words can be substituted that will make the writing clearer, more interesting, more precise? Consider using more active verbs instead of passive ones with forms of the verb "to be," more concrete nouns, and more words that have the positive or negative connotations to create the desired mood in your reader. Think about ways words, sentences, and paragraphs can be rearranged to make the ideas unfold more smoothly and make the thoughts less unambiguous, more interesting, and more inviting to consider. What does the audience need to know before making a decision? This is why skillful informative writing is important.
- *Expunge*—get rid of distracting or weak words, phrases, and sentences that cloud writing and prevent ideas from shining through, glowing with authority as the writing informs, convinces, persuades, and even entertains.

Writing That Shows and Tells

One of the ways to help students expand their writing without simply blowing it up with frivolous air is to have them show and not just tell what they think or believe about their topic. Naturally, confident writers may resist at first when they are asked to write about a topic you have chosen, but when reminded that whatever they write reflects their thinking, students usually become more conscientious. This is another time to remind them about the I in PIE writing. They usually are comfortable with P, stating their own position, telling the reader what they think or believe. But it is the I that brings in illustrations—examples, anecdotes, facts—that help the reader to see what the writer means. Then the E explains with reasons how and why the illustrations show or prove the point the writer is trying to make.

Sample template (note transition words in italics):

> State your **POSITION** (or opinion on the topic). *For example*, (**ILLUSTRATE** with quotations, facts, or examples from literature or from life). *This shows* (In two or three sentences **EXPLAIN** or expand the link between the illustration and the point). *Furthermore*, (another **ILLUSTRATION**). *This shows* (In two or three sentences **EXPLAIN**). *Moreover*, (another **ILLUSTRATION**). *One can see how* (In two or three sentences **EXPLAIN** or **SUMMARIZE**).

Sample paragraph:

> [P]Learning to write is an important skill for anyone to develop whether a teenager or a grownup. [I]For example, teachers learn what students understand from what they write. [E]High school students must write well on SAT tests to get into top colleges. This shows that young people who want to get good grades in school will have to write well enough to show what they know. Furthermore, people use writing to help take care of problems in their personal and professional lives. Some adults write letters to apply for a job; others write letters to explain why they are behind on their payments. Sometimes a person loses his job and just can't keep up. A well-written letter may be just what is needed to get an extension so he can pay the bills latter without penalty. One can see that both young and older people have good reasons to be able to express themselves clearly in writing.

Some students respond well to this formulaic approach to developing paragraphs when you offer a template or suggest a required number of sentences for each paragraph. In the early weeks of the school year, you could require five-sentence paragraphs in their drafts; then raise the number up to seven or nine. Each sentence in the draft should fulfill one of the PIE structure's functions. Also remind the students to add transitional words and phrases that show the relationship among the sentences. By the final draft, the number of sentences may well be fewer or more, and some of the transitions may be deleted without losing the flow of ideas, but requiring specific components in early drafts pushes students to organize and expand their writing in a meaningful way.

WRITING EVALUATIONS OF PUBLISHED WORKS

Adolescent readers sometimes wonder why teachers get so excited about books, plays, poems, essays, and films that do not seem all that appealing to young people. They may not understand until you point it out to them that each reader has his or her own standards to decide what is interesting or worth reading. You can demonstrate this fact by sharing a set of criteria for evaluating literature[5] and thus establish another prelude to students for writing a different kind of persuasive writing—critiques of literature and film. The results will provide evidence your students are reaching the standards that measure that they know how to write their own thoughtful considerations of different aspects of print, digital, and film media.

Working as a class, ask your students to score their response to a piece of literature you already have studied together. Have them create a scorecard with space for nine responses. Then ask them to think about the specific reading and consider

- how difficult the text or film was to understand when they read on their own.
- how much they found themselves drawn into the story and away from their everyday life as they read the text or viewed a film.
- how much the people and places seemed familiar, believable, or, at least, somewhat reflective of life as the student knows it.
- how artistically or creatively the author or director used various elements. Though difficult to understand at times, was the writing or filming intriguing enough to be reread or rewound? Did they want more time just to bask in the beauty of the setting or to relive the terror created by the author's skillful use of sparkling vocabulary, fresh images, realistic dialogue, and images in a fresh and engaging way? Were they curious about the director's use of camera angles and shots, lighting, and music?

- how well the text and film flows and how well all parts seem to fit together in a meaningful way or how often the story line seems disjointed or has scenes that could be deleted without being missed.
- how the reading or viewing made them feel. Sometimes readers respond positively or negatively to something read or viewed because they appreciate how well an author's tone, personal style, or attitude comes through the writing. That may be one of the reasons adolescents enjoy book and film series so much. They know what kind of tone to expect and look forward to experiencing the work of one who clearly reveals his or her feelings about a topic.
- how strongly they respond emotionally—positively or negatively. Do they think the mood created is lasting and universal, fleeting or unique?
- how closely the text or film confirms or contradicts their personal beliefs. Even if they cannot put it into words, novice as well as veteran readers and viewers are influenced by values and beliefs relating to religion, politics, social issues, and attitudes about what is moral or immoral, right or wrong.
- how much new information and understanding about oneself and about others is gained from reading or viewing. Perhaps the quality of literature and film that is more difficult to articulate relates to its ability to provide insight. Either may be a mirror that reflects the reader's or viewer's truths about herself that she had not considered before. The experience in reading or viewing could also be a window, offering new insight into other individuals, groups, places, and situations. Some text and film compels those who experience it to consider their own behaviors and thoughts about life and death, good and evil.

Works that unveil what is true and beautiful and prick our conscience to become better people often are those texts and films that continue to be read and viewed for years and years. Even though young students seldom appreciate the works' value until years later, it is the significant insight derived from published works that spurs educators to teach the classics for generation after generation.[6]

Seeing how others write persuasive literary critiques helps students learn. Invite students to bring in samples found on the back of paperback books, in library leaflets, and on websites that sell books. Using these as models may be a good start for your students. They will see professional reviewers and film critics include references directly or indirectly to many of the criteria you are asking your students to consider.

You also could provide samples of student reviews and critiques that are posted on websites such as the Scholastic Book Clubs and the Spaghetti Book Club—Book Reviews by Kids for Kids. Print out a few reviews and ask your students to circle the words or phrases that suggest the different criteria these writers have considered as they indicate what they like or dislike about the books and film. Seeing how well they can tell what these reviewers value and that many reviewers use lenses similar to the nine you are teaching will let your students know how common it is for even very young writers to express their opinions articulately in writing for the public to read.

Charting Responses Provides Facts for Writing

You and your students may come up with more sophisticated terminology for evaluating literature and film, but you can trigger their thinking by getting young evaluators started using the phrases that follow. They can look through these nine lenses and then organize their thoughts on the value of what they read and view. Ask them to rate a piece of text or video on each criterion using a scale of one to five (low to high):

1. Easy to understand
2. Takes me away from now
3. Seems like real people and places
4. Creative writing or filming worth revisiting
5. Parts fit together well
6. Author or director's opinions seem obvious
7. Creates strong feelings
8. Morals match mine
9. Opens my eyes and challenges me to think about others
10. Other

As students record their responses, remind them to include in their notes specific references to what they read or view. They will need those examples to flesh out their evaluative review. During the whole-class mini-lesson, you could set up small, informal groups and assign students to find a quotation, a short phrase, or a sentence, suggesting key words as examples, and to record page numbers, paragraph numbers, or reference to specific scenes from the literary work under the microscope of their focused thinking.

Once you have introduced the idea, done a whole-class discussion of a commonly read or viewed published work, and analyzed critiques by students and professional reviewers, then assign the students to write evaluations of their independently chosen books using the criteria you have chosen. Direct their attention to names of award-winning authors on the Newbery, Orbus Pictus, Coretta Scott King, and California Young Reader Medal lists. You know your students will be reading work by quality authors whom they still may not like. That's perfectly all right. You are inviting your novice critics to convince their readers that they have given serious consideration to various aspects of the work and can support their responses with clearly organized ideas that reflect their personal opinions.

Organizing Notes into Revealing Critiques

Once they have their prewriting notes, your young critics are ready to plan ways to arrange their responses into a well-structured piece of persuasive writing that explains why they evaluated the reading or viewing experience the way they have. Questions they should consider:

- What is your *general response* to this piece of literature or film? Strong, moderate, weak? Impressed? Neutral? Unimpressed?
- Why have you *ranked* the work as you have? More low points than high points?
- What specific references from the literary work or film can you *cite to explain and support* your opinion?
- Which quotations will best show what you want to say?

Next, your students decide the best way to organize their thoughts. They could write about

- strong qualities to weak—those they rate highest to those that rate lowest

- more personal qualities to less personal ones—personal beliefs to parts fitting together
- vice versa
- some other way

The class may need to be reminded to include in the opening paragraph the title and author of the work as well as a general response to the literature. This can be an opinion word, an adjective or adverb that will guide students' writing and alert their reader about what will follow. Awkward? Believable? Clever? Memorable? Challenging? Sloppy? Stereotypical? The evaluation could begin with a carefully selected quotation that reflects the strong point the student writer will explore and expand in the remainder of the critique.

For this kind of assignment to be successful, students must believe beyond a shadow of a doubt that you will accept their honest opinion. As long as they include responses to each criterion and support their answers with specific examples from the text or film, they are on the right track. Let them know there are no wrong answers, just unsupported claims. Then and only then will they eagerly submit fully developed essays that persuasively show their deep reading and careful consideration of many aspects of a published work they have read or viewed.

READING CLASSMATES' WRITING INSPIRES BETTER WRITING

Once students' drafts are written, your students know they have several steps to take before submitting their work for evaluation or critique grades. One strategy for inspiring better writing is to have students read and respond to the revised, but not final, drafts of their classmates. Working on their computers, students can be instructed to insert comments but not correct the writing of their peers. Correcting, you already have taught them, is the responsibility of the writer who can choose to use or ignore the commendations and recommendations made on their compositions. See "Teacher Resource F" in the appendix for ways to structure this one-period, in-class assignment.

Is it worth the class time to have students read and respond to peer drafts? Here are sample student reflections after a class period spent doing this task.

Student A: I think I learned a lot with this project. It helped me realize that other people have better and weaker strengths than I do. To sum up my commendations, I need to make my title more appealing, make the paper less confusing at times, and add in some information. I think that I also learned that if I take time to look at my writing, it could be a lot better than just having the teacher do it for me.

Student B: I learned that everyone makes mistakes, even people I perceived as smart.

Student C: I did a good job on giving a lots of detail and was good at staying on topic. I really need to work on making my paper less boring. I also need to explain stuff that isn't commonly known. Reading other people's work made me realize I should make my paper a little more exciting and add more emotion. I also want to try and organize a little better.

Student D: I'm glad that we did this because I know some things I can correct on my biography that I didn't notice but my friends did notice. I think this was a really good idea to do this. It helped me a lot!

ASSESSING WRITING: INFORMALLY OR FORMALLY?

Periodically during the school year, teachers are required to assess student learning and submit the results to people outside the classroom. In some schools, this reporting is done totally in-house with only administrators, parents, and students seeing the results. In other school settings, there are state exams, and in numerous districts, the results of standardized tests impact the ratings of the school and the evaluation of the teachers. The question arises, "How can I prepare and inspire students to write their best in any testing situation?" No easy answer. As often is the case, the kind of preparation depends on the reason for testing.

Students usually write well when they know what is expected. The challenge is to resist making the prompt so specific that there is little room for creativity on their part. When you have a choice, make formal writing assessments opportunities for students to shine. No, this does not mean writing easier tests. It does mean writing tests that measure in a variety of ways what you have taught as well as what students are expected to know.

As you instruct your students that writing can be a place to explore what they think, they may not be thrown off when they see a test question on a topic that is relatively unfamiliar. Instead of giving up because they are not sure of an exact answer, the student writers feel confident enough to begin writing. They will have experienced that the act of writing sometimes unlocks their thinking and that they sometimes begin not knowing but end up showing they do know . . . a little. Partial credit is better than no credit. So continue to remind your students of the different purposes for writing and that learning different ways of writing is a process during which the students discover what they want to say and then, under teacher guidance, learn how best to say it.

Since you, the teacher, have very definite skills you are asked to teach and must guide the students toward learning those ways and showing what they know about good writing, it may be useful to work backwards by asking yourself questions similar to those asked when designing long-term writing units and short-term individual lessons.

- What skill are you trying to measure in this assessment? Is it
  - how well they understand the texts and topics you have studied together?
  - how well they can show what they know about analyzing a character or a piece of writing?
  - how well they can write—organize and develop their response?
- What will you need to see in their answers or writing to know their level of understanding or skill? Is it
  - reference to the text?
  - use of literary language?
  - organization?
  - development of ideas?
  - correct use of vocabulary and grammar?

If it is all of these, consider some step-by-step test preparation during which students

- review the literary language you've been teaching (direct and indirect characterization, motivation, elements of fiction, text structures, rhetorical devices, or whatever you have been teaching).

- work together, going back to the beginning, middle, and end of the text to find examples of each of the devices and terms that students save in their notes.
- talk together and share their notes.

Those with no notes can work together to create them. It is surprising how much some students recall without having to record what they see and hear. However, they should not be allowed to mooch off those who do keep good notes. As you listen to their talk, you gain insight into what students know or what you may need to help them review.

If you know the formal assessments will require your students to write single- or multiple-paragraph responses, let them practice in class, but without pressuring them with grades. The goal is to help them learn to use their time wisely. Remember the personal story that began chapter 4?

As you teach your imminent test takers how to begin responses to essay questions, invite them to write a statement of their opinion about the reading you assign in which the student writer

- uses some kind of modifier to indicate how well or poorly they think the author has developed the characters or essay topic and
- explains how much the student can identify with the characters or situation and/or
- shows how the student sees connections to everyday incidents in the way one or more characters act or react in the text to which the student is responding.

Their essay will then be an attempt to show why that modifier is true or valid. Then begin writing PIE paragraphs that include ways their illustrations support their position/opinion. This explanation is the most important element because it shows students' level of understanding and familiarity with the text. The students should be ready to write their body paragraph(s) and conclusion paragraph to reflect or summarize what they write.

From the beginning of the school year, plan times to practice within the same time constraints under which the students will be tested. Regularly ask students to reflect on how they used the time.

- Did they finish?
- Are they satisfied with the results?
- What can they do differently to use the time more efficiently?

Keep it light. The purpose is for them to understand how to pace themselves so that they can complete the tasks to the best of their ability. Resist the temptation to burden them with the impact of the test results on them or on you. Encourage them to do their best.

Rather than show them fully polished sample essays, write along with your students, and then show them how you build your essay. Ultimately, students come to understand how to organize and develop a basic essay within a prescribed time period. Knowing this is a different kind of writing for a different purpose should reduce their anxiety about having no time for multiple revisions and deep editing. Some students will be relieved to know they can write the introduction last! It is not when the introduction is written, it's when the grader reads it. Just save space on the top of their paper to come back and write that inviting opening passage to intrigue the grader to keep reading.

WRITING FOR SPEAKING

Speech writing responds to a specific set of realities. Public speeches usually are prepared for a specific audience in a specific place for a specific purpose. This means the speech writer includes features to ensure the audience will retain more of what they hear. Well-crafted speeches have carefully worded signposts to alert the audience of what is to follow, lots of transitions to clarify connections between ideas, more repetition to remind the listeners of key ideas, and spoken citations to acknowledge information borrowed from other people and sources.

In other words, the content and delivery are designed to help listeners know what to listen for and to provide spoken cues to remind them of what they have heard. And since public speaking is viewed as well as heard, conscientious speakers dress for the occasion and they use voice, hand gestures, and physical movement to enhance what is being said.

By spring of the school year, your students are becoming comfortable enough with you and their classmates to give oral presentations with more confidence and competence than in the opening semester. Spring is therefore a good time to have them write and then deliver a formal informative or persuasive speech. Such an assignment offers your students another opportunity to hone their research, writing, and speaking skills for an authentic audience and meet those Common Core State Standards for Speaking that call for students to

- "integrate and evaluate information presented in diverse media and formats, including visually, quantitatively, and orally" and
- "evaluate a speaker's point of view, reasoning, and use of evidence and rhetoric."[7]

Your students may be more tempted to write and practice giving speeches when you tell them about top-ranking leaders in business and government who know how vital it is to their success. To be more effective and inspiring speakers, many hire professional speech writers and speech coaches. It is not that these influential men and women are not smart; it is because they know speech writing is different from report writing. As when teaching other kinds of writing, having your students read and critique samples of written and delivered speeches can help students see the unique qualities of this form of communication.

Looking closely at written speeches, students will notice several distinct features. They will notice that speech writers use more repetition and shorter, more declarative sentences comprising vivid verbs, concrete nouns, graphic images, and also vocabulary chosen for its sound and suggestive power.

As they will have discovered in your lessons on text structures, your students see that speech writers incorporate carefully chosen transitions and signal words to help hold the speech together while keeping the listeners on track with the positions and arguments presented. Ask the students to highlight or underline in different colors the various features they notice as they read or view. Then let them compare their observations with those of a partner.

BRIDGING THE GAP BETWEEN READING AND WRITING A SPEECH

A smooth segue between noticing the text of a speech and writing a speech is showing a speech being delivered. You can get your young speech writers off to a good start by drawing their attention to the vocal and visual characteristics of an effective oral presentation. Ask them to pay attention not only to what the speaker says but also to how he or she looks during the delivery.

Choose a couple of the TED talks on topics your class has been studying this term. To begin, turn off the volume and ask the students to simply observe the speaker.

- How is the speaker using the physical space? Which gestures seem natural; which are distracting? Then turn up the volume and ask students to pay attention to vocal qualities.
- How does the speaker pace his or her presentation? Use pauses? Modulate his or her voice? Articulate words?
- What would the students like to imitate or avoid when they give their own speeches?

Writing for a Specific Audience

Then invite students to choose a topic on something that interests them or that they are studying in another class and write a speech for a specific audience with which they identify themselves. This can reinforce or expand their thinking about this other topic and be an efficient way to spend the next couple of weeks—using language arts skills to improve their performance in another class. What a concept!

Considering the knowledge of a specific audience is an opportune time to remind your students about the kind of language they should use to best get their ideas across. For example, if they choose to talk about reducing injuries in a particular sport and are speaking to a homogeneous group of sports fans, the speaker is right to use sports-specific jargon and slang. To demonstrate this fact, ask your students what this sentence means: "The difficulty of your set could be increased if you do a jam followed by a peach."

Class members familiar with gymnastics will understand the speaker is describing the point value of a gymnastics routine and may go on to show how injuries occur and could be reduced with changes to practice routines or to the equipment. By the way, the sentence means

> The point values you can earn on your gymnastics routine can be higher if you include, in sequence, two particular skills on the uneven parallel bars: the "jam," which leaves the gymnast sitting on the high bar; and the "peach," where the gymnast moves from the high bar to the low bar.[8]

When, on the other hand, the speech is being written to be delivered at a school board meeting comprising neighbors new to this sport, the speaker would choose more general language likely to be understood by listeners less familiar with the lingo of the sport and provide explanations when the lingo is used. The same care in choosing language would be true if the speaker were talking about science, dance, music, or art. In each case, the prior knowledge of the audience with the topic should determine the language the speaker chooses to use in the final text version of the speech. To prove your point, you could have students revise their speech, adapting it for a different audience. What would need to be changed to make a neutral or hostile audience open to change?

Applying Known Persuasive Strategies

If you decide to have your students write the text of a persuasive speech, spend a little time reviewing persuasive strategies, organizational patterns, and ways of determining what the audience thinks and believes before trying to convince them to change. Of course, allot time for students to read their speeches aloud to the class.

Remind your students to be thoughtful speakers who take into consideration what the audience sees as it listens, and so to consider their attire, gestures, and use of physical space in their speech to be given. Will there be a microphone? Distracting activities in the vicinity? Most important, the speakers also practice their speeches ahead of time to develop confidence so that they can deliver their speeches with poise, in a pace that is easy to follow, using pauses, pacing, and volume to attract and retain attention throughout the speech. See more on speech delivery in chapter 9, where you also will find rubrics for student practice and peer and teacher feedback.

WEIGHTING AND GRADING WRITING

Unfortunately, middle school students, like their counterparts in high school, often are more concerned about the grades they are earning than what they are learning. To reduce attention paid to grades, consider giving low weight to grades in the first quarter and increasing the impact on reported grades incrementally during the school year. This does not mean lowering the demands on the assignments. Instead, for example, assign just thirty points for final drafts during the first quarter; fifty during the second quarter; seventy-five during the third quarter; and then one hundred points during the fourth quarter. As the semester progresses, students still are being held accountable for writing well, but they are not penalized as they learn.

Include in each assignment a rubric that clearly states the minimum that is expected in terms of content, organization, and correctness for each grade or point level. The students will see what is required, will ask questions

Figure 6.1.   School Year Journey Has Ups and Downs

when they do not understand, and usually, along with their parents, will be less surprised and disappointed with their grades when they do not earn the highest ones. This done? Move on. Good teaching inspires pride in performance. Trust yourself and your students to delight in doing well.

WRITING FROM RESEARCH—A SUMMATIVE ASSESSMENT

Want to introduce students to different kinds of basic reference resources? Point out how often students see definitions, quotations, anecdotes, personal experience, and references to current events in editorials, essays, and speeches. Middle school students are familiar with dictionaries and stories in newspapers and magazines but may not know about collections of quotations and anecdotes. Young writers know they are supposed to acknowledge when they borrow information from others but may not have had many assignments that ask them to show that they know how to do this. During the second quarter of the school year, design a series of mini-lessons during which your students must utilize a range of reference materials that published writers use.

Consider a short writing assignment that requires that they do just that. They could write an editorial on an abstract term and then present those ideas in a persuasive speech, giving and receiving peer feedback on both. This summative assignment can demonstrate how well they are progressing on meeting Common Core Standards in reading, writing, speaking, and listening. Of particular focus is the writing standard that requires students to "gather relevant information from multiple print and digital sources, assess the credibility and accuracy of each source, and integrate the information while avoiding plagiarism."[9]

Choosing an Abstract Term

In this writing-speaking assignment, students can draw from a hat an abstract term. Then, from the specified resources, they gather information to write an editorial, which can be converted into a short, persuasive speech that is designed to raise the awareness of their readers and listeners about their chosen term. The editorial and speech should give significant reasons

BOX 6. 1 ABSTRACT TERMS

apathy	irritation	satisfaction
beauty	loneliness	simplicity
conceit	misery	surprise
cowardice	optimism	suspicion
dignity	patience	sympathy
elegance	pleasure	trust
failure	regret	worry

to strive to achieve or to avoid an experience with the abstract idea like those in the text box titled "Abstract Terms."

Adjust the list of terms to meet the language skills of your students. Having more than one student working with the same term will make for interesting reading and listening. If it is appropriate in your school setting, have students work in pairs and add a visual component where students include a poster or a set of five or six slides with images to supplement their oral presentation. The primary goals are to learn about and use a variety of resources in a piece of persuasive writing. The final product should include five of the following six kinds of support:

1. Definition of chosen term
2. Quotation using the term
3. Anecdote—could be an example from reading
4. Some sort of statistic or number relating to the term
5. Personal experience or observation of the term in action
6. Contemporary issue or situation illustrating the term

Of course, students will be expected to cite their sources. So this assignment makes for a fine summative assessment of a variety of skills most middle school English language arts teachers are expected to teach. It will be helpful to know which citation style is used in your district high school—Chicago, MLA, APA, or another. Students who arrive in high school with knowledge of citations will be better prepared for the academic challenges they are sure to meet there.

Reviewing and Introducing Reference Materials

To ensure that students are prepared for this complex assignment, several weeks before giving the assignment, plan and present a series of mini-lessons reviewing ways to use each of the resources. Students save their notes for use at the end. Your students may have had experience with some of the reference materials and have simply forgotten a few of the finer points. For example, for the print dictionary, review

- the guide words at the top of the pages that help students determine whether the word they are searching for will appear on a particular page.
- pronunciation guides with familiar words to help decide how to say the vowels and diphthongs. Some digital dictionaries have a link that will pronounce the word so that viewers can hear and practice saying it. Since this assignment includes an oral component, being able to say words correctly and confidently can be the key to a successful presentation
- phonetic spellings in parentheses
- a letter to indicate the part of speech and what the word means when used as a noun, a verb, an adjective, or an adverb
- a phrase or sentence showing how the word is used
- the etymology of the words (good time to mention value of knowing root words)

You should be able to locate a number of websites to help you plan a presentation just right for your students. Some of the websites even have quizzes to measure student understanding before you move on to next reference resource.

If your students do not have consistent access to online resources, borrow print dictionaries and books with collected quotations from the school and community libraries and from colleagues in your building. From the collection of quotations, students should find one that includes their abstract terms and illustrates or highlights the point the students decide to make about their term.

Zoning In on Quality Online Information

Perhaps one of the more critical skills twenty-first-century students need to learn has to do with conducting research online. Consult with your librarian or media specialist, who probably has special training, to introduce students to efficient navigation of resource materials and online databases.[10] As you plan your lessons, consider ways to guide your students in

- searching smarter by using more precise key words;
- choosing search engines that will lead them to prescreened sites with appropriate academic and scholarly articles for middle school students;
- evaluating domains and learning the difference in perspective and bias expected on each. Consider: com (selling), org (clubs, religious groups, etc.), gov (U.S. government), and net (networking within an organization);
- scrutinizing sites to assure they are getting current, reliable information; and
- modeling the strategies you use.

A number of online sites are available to help you design learning experiences during which your students can explore sites and practice their discernment skills. You can help your fellow travelers avoid getting lost in the dead ends along this school-year journey and becoming swamped in the quagmire of worthless websites, wasting valuable time needed to do quality research.

Appealing to the Heart and the Head with Stories and Statistics

After explaining to your students that anecdotes are usually short narrations of an interesting, amusing, or biographical incident, share a couple of your favorites with them. These should be brief enough to be told in thirty to forty-five seconds and can be chosen to appeal to the heart and be convincing examples of the term. Show your eager listeners how these little stories can enhance a speech.

If your students are English language learners, you may find it useful to find a translation of anecdotes in their native languages reflecting something in their specific cultures. Humans in general are storytellers, and most of your students can relate tales of family and friends. During your lesson on anecdotes, do invite students to share some of the heart-wrenching stories their families tell in order to teach them lessons.

Because many readers and listeners are impressed by numbers, using statistics ethically can be a powerful persuasive strategy that appeals to the head. This kind of evidence need not be a challenge for students to use. Students already are familiar with statistics in sports, movies and music, and commercials that relate percentages about the number of people who use or are impacted by certain products.

You can point out how young teens are enticed to do or buy something if it will put them in the group with the majority when advertisers use bandwagoning—the suggestion that everyone is doing it. Your young students soon see how persuasive an appeal can be when it includes specific numbers. From their studies in science and social studies, students already have seen statistics used to make a point in terms of ecology and politics. If statistics will work in their article and speech, encourage your budding researchers to use numbers from one of those commercials or classes. In your demonstration lessons you can show them websites that report demographics and data about people, places, and events.

Connecting to Current Events

Requiring that the article and speech include evidence based on a contemporary issue or situation is a good reason to teach students how to read and extrapolate information from news articles found in either print or digital resources. For this assignment, students should pay attention to current events and choose one that illustrates a reason to strive for or to avoid an experience with their abstract term. Remind them to record when and where they get their facts.

No matter how limited the electronic resources available to your students, it is important to teach them the basics of citing resources as a matter of academic honesty. Whatever they borrow should be acknowledged. For young, inexperienced students, you may simplify the task by requiring that the list of resources consulted list only the websites, books, and articles from which students borrow information for use in their writing or speech.

The minimum list should cite a dictionary, source for quotation, anecdote, statistic, and current event. You can ask them to alphabetize the list by author or title. For the older or more experienced students, teach them how to write endnotes where they include in the text of their writing a number that links what has been borrowed to a specific article or book with the same number. These resources then would appear in the bibliography or list of sources consulted. For less experienced students, consider using the parenthetical citation style that simply has author's last name, key words, or titles that appear in the students' list of resources consulted.

Organizing the Researched Information

After the month or so that you spend introducing and reviewing these resources and giving students time to practice using them, go back and review the abstract term assignment. Remind students to use five of the six kinds of support in their final draft. Here are some guidelines to help them organize their writing.

Introduction
- Dramatic opening that links to the idea of the article or speech—could begin with anecdote, quotation, or startling statistic.
- Transition to signpost—two or three sentences that link opening ideas to their signpost or thesis sentence. Could be "just as . . . so too" or "in much the same way . . ."
- Signpost or purpose statement—suggests that the writer or speaker will follow a specific organizational pattern in the body of the article or speech.
  - Chronology—in order of time. Could be "in the beginning," "then," or "next."
  - Cause and effect—tell about a problem and the effect of it. Could be "Because he neglected to . . . the repair costs skyrocketed" or "If students don't learn . . . they are likely to . . . for the rest of their lives!"
  - Order of importance—most important idea to least or least to most important.
  - Problem solution—describe a problem and offer a solution.

Body
- Incorporate five of the six kinds of evidence listed above.
- Appropriate transitions (direct their attention to your class list of transitions).
- Anything else the writer or speaker thinks will make the article or speech more interesting to read or hear.

Conclusion
- Memorable closing—could save quotation for closing.
- Summary of key ideas.
- Challenge to attain or avoid experience with the term.
- Call for change—urging reader or listener to strive to attain or avoid experience with the term.

Students should be encouraged to draft their article or speech using these guidelines but freed during the revision stage to make adjustments to better fit their personal style.

CONCLUSION

By the final quarter, on the last few miles of the school-year journey, the student travel companions will be more proficient and self-assured persuasive writers and speakers because you have taught them that effective, experienced communicators understand the purpose of different kinds of writing and speaking, appreciate ethics of argumentation, recognize the value of organization, and know the importance of respecting their reader or audience. Equally important, your maturing adolescents will have become more critical readers and listeners, more aware of ways that others may use these skills to convince readers, listeners, or viewers to change their beliefs and behavior.

By implementing a range of lessons and varied assessments, you will have reached your destination with students who are equipped with the knowledge and skill to be literate, contributing members of society who are able to meet many of the Common Core State Standards for English Language

Arts and for the curriculum you have been assigned to teach. And as a bonus, if you have published their work and created videos, you all will have souvenirs to share from this successful and rewarding journey of teaching and learning together.

NOTES

1. Francis Bacon, "Essays of Francis Bacon—Of Studies," Authorama Public Domain Books, http://www.authorama.com/essays-of-francis-bacon-50.html (accessed March 8, 2012).

2. "English Language Arts Standards » Anchor Standards » College and Career Readiness Anchor Standards for Writing," Common Core State Standards Initiative, http://www.corestandards.org/the-standards/english-language-arts-standards/anchor-standards-6-12/college-and-career-readiness-anchor-standards-for-writing/ (accessed May 17, 2012).

3. Benjamin Franklin quotation from Finest Quotes, http://www.finestquotes.com/select_quote-category-Mind-page-0.htm (accessed May 28, 2012).

4. Goran "George" Moberg, *Writing in Groups: New Techniques for Good Writing without Drills*, 3rd ed. (New York: The Writing Consultant, 1984).

5. Walter Blair and John Gerber, eds., *Better Reading Two: Literature*, 3rd ed. (Chicago: Scott Foresman, 1959).

6. Ibid.

7. "English Language Arts Standards » Anchor Standards » College and Career Readiness Anchor Standards for Speaking and Listening," Common Core State Standards Initiative, http://www.corestandards.org/ELA-Literacy/CCRA/SL (accessed April 30, 2013).

8. Raymond C. Jones "Can You Tell What It Means?" Reading Quest. August 26, 2012. http://www.readingquest.org/premises.html (accessed August 21, 2013).

9. "English Language Arts Standards » Anchor Standards » College and Career Readiness Anchor Standards for Writing," Common Core State Standards Initiative, http://www.corestandards.org/the-standards/english-language-arts-standards/anchor-standards-6-12/college-and-career-readiness-anchor-standards-for-writing/ (accessed March 15, 2012).

10. Leslie Harris O'Hanlon, "Teaching Students Better Online Research Skills: Improving Web Research Tactics Is a Priority," *Education Week*, May 20, 2013, http://www.edweek.org/ew/articles/2013/05/22/32el-studentresearch.h32.html?tkn=QWCCgXpStXBSdGy%2BRabLBT9BSWvJPFfQ47w2&cmp=clp-sb-ascd

(accessed May 23, 2013); print version published May 22, 2013, as "Teaching Students the Skills to Be Savvy Researchers."

RECOMMENDED BOOKS ABOUT REAL PEOPLE

Biographies

Coming Home: From the Life of Langston Hughes by Floyd Cooper
   A portrait of the childhood of poet Langston Hughes chronicles his early life with his grandmother and the events, personalities, circumstances, and rhythms that shaped his world and his writing.

Genius: A Photobiography of Albert Einstein by Marfe Ferguson Delano
   Compelling text and archival duotone photographs recount Albert Einstein's life, from his privileged childhood in Austria through the crucial years during World War II, touching on his theory of relativity and the importance it played in scientific development.

The Life and Death of Crazy Horse by Russell Freedman
   A profile of the Teton Sioux warrior depicts him as a shy, sensitive youth who overcame his fears in order to protect his people and their lands from invading white settlers, and follows his achievements in the Battle of Little Bighorn in 1876.

Harvesting Hope: The Story of Cesar Chavez by Kathleen Krull
   A biography of Cesar Chavez, from age ten when he and his family lived happily on their Arizona ranch, to age thirty-eight when he led a peaceful protest against California migrant workers' miserable working conditions.

Promises To Keep: How Jackie Robinson Changed America by Sharon Robinson
   A biography of baseball legend Jackie Robinson, the first African American to play in the major leagues, as told by his daughter.

Starry Messenger: A Book Depicting the Life of a Famous Scientist, Mathematician, Astronomer, Philosopher, Physicist, Galileo Galilei by Peter Sís
   A finely illustrated overview of the life and work of Galileo explains, in simple language and with Galileo's own words, the impact of the astronomer's discoveries on the science, philosophy, and art of Renaissance Italy.

7

VERSING LIFE TOGETHER

Writing Patterned and Original Poems

Robert, Bobby, Bob
Fast, fleet, flown
Baby, boy, grown

—Anna J. Small Roseboro, "Our Son"

Even if your students are on board and initially excited about reading and talking about poetry, you may face a roadblock when you ask them to write it. Why? Perhaps it is because some students find reading poetry such a challenging experience that they may not think they are "deep" enough to write poetry. True, some students are naturally talented poets, but others learn by seeing how others write, being inspired by what they learn, or simply by patterning the work of others. This probably is the best reason to read and study a variety of poetry before assigning all your students to write it. Once they understand the unique characteristics of poetry and experience the joy of word play by others, they eagerly accept the challenge to try versing, writing poems of their own.

You probably have been reading poems and having students write poetry as part of other lessons already. You may have had students write poems in response to literature, to news events, or even to viewing paintings and pictures. You understand what a fine vehicle poetry is for showcasing young writers' understanding of the literature and its connection to their lives. In this chapter, the purpose for writing poetry is different. It is for your students to experiment and conscientiously apply some of the features of poetry to recreate experiences of their own while meeting the curriculum and Common Core State Standards for English Language Arts that ask students to demonstrate anchor tasks such as

- producing clear and coherent writing in which the development, organization, and style are appropriate to task, purpose, and audience.
- developing and strengthening writing as needed by planning, revising, editing, rewriting, or trying a new approach.
- using technology, including the Internet, to produce and publish writing and to interact and collaborate with others.[1]

This chapter takes you and your students traveling into interesting side paths and offers suggestions for trying out different approaches to poetry writing. So feel free to let the students get off the tour bus for a while and play with the language. Invite them to splash around in freshwater streams; to wallow around in the mud a bit—manipulating words, forms, and imagery; to wander through the open markets checking out the collections you gathered to show how published writers craft their poems, sampling the goods, trying on styles; to experiment a bit, tasting different cuisines—all before you begin evaluating the quality of your students' writing.

Some students appreciate being reminded about some of the specific features of this kind of writing. But start with a definition of the genre using the one in your anthology or the one that follows. In either case, dictate the definition and then have the students write it in the poetry section they have set up in their journals.

Definition: "Poetry is literature designed to *convey* a vivid and imaginative sense of experience, especially by the use of *condensed* language *chosen* for its sound and *suggestive* power as well as for its meaning and by the use of such literary devices as *structured* meter, *natural cadences*, rhyme, and metaphor."[2]

Choose from the following activities, those in your own textbooks, or those you have found useful in the past. They all are designed to help your

Poetry is

SOMEONE saying SOMETHING to SOMEONE(S)

Figure 7.1. The Speaker—The Poem—The Audience

students compose a variety of poems that reflect their own personal experiences and observations and to encourage these young teenagers to dig deeper into quality literature. When they recall that poetry is someone (the poet) saying something (the poem) to someone (the audience—reader or listener) and usually a writer recreating an observation or experience, these young writers are eager to experiment in this particular mode of writing. Allot time for students to look back at some of the poems you have read together and consider who could be the speaker, who could be the audience, and what could be the message.

PATTERNING AND EMULATING

Want a compelling way for your reluctant writers to jump into poetry writing? Imitation. Modeling what others write. This is nothing new. Patterning and copying the work of others are traditional ways to learn difficult skills. Consider the painter and musician, the dancer and athlete. In each case, novices try to duplicate the strokes and colors, the sound and technique, the form and movement of the masters. You can give your students similar opportunities during this poetry unit.

Lead the way and model for them. First—choose a poem that you love and, with your curious young teens watching, show how you work through the process of figuring out the pattern and then of imitating that pattern. Ask

BOX 7.1: PATTERNING POETRY

Analyzing sentence syntax:
"Daybreak in Alabama" by Langston Hughes

When I get to be a composer
I'm gonna write me some music about
Daybreak in Alabama

When	I		get	to be	a	composer,
adverb	*pronoun*		*verb*	*verb*	*article*	*noun*

Analyzing rhythm and rhyme pattern:
"I'm Nobody" by Emily Dickinson

/	u	/	u	/	u	/		
I'm	no	bod	y	who	are	you?		*4 beats* A
u	/	u	/	u	/			
Are	you	no	bod	y	too?			*3 beats* A

them to look for rhyme and rhythm; draw their attention to sentence structure; entice them to imitate the kind of imagery; or challenge them to recreate the emotional impact through sound selections and choice of words.

Perhaps you already are familiar with the poems "I'm Nobody" by Emily Dickinson or "Where I'm From" by George Ella Lyon. Use these easily accessed verses to begin, and then let the students pick one or two of their favorite poems from the unit and write a poem that emulates the structure, style, techniques, and rhythm of their chosen poet. See the companion website for this book for specific assignment handouts.

Structured poems may be your choice to introduce this kind of poetry writing. The limerick, the haiku, and the sonnet are traditional patterns of poetry—each with a specific rhyme or rhythm pattern. Many of your students already are familiar with these patterns from elementary school. Here are a couple of traditional patterns to trigger their memory.

Limerick: a five-line poem, usually funny, that follows an AABBA structure.

> There was an Old Man in a tree,
> Who was horribly bored by a Bee;
> When they said, 'Does it buzz?'
> He replied, 'Yes, it does!'
> 'It's a regular brute of a Bee!'

> —Edward Lear

Sonnet: a poem of fourteen lines that follows a strict rhyme scheme and specific structure. There are different types of sonnets, the most well known being the English sonnets by William Shakespeare. You may find your students enjoy exploring the ways Shakespeare uses hyperboles and metaphors in Sonnets 61 and 130. You know how young adolescents feel about matters of love. They may gain more insight into the skill required to write originally as they create their own contemporary exaggerations and comparisons.

Or you may refer them to the narrative poem "Barbara Allen," as modeled in a ballad about my wedding to my husband, William.

The Ballad of William and Ann*

> Oh, it was around Christmas time
> When the marriage, it was planned.
> The family and friends all came to see
> Lord William wed Lady Ann.

> The musicians were seated, all playing their songs
> Awaiting the groom to appear.
> And seated among the guests that day
> Sat his former love, Lady Mear.

> The minister signaled the groom to come out
> To stand with best man at the right.
> The minister motioned the guests to stand
> As the bride marched in dressed in white.

Lady Mear, she stood with hankie in hand
Weeping for the man she had lost.
She'd been too proud to accept the ring
Lord William had gotten at cost.

The bride advanced at a stately pace
By her handsome groom to stand
Lady Mear, near the aisle, could be heard for a mile,
Shouting, "Hey, Lady Ann, that's my man!"

Lord William's response to the lady's outburst,
"You had my heart in your hand.
You cast me aside. Yes, I did love you first,
But today, I'll wed Lady Ann."

So that day long ago about Christmas time,
The guests got more than was planned.
An old love turned mean in quite a wild scene
When Lord William wed Lady Ann.

—Anna J. Small Roseboro†

*Patterned after "Barbara Allen," by Anonymous
†Mrs. William G. Roseboro

How about having your music lovers pattern song lyrics? You may find useful ideas from the *Learning from Lyrics* website of M.U.S.I.C.—Musicians United for Songs in the Classroom.[3]

While you definitely want to spend some time modeling the different poems with or for your students, save plenty of time for them to experiment independently. Remember, your goal is to provide the classroom structure and cultivate a nurturing environment that makes for a safe and comfortable setting in which to learn. Slowly but steadily release some of that control as the students become comfortable with the classroom routines.

The way you spend time shows what is important. During this portion of the unit, play and practice are important. Soon, you can persuade your students to perform self-selected or written poetry for their peers. And just as athletes and dancers who practice a lot feel more confident performing, your maturing teens feel more assured when they have practiced. Just for fun, have them exchange poems and try to summarize who the speaker and audience might be and what the message of the poem is . . . in one sentence.

Pantoums

One pattern that yields successful poems in middle school is a version of the less-familiar pantoum, a poem consisting of eight nonrhyming lines; each line used twice. A pantoum is less intimidating for reluctant poets and works well because it is based more on repetition than on rhyme or rhythm patterns. It also can be used as an alternative book report to capture key events, a memorable scene, or a favorite character from a literary work or from a life experience. Here is a sample poem written when a seventh-grade class finished reading *A Farewell to Manzanar* by John Houston and Jeanne Watasuki Houston, an autobiographical novel about Japanese internment during World War II.

Begin by writing four original lines:

(1) When I was seven
(2) My family was evacuated.
(3) We rode a bus
(4) To Manzanar.

Repeat lines two and four, and add lines five and six to expand ideas introduced in lines two and four, like this:

(2) My family was evacuated.
(5) Only forty-eight hours to prepare, then
(4) To Manzanar.
(6) We rode in shock, but together

Repeat lines five and six, and add lines seven and eight to expand ideas mentioned in lines five and six, like this:

(5) Only forty-eight hours to prepare.
(7) Mama, stressed and frustrated, broke all the dishes.

(6) We rode in shock, but together.
(8) Together, except for Papa.

Finally, repeat lines one, three, seven, and eight in this order:

(7) Mama, stressed and frustrated, broke all the dishes.
(3) We rode a bus
(8) Together, except for Papa.
(1) When I was seven.

The result is a lovely poem that captures the essence of the story. As you read and then write your own sample of this particular pattern poem, you can see how much grammar, usage, and punctuation students must employ to make sure that pronouns are the right number and gender and that the verbs are the right tense to make sense as the writers add more lines!

After sharing this sample pantoum or one you compose yourself, your students are likely to be inspired to write their own, such as this poem written by an eighth-grader about *Locomotion* by Jacqueline Woodson.

We're All Right*

What's that? It's Locomotion
I smell her, I hear her, is she here?
Mother, Father cries fire
Dancing with her, I remember

I smell her, I hear her, is she here?
Honeysuckle yeah that's her Locomotion yeah that's her
Dancing with her, I remember
I have to find God she says

Honeysuckle yeah that's her Locomotion yeah that's her
Momma yeah she's by my side

I have to find God she says
Church, Lily, me I found God

Momma yeah she's by my side
Mother, Father cries fire
Church, Lily, me I found God
What's that? It's Locomotion

—Anthony

* Based on *Locomotion* by Jacqueline Woodson

True, the poem still requires some editing in terms of punctuation and pronoun/noun agreement before being published as a final draft, but one cannot miss the passion and voice as Anthony portrays the conflict, what he understands, and how he seems to relate to one of the themes revealed in this young-adult novel.

Lazy Sonnets

Here is a simple structured format that works well with ninth-grade students and gutsy younger ones. You may assign these "lazy sonnets" after a formal study of poetry that includes lessons on the traditional fourteen-line sonnets or after teaching Shakespeare's *Romeo and Juliet* or another text that includes sonnets. The students can use this exercise to practice poetry and also to summarize their thoughts about the play. The only rules are to use fourteen words and to follow the rhyme pattern of an Elizabethan (Shakespearean) or Italian (Petrarchan) sonnet.

As a culminating activity following a study of *Romeo and Juliet*, the assignment was simply to encapsulate a key idea, to show the characters, conflicts, or a theme of the play; to use just fourteen words and to end with a rhymed couplet. You could divide the class into five groups, one per act, or a number that fits the play you are studying, and have students in each group write about their assigned act. Here is one Kaveh wrote based on Act V of *Romeo and Juliet*.

Act V

Paris
slain
by
Romeo.
Romeo
then
slew
himself.
Later
Juliet
slew
herself.
Madness
Sadness

—Kaveh

What is particularly fun about writing these lazy sonnets is that they are manageable for a range of students. Students who are frustrated by writing other poetry likely can compose a lazy sonnet successfully. Some even include a rhyme or rhythm pattern as well as the couplet! Your creative students may write quickly enough to enter their sonnets on the computer and print out these unrevised sonnets by the end of the period. Quick. Fun. Enlightening for students. Revealing to you.

CAPTURING PERSONAL EXPERIENCES IN POETRY

Much writing is autobiographical, portraying personal experiences. But it can be more. Joseph Epstein writes, "The personal essay is, in my experience, a form of discovery. What one discovers in writing such essays is where one stands on complex issues, problems, questions, and subjects. In writing the essay, one tests one's feelings, instincts, and thoughts in the crucible of composition."[4] This self-discovery is also true when writing poetry.

For their poetry assignments, encourage, but do not require, students to use their personal experiences and observations as they imitate the structure and pattern of published poetry they enjoy. In keeping with the philosophy of the National Writing Project, write along with your students. This keeps you attuned to what it feels like to write "on demand" and also gives you an opportunity to reveal to your students a little of who you are when you are not teaching. The poem opening this chapter is one written about my son's growing up and leaving home.

Initially, you may be uncomfortable writing about your personal experiences in front of or along with your young teenagers, but it is well worth any risk of discomfort. Be prepared; you and your students may be surprised by what comes out in this kind of writing. Occasionally, however, several of you may decide not to show it to anyone or read it aloud. Honor these decisions. You can let them pass.

Revealing about and to Myself—A Personal Story

One year, when a class was modeling the sentence structure, rhyme, and rhythm pattern of Robert Frost's poetry, students were asked to recreate an experience of their own. You probably recall from attending poetry readings that poets often explain the incident that gave rise to a particular poem. Invite your students to do this, and model such an introduction yourself. That was done before reading the draft of the poem evoked by the Robert Frost poem, "I Have Been One Acquainted with the Night" read that day. Here is what I gave as background for the poem.

"In 1996, I was a part of a team of teachers who, sponsored by Rotary International, served as ambassadors of education to Kenya, Uganda, and the French island of Mauritius. I had never been to Africa and was thrilled about the opportunity, and also a little apprehensive.

"Families in Africa who were curious about us and about our country often volunteered to be our hosts. On our last evening in Mombasa, Kenya, our new friends had a lawn party and invited members of the local Rotary groups and their families to attend. After dinner, our host asked each member of our team to speak about our time in Mombasa. When I arose to speak, trying to compose myself and gather my thoughts, I looked up. Seeing the brilliant night sky, all of a sudden it struck me that I could be standing on the soil of my ancestors;

they could have stood in this same place and witnessed such a sparkly navy blanket of a sky.

"As a fifth-generation descendent of African slaves, I don't know where exactly in Africa my family is from. Nevertheless, standing there in the Kenyan night moved me deeply. Tears leaked from my eyes; primordial memories arose and clogged my throat; I couldn't see; I couldn't speak, but somehow I began to sing the old Negro spiritual 'Sometimes I Feel Like a Motherless Child.' To this day, I have no idea why that particular song came to me. Nor did I realize how deeply lodged in my memory that experience had become—until I began patterning Robert Frost's poem "I Have Been One Acquainted with the Night." It was then that I understood Epstein's point that writing is a form of discovery."

Describing my African experience did help my students understand that we humans often do not know what we think or feel until we read what we write. I encourage you to write with your students. You, too, may unlock something memorable about an experience you have had and may write a poem you are willing to share with your students. Here is mine.

Acquainted with That Song*

I have been one acquainted with that song.
I've sung the song in tune—and out of tune
I have held that high note oh so long.

I have sung the song—clear like a loon.
I have kept within the music's beat
And swooped down low, yet staying right in tune.

I've sung that song and let my voice just soar
While deep within my soul the words brought tears
That slipped right down my cheeks; my heart just tore.

That song, reminding me of trials sore
Experienced by people who did so long
For freedom, justice, rights, and so much more.

Freedoms they'd awaited for too long.
I have been one acquainted with that song.

—Anna J. Small Roseboro

* Patterned after "Acquainted with the Night" by Robert Frost

Converting Prose to Poetry

Another practice activity is transliteration—the act of converting from one genre to another. Young teens love knowing and using such sophisticated words. You could give this assignment after reading together Gordon Parks's poem "The Funeral," where he describes things that appear to have changed since he left his hometown many years ago. You could ask your young teens to write about places that seem different to them now that they are middle school students. They first write a paragraph in prose and then recreate the experience as a poem by condensing the language or creating word images. The move from prose to poetry reiterates the concept of condensed language or the use of sensory and figurative imagery that you talked about earlier in the definition of poetry.

The following is Kristin's paragraph and then her poem, in which she experiments with hyperbole and rhyme:

> Since I've gotten older I have realized many things have changed. The school looks a lot smaller than it used to. My home used to feel roomier and it felt like it had more space. My bed even seems smaller. The walls and sealing feel closer but my sibling seem the same.

Her poem:

Changes*

The walls and the ceiling have started to shrink
While I get taller and taller
And the schools must be fooling my eyes
They're growing smaller and smaller!

My room is getting less roomy.
I can't stretch out in my bed.
I wonder what will happen?
Opps, I've just hit my head.

* Modeled after "The Funeral" by Gordon Parks

A second poem that students seem to enjoy reading, discussing, and patterning is Langston Hughes's "Mother to Son." His poem begins,

"Well, son. I'll tell you:
Life for me ain't been no crystal stair."

Here is Kristin's patterning of Langston Hughes's "Mother to Son"

Life Is Not a Perfect Picnic*

Life is not a perfect picnic
There are many bad conditions like
Ants
And seagulls
And wet grass
And even places without a blanket
Cement
But there is no way you can give up
Or go back
You have to keep on waiting for the grass to dry
And looking for a spot to sit
And eating the food
And sometimes going in the shade
But don't give up
Keep searching for the perfect spot.

—Kristin

* Patterned after "Mother to Son" by Langston Hughes

You may need to remind the students about acknowledging their sources. When students pattern a poem, they should indicate somewhere on the page the title and author of the poem they are modeling. This teaches them academic honesty and also lets them know that patterning is an acceptable way to write, as they notice when reading collections of limericks, sonnets, and haiku. Same patterns. Different personal experiences.

EDITING POETRY

> *The difference between the almost right word and the right word is really a large matter--it's the difference between the lightning bug and the lightning.*

> —Mark Twain in Letter to George Bainton, 10/15/1888[5]

Your students may be curious about ways they can apply to poetry writing what they've been learning about editing prose. Yes, remind them that the genre of poetry represents a more condensed form of writing in which words often serve multiple purposes, and for economy, conscientious poets choose words for their sound and suggestive power. Those poets writing structured poetry have the additional constraint of selecting words that also fit their rhyme and rhythm pattern. Since poetry is designed to recreate incidents, your students could check their drafts to see how many appeals they make to the five senses, the way we experience life.

Invite them to check for the gustatory joy in their work. Consider substituting more interesting words that just feel good in their mouths when they say them. I like *moiling, roiling,* and *cacophony*! The editing stage is a good time to direct your fledgling poets' attention to the thesaurus feature in many word-processing programs and supply them with a copy of a rhyming dictionary, reminding them to keep in mind not only the definition but also the connotation of words they choose.

WRITING ABOUT POETRY

Responding to poetry through essay writing is an important component of poetry study. You can combine writing poetry and writing about poetry in the same unit. If so, it would be beneficial to begin using the poetry analysis strategy called Poetry TIME as outlined in "Teacher Resource B" in the appendix. Then select an appropriately challenging poem, and so the whole class can focus its attention up front, project the poem on a screen and have the students conduct a TIME analysis of it.

You can ask the students to read the poem silently and then listen to you read the poem aloud. Then invite a student to read the poem according to the punctuation, rather than just stopping at the end of each line. This third reading helps the students focus on the fact that poems sometimes include punctuation and that the punctuation serves the same functions as when used in prose, clarifying the meaning of words organized in a particular pattern. It still is beneficial to have a fourth reading of the poem by another student who, by this time, may have an idea of what the poet may be trying to express, and this student may choose to emphasize different words or read at a different pace and thus offer another level of understanding. By the fourth reading, students begin noticing the elements of imagery and music, and they also may sense some emotion—either expressed by the author or experienced by themselves as readers.

If you provide students copies of the poem, also give them a couple of colored pencils. In this case, you have the students underline what strikes them as they read the poem to themselves. On the first reading, encourage the students to underline appealing or thought-provoking words and phrases. Then, before the second reading, have them change pencils to another color and mark what attracts them on this second reading. It is fine to underline the same word or phrase in a second color. Then conclude this version of multiple readings by asking students to read aloud the words and phrases they have underlined. If one student reads a line first, it is all right for another student to repeat it. It is likely that the repeated words and phrases reveal the theme or main ideas of the poem.

Next, after whatever opening reading strategy you choose, have students complete their TIME worksheets on their own, answering questions about the title, thought, theme, imagery, music, and emotion. Then have them turn and talk about their observations with a partner, using their six-inch voices. Finally, conduct a full-class discussion of student reactions and responses. Remind them to use the PIE format—oral practice for writing an analysis of the poem. Ask them to state their point or observation about the poem, illustrate that observation with a direct quotation from the poem, and explain the significance of that illustration. They then are ready for an assignment like the one that follows.

In-Class Writing about Poetry—Telling the TIME

The assignment for students: Carefully read the assigned poem, noting the structure, imagery, and meaning or message for you. Then in response to the poem, write a fully developed essay that includes the following:

- Summary of the poem—What is it about?
- Structure of the poem—What poetic devices does the poet use?
- Personal response to the poem—What poetic devices help create this personal response?
- A thesis statement that indicates the kind of poem it is and your personal response to it.
- A body that explains ways the structure of the poem influences your response.
- Quotations that support your observations.

For homework or during the next class meeting, assign the students to write a three-part essay in which they write the analysis of that poem or one of their own choosing. They should use the information they gathered while "telling the TIME" of the poem.

Another way to have students write about poetry is to invite them to make connections based on their own experiences, a text-to-self response. In the Gordon Parks poem "The Funeral," Parks writes about returning to his hometown after years of absence. The assignment instructs students to consider how a place they knew as a child seemed different when they returned as a young teen. Warren's one-paragraph response follows.

Response to Gordon Park's "The Funeral"
When I was younger I would go the YMCA and for the camp we would go to Discovery Zone. Everyone I knew would go down this slide that was called the black hole. Now I was about 6 then and still disliked the dark and it wasn't just the dark that made the slide scary. It was that I would always create so much friction that it would spark and pop on my skin. I was much shorter

then also, so the slide seamed much larger that it realy was. *3 years later one of my friends had a birthday party at Discovery Zone and amazingly I had gone throw a couple of growth spirts so I was much taller. I went up to the "Black hole" which apparently wasn't so dark as I had previously found. So when I went down it had seemed to extremely short as well.*

Assigning the Poetry Project or Notebook

An effective way to reinforce the interests raised and skills developed during a poetry unit is to have the students assemble a poetry notebook. The collection should include poems students have read and enjoyed as well as poems they have written themselves. Decide how much time you have to devote to this project and activities that allow students to organize their choices around one of the following:

- poems by a single poet;
- poems written on a single idea or theme (family or hobby, love hurts, seasons that reflect life's journey, etc.);
- poems employing common poetic devices; or
- poems reflecting a specific culture or nationality.

If you decide to assign a poetry notebook, it is imperative to inform your students at the beginning of the poetry unit. In this way they can think about and collect poems throughout the weeks you spend on direct poetry instruction. Encourage students to use available digital devices and computers to search for, write, and save their poems; some students may decide to create video, digital, or audio components in their poetry notebooks that can be shared live or online. Remind them to keep a record of their sources, including URL addresses and dates viewed.

Assigning a poetry project is a good way to incorporate a research component into your teaching, too. Your school librarian can help students find background and biographical information on their selected poet and, if access to the Internet is available, refer students to preselected age-appropriate websites. You may even ask your students to read and comment on a critical review written about one of the poets whose work the students include in their notebook. The prompt could be, "In what ways do you agree and/or disagree with the opinions expressed in this review of your author's writing?" Student replies could be just a half-page of word processing in which they also cite the review to which they are responding.

In your planning for the project, check online sites with safe environments where students can post their writing. Some teachers you know may have produced class anthologies using www.lulu.com, a free site for composing and, for a modest fee, that includes an option to print booklets that others can purchase. Some sites require parental permission to post online.

Your colleagues may be familiar with such sites, or you can ask online teacher communities such as the NCTE Connected Community for recommendations.

The choices students have to make for this project, conducting research, writing and selecting poems, deciding formats, creating order, using technology, and collaborating with classmates all are part of an authentic assessment where students are showing what they know and are able to do based on skills they bring and those they learn under your carefully designed tutelage.

RECITING—POETRY OUT LOUD AND IN CHORAL FORM

Words, Words, Words

Words stir me
When I hear them,
When I read them,
When I write them,
When I speak them.
Words urge me
To keep listening,
To keep reading,
To keep writing,
To keep speaking.

Let me hear you so I can know you.
Let me speak so you can know me.

Prodigiously stirring words help me know you.
But viscerally urging words help me know me.

—Anna J. Small Roseboro

Invite local poets or professional groups such as Poetry Alive! to come read or perform for your students, and include time in class for students to prepare and perform poetry for one another. This can be a powerful experience for speakers and listeners as evidenced by the opening poem of this section. That is a poetic response to a performance of student poets. Consider, too, some of the online sites that show poets reading and performing their own work.

When teaching *Romeo and Juliet*, for example, you could require students to memorize the prologue to act 1. To aid the students in learning these fourteen lines, on the day you introduce the play, perform the sonnet yourself, and then have the students echo it back to you, line by line. On subsequent days, begin the class period with the class standing and reciting the sonnet together. Since the prologue previews the plot of the play, this oral, auditory activity provides a regular reminder of what happens as the drama unfolds.

Performing poetry is an occasion to use hand gestures to help the students see and remember the lines and the ideas. Think of the line, "A pair of star-crossed lovers take their lives," when you could begin by holding up the pointer finger of each hand and then bring the fingers together, forming an X, by the time you reach the end of that line of the poem. Logically, when you reach the closing couplet, "which if you with patient ears attend / What here shall miss, our toil shall strive to mend," just point to an ear.

Some days, conduct the chorus of students by beginning the first stanza as a solo, direct one side of the room to recite the next stanza, then have the other side speak the next one, and conclude by saying the closing couplet together. On other days, you might divide the poem into parts and organize speakers by gender. By the second week, when most of the class knows the sonnet by heart, invite individuals to recite a line alone, or with a student "director" while you stand aside or sit as their audience. On the test for the play, offer extra credit for the students to write as many lines of the prologue as they can. Most are able to write the whole sonnet!

You should not be surprised, either, if you see students you taught this way standing around challenging one another to perform this sonnet . . .

with the hand gestures! Repetition and physical movement are powerful reinforcements to learning.

In another lesson, you could assign a poem and then ask small groups to develop their version of a choral reading to perform for the class. A classic performance piece is "The Highwayman" by Alfred Noyes. For a chilling end, suggest that the closing line be spoken by a single, soft-voiced student.

A modern favorite is Maya Angelou's "On the Pulse of Morning," which she recited at the presidential inauguration ceremony for Bill Clinton in 1993.[6] Not surprisingly, no two groups develop the same script. That is just fine. Seeing and hearing different "versions" of this poem expands the students' understanding of and appreciation for the ideas, sounds, and images of the diverse groups Angelou mentions in her memorable masterpiece.

Your teaching colleagues may even welcome an opportunity to have their students witness poetry out loud. So, on performance day, have each class decide the group that gives the most powerful or interesting performance, and then commission this group to represent the class and go "on the road" to recite its rendition of the poem to other classes that meet in your hallway. What pride students feel performing poetry for classes of older or younger students!

CELEBRATING POETRY

By this time in the poetry unit, you and your students have read, written, and performed poetry in class, so you are ready for a special poetry celebration. See "Teacher Resource E" in the appendix, which has ideas for student preparation. It can be simply a special time during the regular class period or a bigger event to which family and friends are invited to come for a program in the cafeteria, auditorium, or library.

For the celebration, invite all the students to memorize and perform a selected poem—one that they have read or one that they have written. If you have multiple classes celebrating together, you could hold an "open mic" time where volunteers come forward to perform their chosen poem. To assure that someone "volunteers," ask students to sign up ahead of time. On the day of the celebration,

- have all students display their notebooks laid on tables like a science fair exhibition;

- invite guests to leave sticky notes with commendations on poems they like;
- have one student master or mistress of ceremonies who welcomes the guests;
- have a second master or mistress of ceremonies who calls on the volunteers to recite their poems; and
- invite everyone in attendance to share the light refreshments.

Be prepared for on-the-spot volunteers who see the joy of performing and want to share the spotlight.

All of this means planning well ahead to reserve the space, to invite administrators to attend, to have microphones in place, and to have refreshments bought or brought and laid out. Students should be recruited to help set up and clean up. Parent volunteers may be available to assist, too.

If you work together with other teachers, you may be able to turn this celebration into a school-wide event. Post student poetry in the halls. Write it with colored chalk on the sidewalks (with permission of the principal, of course). Encourage the students to enter their writing in local, state, and national poetry contests in print, audiovisual, or digital formats or to perform in age-appropriate poetry slam venues.

The poetry celebration is the perfect time to invite students to recite poetry of their nationality, culture, or home language. Since poetry is written to be heard, it does not matter whether everyone in the audience understands every spoken word. Just invite these students to recite a favorite poem, and let them bask in the pleasure of sharing themselves in a language close to their hearts. To enhance the experience of the listeners, though, encourage those students who are comfortable reciting the poem in a language other than English to first give a brief synopsis of the poem—in English.

CONNECTING BEYOND THE CLASSROOM

Many educator websites provide online opportunities for students to expand their knowledge of topics addressed in the books used in language arts courses across North America. You might want to ask students to share their poetic responses to the novel with other classrooms across the nation and around the world via the Internet. If you meet teachers from other schools, counties, or areas of the country, consider a joint project. For instance, a teacher from Florida and another from California set up a "Coast to Coast" project in which students wrote to each other about the poetry that both classes were studying. The instructors posted selected works by a poet from their own state and invited the students to discuss their responses online. The resulting conversation offered the students insightful peer perspectives while affirming that students on both coasts have to learn and apply the same kinds of analytical and evaluative skills. Participants in online social networks for teachers often are seeking collaborators for projects like this.

Consider posting an invitation for other teachers to join your class in this type of assignment based on a commonly read novel. You may decide on other modern favorites such as *The Skin I'm In* by Sharon Flake or *Among the Hidden* by Margaret Peterson Haddix. Use an education site such as edublogs.org, or launch your own on a social network like the National Council of Teachers of English Connected Community website, inviting other teachers who may be teaching the same novel simultaneously. If you begin planning early, you are sure to find other educators willing to coordinate assignments and due dates. Collaboration is invigorating for both students and teachers. As you search for online communities where teachers share resources, visit sites of reputable ones that vet what is published, such as ReadWriteThink.org.

CONCLUSION

Poetry writing need not lead to student defeat or frustration or be a hazard that sends your tour bus into a ditch. Your creative, well-structured lesson planning and nurturing instruction can create an environment in which students compose and recite poetry with pleasure, poise, personality, and pride. Their original poems are likely to become valued souvenirs of this portion of the trip.

You can confirm the fine work of your students and encourage them to submit their poetry for publication in print or on safe Internet sites. Of course, support students who decide to enter local poetry slams, and attend them if you can. While using the experiences of a fictional character can

Figure 7.2.   Give Students the Key to Unlocking Poetry

provide a firm bridge toward students writing about their own lives, writing about personal experiences should not be an assignment requirement. We must honor students' need for privacy.

Celebrate poetry with your students and watch how what they learn about the power of careful word choices, deliberate crafting, attention to organization, and impact of appearance carries over into their reading and writing about other texts. With your help of providing them a key to unlock the poetry of others and to release the poetic endowments of their own, your students look forward to "versing" their lives in poetry, the way I learned to turn my prose thoughts about my son, Robert, into the verse that opens this chapter.

NOTES

1. *Common Core State Standards for English Language Arts & Literacy in History/Social Studies, Science, and Technical Subjects*, http://www.corestandards.org/assets/CCSSI_ELA%20Standards.pdf (accessed May 17, 2012).

2. *Houghton-Mifflin College Dictionary*, s.v. "poetry."

3. *Learning from Lyrics*, http://www.learningfromlyrics.org/ (accessed April 21, 2012).

4. Joseph Epstein, "The Personal Essay: A Form of Discovery," in *The Norton Book of Personal Essays*, ed. Joseph Epstein (New York: Norton. 1997), 15.

5. Mark Twain, letter to George Bainton, October 15, 1888, quotation from TwainQuotes, http://www.twainquotes.com/Lightning.html (accessed May 7, 2013).

6. The text of Maya Angelou's poem "On the Pulse of Morning" can be found on a number of Internet websites.

BOOKS AND WEBSITES TO SUPPLEMENT THE TEACHING OF POETRY

Blum, Joshua, Bob Holman, and Mark Pellington. *The United States of Poetry*. New York: Henry N. Holt, 1996.

Brenner, Barbara, ed. *Voices: Poetry and Art from Around the World*. Washington, DC: National Geographic Society, 2000.

Clinton, Catherine. *A Poem of Her Own: Voices of American Women Yesterday and Today*. New York: Abrams, 2003.

Creech, Sharon. *Love That Dog*. New York: Harper Collins, 2001.

Dunning, Stephen. *Reflections on a Gift of Watermelon Pickle*. Glenview, IL: Scott-Foresman, 1995.

Goldstein, Bobbye, ed. *Inner Chimes: Poems on Poetry*. Honesdale, PA: Boyds Mills Press, 1992.

Holbrook, Sara. *By Definition: Poems of Feelings*. Honesdale, PA: Boyd Mills Press, 2003.

Hollander, John, ed. *Committed to Memory*. New York: Academy of American Poets, 1996.

Janeczko, Paul B., ed. *Seeing the Blue Between: Advice and Inspiration for Young Poets*. Cambridge, MA: Candlewick Press, 2002.

Levine, Gail Carson. *Forgive Me, I Meant to Do It*. New York: HarperCollins, 2012.

Peacock, Molly, Elise Paschen, and Neil Neches, eds. *Poetry in Motion: 100 Poems from Subways and Buses*. New York: Norton, 1996.

Rochelle, Belinda, ed. *Words with Wings: A Treasury of African American Poetry and Art*. New York: Amistad, 2000.

Strickland, Michael, ed. *Poems That Sing to You*. Honesdale, PA: Boyds Mills Press, 1993.

Vecchione, Patrice, ed. *Revenge and Forgiveness: An Anthology of Poems*. New York: Henry Holt, 2004.

Vecchione, Patrice, ed. *Truth and Lies: An Anthology of Poems.* New York: Henry
Holt, 2001.

Websites

- *The Academy of American Poets*
- *American Poems*
- *Favorite Poem Project by Robert Pinsky*
- *Poems Daily*
- *Poetry 180: A Poem a Day for American High Schools*
- *ReadWriteThink*

8

ENTERTAINING WRITING

The Short Story

Short stories should be written to entertain the reader.

Jeremy Hubble[1]

Storytelling is a fundamental activity in many families used to entertain, admonish, persuade, or simply pass along the history and heritage of a culture. You may find that moving from listening to stories, to reading and analyzing stories, to writing stories of their own can be an empowering experience for middle school students. They have stories to tell, and inviting your students to write their stories is a natural way to reinforce their academic skills while you encourage and affirm these adolescents personally.

Writing about real or imagined experiences by modeling the elements of fiction they already are learning inevitably helps students develop a better understanding of themselves and the world around them. Students who have learned the basic elements of narrative fiction are well prepared to write easy-to-follow stories of their own. Some are eager to begin regardless of whether or not they understand plot, point of view, and theme. Writing, reading, and responding to their peers expands their understanding of this genre of literature, too.

Including units on short-story writing offers several opportunities to learn about one another while fulfilling curriculum standards guiding most school English language arts programs as well as the Common Core State Standard that students should be able to "write narratives to develop real or imagined experiences or events using effective technique, well-chosen details, and well-structured event sequences."[2] The early drafts your youngsters write using some of the ideas in this chapter should give you a good sense of specific elements of fiction to review along the way, as students are being encouraged to model what they have read. After experimenting with different ways to draft, invite your student to flesh out their stories and submit them for evaluation and publication.

CHANNELING THE MASTERS

This term *to channel* simply means to consider the guidance of those who have come before and also to provide a protective passage from one source to another. Edgar Allan Poe suggested that a short story should be written to be read in a single sitting and be so focused as to produce a unifying effect. To help your students focus their attention and to create a unifying effect in an entertaining way, consider having them work with a single protagonist in a limited setting who strives to resolve a single conflict. Also refer them regularly to storytellers whom they enjoy and writing you have studied together.

Beware: Bumps Ahead

Since some students are not keen about this assignment, allot just enough time for all students to draft a brief story—not so long that you cannot maintain enthusiasm for the task. Be observant as you coach the students through this process, and adjust the teaching pace as needed. Initially, plan to spend about two weeks.

Hint: Tell students that it might help them to tell the story to themselves, in their heads, before writing. If they can describe to themselves a problem to be resolved in a few sentences, they probably have a story. Stress the ideas of conflict and resolution so that they create stories that have real plots rather than just a series of incidents. Set up pairs of students and encourage the partners to tell each story to each other. Or assign the students to try out their story at home or with their seat partner on the bus.

KEEPING IT PERSONAL WITHOUT BEING INTRUSIVE

Experienced authors know that using personal experiences lends authenticity to their writing. But asking students to do this may cause resistance if they feel they are being asked to "spill their guts." So you may find it better to take it slow. Allow distance between what you require them to write based on their personal lives. You could suggest they put themselves into the "story" as a friend or foe of the person they are writing about or by becoming the protagonist in the setting they describe based on a picture or photo they have selected, as demonstrated in an activity below.

In other words, when assigning the narrative, move step by step from the impersonal to the personal, encouraging students to use their experiences to flesh out their narratives but not requiring them to write about their own specific experiences.

CREATING A CLASS STORY

Plan a brief class lesson for which students create a basic plot outline.

- Ask for a protagonist.
- Ask for a setting (any setting!).
- Ask for a conflict likely involving an additional character.
- Ask how the conflict might be resolved.
- What attempts would the protagonist probably make to solve the problem?
- Who cares? This is the toughest question but one that pushes students to create more interesting stories with some intrigue.
- Be visual: to help visual learners, diagram the plot on the board or screen as you create the story and have students fill it in as they respond to prompts. Order is not important at first. They may work backwards and still come up with an intriguing tale.

In other words, do your best to ensure that students are thinking "story" before they begin writing their narratives. You may find the "Entering Art" activity described later will provide a rich experience that could be expanded into dramatic narratives. Encourage interested students to use their ideas for prewriting. Some could graph their own plotlines and draw character "sketches" before they try to express those creative thoughts formally in writing, in another medium—in this case, the short story.

CROSSING CURRICULUM BORDERS FOR WRITING INSPIRATION

Middle school students value opportunities to use what they learn in one class to enhance the work they do in others. Why not invite your students to use information from history or social studies as fodder for short-story writing? You could even collaborate with your colleagues in other content areas to arrange units to be taught concurrently or subsequently. For example, after the students have studied a particularly rich historical period with lots of intriguing characters or action-filled adventures, plan for your students to write stories inspired by those people, places, and events. After all, there is an entire subgenre of historical fiction. After students have studied particular units in life science or physical science in which they have investigated concepts in biology, geology, chemistry, or physics, invite stories that incorporate that information. After all, there is an entire subgenre of science fiction.

Students can do the same kind of cross-curricular writing by incorporating their newly gained experiences in art, music, math, and physical education. The specific details about a piece of music, or solving a math problem, or rules in a sports game can make a story more entertaining and believable. After all, there is an entire subgenre of . . . you get it. Fiction writers utilize what they know about all kinds of subjects, so encourage your students to draw on their studies to enhance their short story writing, too.

HELPING "STORYLESS" STUDENTS

Sometimes students still have difficulty coming up with a story to write. What to do?

1. Ask them to model a story they already have read for class but with characters and settings that are familiar to them. Following that pattern reminds them of the elements of fiction.

   Have students bring to class pictures from print or online publications and then write stories to accompany these images. For example, a week before beginning the story-writing assignment, assign students to bring in three pictures—one of each which meet the following criteria:
   - only one person in the picture
   - a group of people in a specific place
   - scenery only—a place, with no people

You should discourage the students from choosing pictures of easily identifiable persons or celebrities to reduce the temptation for the students to limit their imaginations and have their story characters become exactly like celebrity personae.

Organize and store the pictures in three labeled envelopes until it is time to start the story writing a few days later. It is good for students to forget about the article, magazine, or setting from which they took the pictures, so ask them to bring in the pictures about a week before you plan to use them. Let those who may not have access to magazines at home come before or after school to search through the box of magazines you may keep in your room, or have students print out pictures from a neighborhood library or school computer.

Here's a way to set up this prewriting assignment based on pictures:

1. Before the class arrives for a day of story writing, write the prompts on the board or another classroom medium, such as digital slides.
2. Arrange the pictures in the three categories, face down on a tabletop.
3. Ask students to have paper and a pen or pencil on their desks or their computers opened to a blank page in a word-processing program.
4. Invite them to come forward in a logical fashion to take one picture from each pile before returning to their seats. You might even play a lyric-free song and ask students to march up to the music, pick up the pictures, and return to their seats before the tune concludes. Yes,

there may be clowning around. But as long as students are orderly, ignore it.

5. Give students two minutes to look at the pictures they have and decide which one they would like to write about and return the rejects to the table so that others might use them. Complete the selection in ten minutes or so. Then urge students to keep what they have and see what happens. Few students fail to come up with a workable story.

6. Set a timer for five minutes for a "quick-write"—nonstop writing until the timer goes off.

7. Encourage students to write as though their chosen picture illustrates the story they are drafting.

8. Suggest that they begin writing either in the first person as a character in the story or as an omniscient writer who reveals the thoughts and feelings of the characters.

9. If students cannot think immediately of what to write, direct their attention to the posted instructions, or distribute a handout with the following prompts:

If using the picture with one person, write as though you are that person. Write about:

- why you are in this place;
- what happened just before the picture was taken; and
- what's on your mind.

If using the picture of a group of people, choose one of the people and write in that persona. Talk about:

- why you are here with this person or these people.
- how you feel about the others.
- what happened just before the picture was taken.

If using the scenic picture of a place, make this the setting of the story and describe it using such strong, vivid images that an artist could draw the scene using only your writing. Reveal:

- the time period (day, season, historical period).
- what happened just before the picture was taken.
- what is going to happen in this place.

When the timer goes off, invite the youngsters to reread their prose and circle any ideas that might be developed into a story that has characters in a specific place, confronted with and attempting to overcome some specific conflict. Remind them that short stories usually take place in a short period of time, often within a single hour, day, or week. Give your young authors-to-be the remainder of the period to expand on the ideas evoked by this quick-write.

As the students continue writing in the coming days, encourage them to include at least three increasingly difficult obstacles to overcome. Remind them that in a successful story, the protagonist solves the problem in a logical way or decides that there is no solution and, after valiant attempts to solve the problem, ceases the struggle. Discourage "and then he woke up." Push students to consider alternatives that lead to a thoughtful, insightful, and even surprising, but satisfying conclusion.

Exploring Visual Art

Just as travelers often visit art museums to learn more about a community, town, or culture, you can invite your students to view and write about art as a way of learning, too. Ask students to choose a painting by one of the artists mentioned in a historical novel such as *I, Juan de Pareja* or one from the period or book you are studying or they are studying in history. Selections may be by artists you have studied together or chosen because they reflect artistic styles and cultures similar to those students already have seen. The goal is to offer a variety of paintings for students to view and make connections between experiences the students have had reading the literature or just living life. Begin with a common viewing experience, and then let students choose and write about their piece of art.

The following activities are based on notes from a workshop, "Entering Art," led by Terry and Jenny Williams at the Detroit Institute of Art.[3] Variations on these suggestions work to evoke inspiring student poetry as well as essays because art invites imaginative entry into its drama, mood, theme, locality, texture, and space. Both representational and abstract art can lure viewers into the artist's original act of creation. By all means, consult with the art teachers for suggestions appropriate for middle school students.

This imaginative entry evokes all five senses, memories, and dreams as students look and allow themselves to feel and imagine. Allow a full period for this assignment to give time for an experience that is personal and uniquely students' own and time to put experience into words that enrich both their own viewing and the work of art itself. And so that you can write along with your students, set the timer to ring five minutes before the end of the period to have time to debrief.

1. Have a large, sharp copy of the artwork projected when the students arrive in the classroom.
2. Play soft, lyric-free instrumental music as a mood-creating background while students take their seats and you do that beginning-of-the-period record keeping.
3. Invite the students to join you, and all of you view the artwork silently for three minutes. Yes, three full minutes.
4. Then distribute the handout with the prompts you choose for the art you have.
5. Read each step aloud slowly and softly, pausing between prompts to allow time for students to look at the art and to mentally respond.
6. Finally, invite the students to choose the kind of "entry" they would like to write about, and let them write for the next twenty minutes or so. Join in the experience; write along with your students.

Invite your students to turn to a partner and read what they have written. It is revealing to have students who have viewed the same picture read what they experienced as they entered the work.[4]

You could extend this kind of exploring and writing and have your students use preselected website collections of art or photos like those at the Google Art Project or 24 Hours in Pictures. In the second instance, students could locate the photos taken on their own birth date. View all, choose one, and write about it. This writing could be developed into a story, a poem, a dramatic scene, an explanation, a protest, a news article, a letter, or a speech. With the final draft, a copy of the art or photo could then be shared with the class, posted on the class website, and evaluated by you, using a customized Six Traits rubric created by student(s) doing the same genre to respond to the visual images. Their creating the rubric gives them ownership but also reminds them of qualities expected in effective and interesting writing.

BOX 8.2: ENTERING ART

1. Step inside the artwork. Let its space become your space. What does it feel like as you journey into the painting? Where are you? What do you hear? Smell? What do you notice under your feet? Imagine you can touch something in the painting. What would that be? How would it feel?

2. Write about the artwork as if it were a dream. Bring the scene to life and leave us in that moment. Use "In a dream, I . . ." or "Last night I had the strangest dream . . ." or simply, "I dreamed . . ."

3. Write about the scene as if it were happening now, using present tense and active verbs. Begin with "I am . . ." Move around inside the work and make things happen. Begin a line with "Suddenly . . ." in order to create surprise, moving into something unexpected.

4. Write about the work as if it were a memory. List short, separate memories or one long memory. Both invent and remember as you write.

5. Imagine the art as something you see outside a window. Begin with "From my window, I see . . ."

Art illuminates
lessons we teach our students
and they understand.

—Anna Roseboro

By the end of the picture-writing activity, most students are excited about developing their stories, so you can assign them to continue drafting their story for homework or to leave their quick-write and notes in their classroom folder so that they can resume writing at the next class meeting. In the interim, encourage them to listen to the rhythm of conversations to attune their ears to writing realistic dialogue. You should not be surprised when many students return to the next class meeting brimming with ideas of how to continue their story.

Fleshing out Flat or Skeletal Characters

If students need models, refer them to characters in readings that they have already studied. Ask them to pay attention to the way the authors revealed the characters' personality and motivation. As with fan fiction, modeling a favorite author can effectively jumpstart students' writing. Remember the annual Hemingway imitation contests? Encourage students to use direct and indirect characterization to add depth and breadth to people in their stories. Just from the written descriptions, could an artist accurately draw their characters?

Building Suspense

Ask students to

- circle the sentence in their story that indicates the conflict the protagonist is facing. No such sentence? Time to add one!
- put a rectangle around the sentence in the story that identifies the antagonist.
- diagram their story with a plot line to verify that their protagonist is faced with a believable problem and is making logical choices while facing increasingly complicated obstacles in an attempt to resolve the conflict. Remind them of the image of a roller-coaster ride.

Encourage students to revise so that their stories flow to a suspenseful climax and to include the thoughts of the protagonist as he or she considers the final step to solving the problem. The final attempt to solve a problem often is an internal conflict during which the protagonist struggles with issues of right and wrong, safe and unsafe, advantageous and disadvantageous. Remind students that dialogue can reveal inner thoughts when one is writing in objective or third-person point of view.

Complete the first draft for homework, a word-processed copy for class in two days. If this homework assignment is not a realistic expectation for the students you have, arrange time to use the school computers for a couple of class periods. Encourage students to use the rubric the class creates or that you provide to evaluate the draft of their own story before submitting it for peer review.

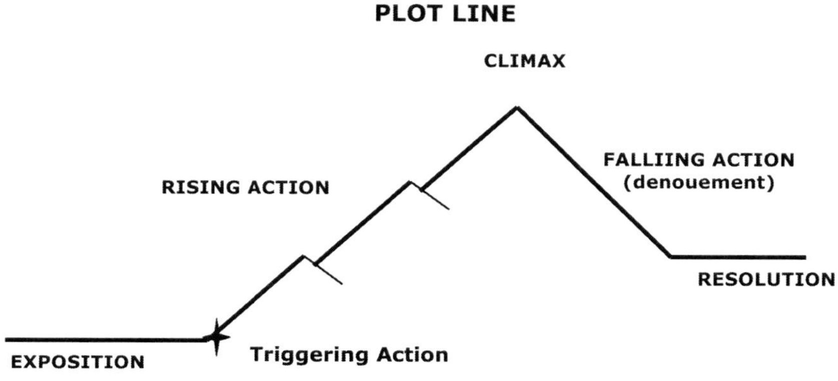

PLOT LINE

CLIMAX

RISING ACTION

FALLIING ACTION
(denouement)

RESOLUTION

EXPOSITION **Triggering Action**

Figure 8.1. Plot—Series of Events in a Story

PRACTICING PEER RESPONSES

Professional writers have editors who read their drafts and offer suggestions for revision. Even before sending their manuscripts to a publisher, many professional writers participate in a writing group or simply ask friends or colleagues to read drafts and give them useful feedback. Allay adolescent skepticism by letting your fledglings know that no one publishes fiction without editors who check everything from storyline to grammar. No writer is that good.

Now is the time for students to serve one another as helpful, encouraging peer responders. Establish either writer-responder partners or small (three to four students) writers' groups within the class to review each other's drafts and make suggestions. The purpose is to give positive feedback in tune with the basic rubrics the students have already created. Positive: "What a vivid descriptive passage. I can almost feel the wind blowing across the meadow." Encouraging suggestions: "Wow, have you thought about telling what the character is thinking right here?" Professional writers frequently have brittle egos. So do amateur writers of any age.

Students usually have good ideas for improving stories. However, in order to keep the peer comments on track, provide the criteria they are to consider on a printed peer-response sheet with a rubric in chart form that includes those statements about what constitutes an effective story. You may create your own or invite your students to help develop these criteria statements with statements about content and creativity, organization and flow, as well as quality of vocabulary and correctness relating to mechanics, usage, and grammar. Your budding authors then can share the assessment standards and presumably the stories with parents or guardians, too.

A number of teacher websites, such as Rubistar, have templates and programs for creating and modifying rubrics to meet the specific requirements of a variety of language arts assignments.[5] See "Teacher Resource C" in the appendix for other ideas to supplement the one that follows.

Once the students understand the rubric, let them have a go at it. Provided you have given the writers enough time and feedback to do their own revisions first, the peer review process should go smoothly and helpfully. Here are two ways to conduct either the partner (or small group) workshop responding sessions.

Option A: Working in Pairs—Desk-Touching Exercises

Ask students to pull desks together to work in pairs. Touching desks suggests sharing a common work surface, physical permission to collaborate. Or if your room is furnished with tables, you may have students pull their chairs together so that the conversation between two students can be private, without distracting or disturbing their other table mates. The rest is gloriously simple but effective:

- Remind students to speak in six-inch voices so that only their partners can hear them as each one reads his or her story to the other one. Let the partner hear how the story sounds as narrated by the author. If there are an odd number of students, serve as a partner yourself, using the story you have been drafting along with the class.
- Encourage students to listen for consistency in point of view and verb tense.
- Then, as students respond to authors, have the authors take a few notes on their own drafts.
- Once the comments are concluded, allow time in class for authors to begin making corrections and revisions as they see fit. Assure them that their stories are their own works; they do not have to make the suggested revisions. But they do need to address grammatical issues and should correct other problems that may cloud communication.

Figure 8.2. Peer Response Groups Can Be Effective

Sometimes it is necessary to modify your teaching timeline based on what you overhear during the desk-touching exercises. If the majority of the students sound as though they need another day of writing before sharing in groups, extend the due date. Good writing takes less time to grade. Keep students on task by making your presence felt and coaching their understanding as needed.

Option B: Working in Groups—Writers' Workshop

Once the students have worked with a partner and revised their stories, it's time to hold a workshop for their stories in a format recommended by the National Writing Project.[6]

1. Ask students to group themselves into three circles (ten to twelve students)—A, B, and C.
2. Instruct them to pass their drafts to a volunteer group leader in the circle.

3. Collect the stacks of papers and redistribute group A papers to leader B, group B papers to leader C, and group C papers to leader A. (Students will be less distracted if their own paper is not in their circle.)

4. Set a timer for two minutes.

5. Once the leader passes the stories to group members, each student should read as much of the story as possible until the timer goes off. Then pass that draft to the right.

6. Repeat reading and passing papers to the right until all but one of the drafts has been read.

7. Distribute the blank copy of the peer-response worksheet, and ask the students to write the name of the student writer and complete that sheet for the last draft they receive to read. Set the timer for five minutes to allow to time to read and write.

8. Next, encourage them to talk among themselves about the general strengths they see in the set of drafts and the problems they recognize they have made themselves and plan to correct to improve their next draft.

9. Take some time now to have a general class discussion and list on the board what seems to be working in the stories so far and what are the main areas on which students need to focus their attention during revising.

10. At the end of the period, return the draft and peer-response sheet to each author and assign a revision to be due in two or three days.

Before the final draft is due, take the time to review the grading rubric with the students so that they can once again assess their own work before you grade it. If they notice something that should be corrected, ask them to do so neatly. You want to see what they know, not a photo-ready version of the story. When students have a clear idea of what is expected of them, they are more likely to meet those expectations. The fewer surprises, the fewer challenges to grades.

You may decide to schedule a second read-around session when the students have finished their stories and are ready to submit them for publication outside the school. In this case, if this has been a generally positive and supportive group of students, you could ask them to rank and rate the stories of their peers. If so, you may find it useful to use "Teacher Resource C" as a guide to set up an assignment which suggests that students work with papers with no names on them and from a different class period. This gives students a little more anonymity and makes for more objective reading.

GRADING DURING STORY COMPOSITION

Monitor student work, but resist the temptation to grade drafts based on final content criteria. Each day that you expect the students to come prepared with work on their stories, consider rubber-stamping the last page written and record checkmarks in your grade book to indicate that the students are completing the drafting assignments. If they are working on computers, they should post a copy in the class folder set up for student storage, not one from which they can delete files. You then can view them before, during, or after class and get an idea of how stories are coming along. You also can post a general commendation or recommendation.

It really is too early to begin grading the quality of their work. Why? Because these early drafts are like practice sessions or training drills. For sports, it is the scores of the games that go in the record book to determine the success of the season.

Now is the time to serve as the students' model and coach. Your attitude is important and more empathetic if you draft a story with your students and offer yours for comments, too. Model making appropriate comments or suggestions, offering positive statements even as you point out a weakness that needs to be addressed: "Great idea for a setting." "Do you think you have enough conflict?" "Is that enough description of the protagonist so that readers could get to know her better?" "This section suddenly changes the story's point of view. How about staying with first person so the reader doesn't get confused?"

Whenever you respond to students' creative work orally or in writing, you run the risk of unintentionally deflating their enthusiasm. You can often get at story problems simply by asking questions. If a student needs more direction than what you can provide with general questions, try more directive questions: "What do you think about rewriting the scene so it seems more realistic—something that might actually happen?" "How do you think adding some thought shots that tell or show how the characters are thinking can increase the suspense?"

Recording daily checkmarks in your grade book provides support for student progress, letting them know that writing is a process and that drafting is a step that counts. If, during this drafting period, you have to report to parents or an administrator about students' performance, you can rely on the comments you have made in the journals along with any other notes you make about students' active involvement in the daily assignments.

GUIDING STUDENTS TOWARD FINAL DRAFTS

Just as professionals submit their work following their publisher's guidelines, require your students to do the same. Your guidelines could be like those that follow.

1. Print final drafts double-spaced on white paper with one-inch margins, using a ten- or twelve-point font. Times New Roman, Arial, or Bookman are most readable (avoid unusual fonts).
2. Drafts should be three to five pages long.
3. Add a title sheet with the story title with no quotation marks, your full name, the class and time period it meets, the teacher's name (spelled correctly!), and the due date arranged neatly on the page.
4. Use the picture from the first classroom exercise, an original drawing, or a computer-generated image as an illustration with final draft if desired. Be sure to give credit if using an image from a website. (Write the web address in small letters under the image. See the "Insert Caption" option.)
5. Submit all of your work on the story, stapled together. Include a handwritten label on the bottom for each section: Draft 1, Peer Response, Draft 2, First Plot Line, and Final Draft, and any others that show evidence of the process. The packet is visible and tactile evidence of what it takes to write a good story. (If students are submitting stories online, earlier drafts still can be included in the final file. You could ask students to save each day's work as a separate file that includes the date.)

6. Celebrate! When all of this work is organized and stapled together for submission with title page or saved and sent, do something fun.

Do follow through with a full class celebration—such as an authors' reception or a book-publishing party in class. Invite students to bring in "neat to eat" treats. (Be cautious about treats with nuts, to which some students have severe allergic reactions. Cold water is a lovely beverage, especially if you add slices of lemon and serve it in small paper cups with decorations on them; and water doesn't stain if spilled!) You might randomly select stories to read aloud to the class yourself or to invite the authors to read—as dramatically as they would like to do. Let the authors embellish their reading if they are comfortable. Join the fun by reading something that you have written.

BOX 8.1: BLOG IT! PUBLISHING ONLINE FAN FICTION*

Another way to encourage students to publish is to offer credit for students' contributions to online "fan fiction." These "works in progress" are essentially readers' own writings designed either to extend novelists' printed prose or sometimes to comment on novelists' works using "drabbles" (short, hundred-words-or-less vignettes that rely on characters or settings from the original works).

Fan fiction is like blogging (web "logging," or commenting on subjects and experiences). Fans write on special fan fiction websites rather than on their own blogs or social networking pages on Facebook, MySpace, and the like.

* Fan fiction is still emerging as a valid educational activity and has not been addressed comprehensively in the educational literature, so be sure to check out the sites before recommending them to your students. See FanFiction.net as a sample.

PUBLISHING STUDENT STORIES

The truly final step for some students might be publishing their story on campus—in print form, in digital form on your pages of the school website, or in an off-campus printed periodical or on one of the websites that publishes student work. Carefully choose from the myriad sites now available on the internet, sites like Edublog and Writing Fix, avoiding those with inappropriate advertising and those that do not provide for privacy of students' personal information.

Consider collaborating with other teachers of your school and creating a school anthology to publish by the end of the school year. Offering students a few points of credit is enough for simply submitting their work to an out-of-school publication. It is a big step for some of your adolescent writers. And do not be the least surprised when one or two students who submit their work each year have it selected for a print journal or anthology. This simply encourages others to try the next time.

Your librarian may agree to display in the library a loose-leaf binder with the stories your students write. Just get one of those white binders with a clear pocket cover and slip in a student-designed or computer-generated cover, and then add a table of contents of the stories arranged alphabetically by author. Other students tend to respect peers' work and enjoy reading it—especially the older students who remember when their writing was similarly displayed. Or you can publish using one of the online sites on which you can create an electronic literary magazine, using www.lulu.com, a free site for composing and one that, for a modest fee, includes an option to print booklets that others can purchase.

CONCLUSION

Just do it! Go ahead and allot class time to write, and offer students an opportunity to publish their own stories locally in your classroom or library, in a printed periodical, or in a digital magazine. All this will validate that what your budding authors have to say is important enough to revise and edit, to polish and share with others. These publications will be like photo albums of your journey with your fellow travelers, working together to meet the curriculum targets or Common Core Standards for Reading and Writing.

NOTES

1. Jeremy Hubble, "'Here We Are Now, Entertain Us': Poe's Contributions to the Short Story," April 7, 1996, http://geocities.jeremyhubble.com/poe.html (accessed April 16, 2013).

2. "English Language Arts Standards » Anchor Standards » College and Career Readiness Anchor Standards for Language," Common Core State Standards Initiative, http://www.corestandards.org/the-standards/english-language-arts-standards/anchor-standards (accessed July 12, 2012).

3. Terry Williams and J. Williams, "Image, Word, Poem: Visual Literacy and the Writing Process," workshop presented at National Council of Teachers of English Annual Convention, Detroit Institute of Art, 1997.

4. Williams and Williams, "Image, Word, Poem."

5. RubiStar, http://rubistar.4teachers.org/index.php (accessed June 13, 2012).

6. Harvey Daniels and Steven Zememan, "Conferences: the Core of the Workshop," in *Teaching the Best Practice Way: Methods that Matter, K–12*, Harvey Daniels and Marilyn Bizar (Portland, ME: Stenhouse, 2005), 182.

9

PLAYING IT RIGHT
Reading, Writing, and Performing Drama

I order you to be silent! And I issue a collective challenge! Come,
I'll write down your names. Step forward, young heroes! You'll all
have a turn; I'll give each of you a number. Now, who wants to be
at the top of the list? You, sir? No? You? No? [Silence] No names?
No hands. . . . Then I'll get on with my business.

—Cyrano speaking in *Cyrano de Bergerac* by Edmond Rostand[1]

Cyrano's rousing speech may not have been as successful as he would have liked, but he certainly delivered it with enthusiasm and passion. You need the same passion to draw your students into reading and writing drama. Drama permeates teachers' and students' lives via TV, movies, school productions, YouTube, and so many other venues, making it a challenge to teach dramatic literature simply by reading it or writing drama without reading it. But that is exactly the way some drama is handled in middle school English classes. That need not be the case with you.

Middle school students really thrive in classrooms where they can stretch their dramatic creativity, imagining what words could sound like spoken onstage and what characters and scenes could look like onstage. And teaching a work of drama is a superb opportunity to broaden your students' experience with literature and to expand their understanding of the unique features of this literary genre. Here are ways to help your young teens further develop their own expressive oral reading and their creative writing skills, as well as those Common Core State Standards Anchor Skills to "analyze how two or more texts address similar themes or topics in order to build knowledge or to compare the approaches the authors take."[2] In this chapter are techniques that can produce a far better response to drama than poor Cyrano elicited.

Come explore lessons based on *Cyrano de Bergerac*, *Romeo and Juliet*, and an in-depth unit on playwriting. Even if you select other plays traditionally taught in middle school like *The Diary of Anne Frank* by Frances Goodrich and Albert Hackett or *A Midsummer Night's Dream* by Shakespeare, you can adapt these ideas for your setting. The list at the end of the chapter recommends plays to consider teaching your students in addition to or in place of what already is in your curriculum. Reading any of them will better prepare your students for writing pretty good one-act plays.

Drama, like other narrative literature, is written about characters facing conflict. In this genre, dramatists create their scripts to be performed by actors who assume the roles of characters in the story. In drama, however, the setting—the time and place—is revealed primarily through sets, lights, props, and costumes suggested in stage directions, and readers must rely more heavily on the dialogue that reveals character and advances plot. Unfortunately, middle school students are tempted to skip those important instructions; inexperienced readers tend to jump directly to the dialogue and experience confusion, even frustration, when they do not understand what is really happening. Consequently, the aspects of drama to teach first are its unique features. Begin the unit pointing out those distinctive elements as you remind your maturing readers that characters and conflict are common to fiction in general.

PLANNING AHEAD

Plan your assignments so that students can read aloud each day and so that all who want to do so have an opportunity to read one major role at least once. If students can be depended upon to study the scenes ahead of time at home, assign parts as homework so that students can practice reading aloud. Otherwise, allow class time for silent reading so that your students can be familiar with the lines and are able to read them expressively in character. Few things dampen enthusiasm for studying drama more than poor oral reading. To interpret the roles effectively, your young actors need to know what is going on and what the lines portend.

Keep in mind, too, that plays are written to be viewed in a single theatrical sitting (perhaps with intermissions). Therefore, if you stretch out the initial reading over too many days or weeks, you lose the essence of the drama. So once the class has read the exposition of the play and is familiar with the main characters and the problem(s) to be solved, keep the action alive by moving as quickly through the play as possible. Then, after you have read the entire play, go back and have students practice and present scenes, and talk about the effectiveness of the literary devices the dramatist has used to create this play.

This doubling back reinforces and clarifies what may have been missed on the original reading. Even as skillful a reader as you are, you are not likely to have come to the level of understanding you now have from just a single read of the play. To enhance the conversations and enrich the discussion, a complete first reading is needed before discussions, writing assignments, and small-group performances. Later in the unit, when you have the students begin writing, allot time for reading aloud their drafts to help ensure their final scripts sound more like real dialogue.

Small-Group Performances

As students begin working in groups to make decisions on how to act out the play, anticipate the four natural stages of development: forming, storming, norming, and performing. Be prepared for students to grumble that their part is too large or too small; encourage staging that includes simple costumes and/or props; consider naming as the director "whoever is creating the biggest stink!" Most of all, keep in mind during this time of middle school students preparing to present scenes that the best-laid plans often are better modified than forced.

The keys for success are to have a goal, explain the goal, and then let the students plan how to implement it. However, they still need you there. Be observant; step in firmly so that students use more of the class time practicing than bickering. Setting your kitchen timer to ring ten minutes before the period ends helps you use these final minutes to rearrange the room, to reflect on what went well, and to remind the students of the next day's assignment. But the sooner they begin planning and practicing, the more likely your young thespians are to learn and enjoy drama. Oh yes, this is a noisy activity!

Attending Live Performances

Check to see whether a local theater company is scheduled to perform the play your students are to study, and try to attend it. Preparing to go see the performance provides another occasion to talk about the difference between reading a play and seeing it performed. Even if it is not convenient to take a whole class to a play, you may be able to invite members of the cast to visit your school. If a different but appropriate play is being staged, still consider taking your students to see it. Experiencing good live theater performance enhances your teaching and extends students' learning.

What if performance prices are high or your school is not near a college or civic theater program that may offer lower rates? Ask around. Or consider community theater groups with educational outreach programs established to introduce students to live theater. Put out the word that you are looking for someone in the area with stage experience; you might find a terrific and inexpensive guest speaker thrilled to come. Also, investigate organizations that might help underwrite the cost of bringing in a touring group; service organizations such as the Kiwanis, Rotary, Lions, and Optimist Clubs, local foundations, and arts associations are possibilities, too.

Planning the Field Trip

If you are new to your school or district and you decide to plan an outing to the theater, consult with your administrator and seek advice from other teachers who have experience with field trips. Trips can take weeks of planning: coming up with the finances, raising the funds for those who cannot afford tickets, transportation, chaperones, and permission slips. But do not be dissuaded by naysayers. Attending a live performance can be an eye-opening experience well worth the effort you expend. Careful planning can make it a pleasure.

Young students enjoy being known as a respectful audience, and you can help them become one! Ushers at school-age performances of plays know which schools and which teachers at those schools have well-mannered students. You can inspire commendable behavior even in rowdy young teenagers. Believe it or not, what they wear makes a difference, but no need to tell them how important it may be to you. Instead, urge students to dress for the occasion with special attire appropriate for your community. When teenagers are dressed well, they seem to behave better.

The public talks. So do what you can to prepare your students to confirm your school's good reputation or to surprise others that your particular class is better behaved than expected. For some students, this may be their first experience with live theater. It is exciting for them. Some will be awed by the ambience. You can allay their anxiety and reduce their squirrelly behavior if you can show them pictures of the interior of the theater and a layout of the facility. This will increase their curiosity and prepare them for what to expect. Encourage them to talk about the experience before, during the ride to and from the theater, and afterwards in the classroom. For young teens, this entire process may be a highlight of the school year. They may even decide to write a play about their going to see one!

LITERARY DEVICES AND VOCABULARY IN DRAMA

Studying a play is an excellent venue for expanding or reinforcing the list of literary terms taught about the elements of fiction and of poetry. For example, as you study *Cyrano de Bergerac*, this list could include those elements that Rostand used so brilliantly, such as:

- allusion
- ballad
- dramatic irony
- mood
- verbal irony

If the play is in your anthology, you may rely on the literary terms and vocabulary featured in the text. The editorial staff usually does a fine job of selecting words middle school students need to know to understand the play, along with some vocabulary that would be good for them to add to their speaking and writing vocabularies. Of course, take time for students to look up and talk about any other words that interest them or trip them up when they are reading or talking about the play. By the second semester, when many course outlines suggest teaching drama, the students are comfortable with each other and with you, are open to acknowledging gaps in their understanding, and are accustomed to looking up words they do not know.

GETTING INTO READING THE PLAY

Staging Tableaux

The best preparation for attending an off-site performance is a good in-class experience reading a play. Start right with the list of characters, the author's description of setting, and the stage directions. Encourage students to predict. For example, if there are family members, ask the students what

BOX 9.1: PROJECT IT! ESTABLISHING VISUAL HISTORICAL CONTEXT FOR A PLAY

Dramatic scripts tell the readers as well as the director when and where the action takes place. If the time and place are unfamiliar to students, show them photos or video clips to help them visualize the setting as they read the dialogue. Websites such as YouTube and Vimeo, along with video archive sites sponsored by the American Film Institute and the UCLA film archives, provide tens of thousands of short clips that (1) were shot in historical locations, (2) recreate historical settings and locations, and (3) illustrate both costuming and dialogue for historical periods. These sites are not always easily searchable by keyword, so it's best to search concretely by the names of films that you have already linked to a period. Preview everything.

conflicts they anticipate among those persons, considering their age and gender. Think about the setting. What is likely to occur in the time and place the author has chosen? Based on the stage directions, where should the characters be positioned when the curtain opens?

To help students get a feel for drama, ask students to read the opening scene silently. Then, with no explanation from you of what they have read, invite one student to come silently to the front of the class and stand where a specific character would stand if he or she were onstage. Then, one at a time, beckon other students individually to assume the personae of particular characters and to take their places in relation to those already positioned there in the front. Ask the rest of the class to observe silently until all characters in the scene are positioned. At that time, call for a freeze—students silently stand in place—to create a tableau, montage, or representation of that scene.

Now ask the class its opinions of the character placement. Before those in the tableau lose their concentration and begin squirming or melting, unfreeze them so that they can return to their seats to join the discussion. Invite participants from the tableau to identify lines from the play that support their own choice of position. Invite them all to look at the script to determine the passages that justify the tableau just presented or to propose an arrangement more accurate to the text. Of course, those who disagree should be asked to quote from the text to show why an alternate placement seems more accurate. Taking time to consider placement on the stage will help your students write more realistic drama when they begin their own playwriting.

Your well-taught students know to pay attention to what happens in the opening sections of any work of fiction, whether short story, narrative poetry, or novel. As they continue reading the play on their own, they are able to follow the plot line and to answer in their journals such "five Ws and H" questions as

- Who are the protagonist and antagonist(s)?
- What is the conflict?
- When does the main action occur?
- Where does the main action take place (other than onstage)?
- Why do characters act the way they do?
- How does the writer have the characters solve the problems raised in the play?

Assigning this writing activity about the opening act focuses students' attention on the main characters as they are being introduced as well as on the conflicts, which playwrights reveal early in the exposition of their works. Yes, the script lists the names in the cast of characters; some dramatists even mention the relationships among the characters, but the reader or viewer usually does not know the personality or motivations of these characters until the play begins. Since you want your students to be able to follow the play without having to go back too often to figure out who's who and what's what, assign this "five Ws and H" journal entry right away.

Begin the play slowly enough for them to get a firm handle on these relationships; it makes the rest of the reading go more smoothly. Then you can spend your time inviting students to read aloud, in character, and to discuss their understanding of the plot while paying attention to character development, plot advancement, and theme revelation. But don't get bogged down in analytical mud. The students do not have enough insight yet to hold insightful discussions about structure. They still are trying to figure out what happens next. Save those conversations for the reread.

After closely reading act I, trust the author to show what is going on among the characters such that the members of the audience can understand the personalities and conflicts themselves. By this time in the school year, most of your students already are active readers, so there is no need to plod through the entire play, stopping to identify this basic information. But answer questions as they arise. Yes, remind students to mark their texts, use their sticky notes, or record in their journals the words or phrases that reveal specific facts about characters, especially motivation. Quick reading is in keeping with the idea that plays are written to be viewed in a single theater visit.

Taking Notes While Reading

While a quick read is usually best for overall narrative comprehension, because they cannot see them, many film-oriented students have difficulty keeping track of characters. These students may benefit from a simple graphic organizer. If your students are not permitted to write color coding in their books, ask the students to keep character-related notes in their reading journal. They can make three columns:

- Column One: Character Name
- Column Two: Character Traits
- Column Three: Page Number

You may find that some students visualize better when they draw a diagram of the set or create charts with arrows, boxes, and circles. Periodically invite your youngsters to share with their classmates the strategies they devise themselves to help them make sense of the text. Shared peer perceptions increase peer comprehension.

These notes and drawings can prepare students to participate actively in discussions about ways the playwrights unveil the personalities and motivations of the characters. Writing and graphically representing these facts and impressions slow the readers, and they pay attention to the crucial information the dramatist reveals in the opening scenes, thus reducing confusion and frustration later. Once these details are firm in their minds, students can read more confidently and understand more deeply. Nevertheless, you'll probably have to remind your students that reading a play is different from watching one. As readers, they must use all the clues the author gives in the dialogue and in the stage directions to imagine what the characters look like and what movements they may be making onstage.

GETTING THROUGH THE PLAY—ART, ACTING, AND VIDEO

Using Props and Making Masks

Young people are more inclined to assume a persona when they have something to hold or when they feel they are disguised. Begin with a brief talk about which props or items of clothing would be appropriate for each character. If bringing props from home is unrealistic, ask to borrow some from the drama teacher and provide them yourself. You know to keep props simple and to avoid realistic-looking weapons—just much too tempting for shenanigans from mischievous adolescents.

To get the students to think more seriously about the personalities of the characters, have them make character masks using inexpensive paper plates and colored markers or crayons. Once you assemble the materials, students can complete the assignment in a single period, choosing colors and symbols that reflect the specific traits of their assigned characters. This creative artistic assignment appeals to those who learn through drawing and seeing.

This assignment also sends students back to the text. When they show their masks to the class, each student should neatly write on the back of his or her mask the lines from the text that substantiate their choice of color, symbol, or the pattern of images on their mask and then read these lines when presenting to the class. Students often are surprised when peers choose the same color to symbolize different personality traits. With textual support, those differing choices are validated.

For example, with the play *Romeo and Juliet*, one student may choose red to reflect the love between Romeo and Rosalind, his lady love before Juliet. Another may use red to show the fiery temperament of Mercutio. A student may use black to represent Juliet's despair while another uses black to represent the stubborn stance the Montagues and Capulets take on keeping their children apart.

The same holds true for symbols. When students support their choices with the text, most results make sense. One student may decorate her mask with birds to represent literally the swan and crow mentioned in the script and also to represent figuratively the flightiness of the characters. Another may use dog-food bones to reflect Mercutio's speech about "a dog" and the "house of Montague." Neither the colors nor symbols students select are as important as the reasoning they offer based on the text. So much is revealed to them, to their peers, and to you.

Drawing and Playing with Childhood Toys

Some teachers ask students to draw or bring in pictures to represent the play's characters. Others ask students what movie or television actors and actresses could be cast for certain parts. Each of these assignments should require the students to find evidence from the text of the play to support their selections. They may even design a playbill or suggest music for the dramatic work you have them read. If this play were a musical, what style of music would be appropriate? Why? If it were a ballet, what would it look like? These assignments call upon students' imagination and help students to connect and contribute to the discussion inspired by their own creative ideas and their own artistic skills.

Further involve students and invite their input by suggesting that they bring in childhood toys and dolls to represent characters and scenes, or spend a class period making sock puppets to use when reading a scene. What about using children's building blocks to recreate sets? Remember, these are young teens, bridging the gap between childhood and adulthood. Playing with appropriate toys that they bring to class while studying a play may be just the thing to revive a play that may be dying on the vine.

Such activities reinforce learning by seeing, hearing, and doing. Writing in their journals the words from the text and discussions, experiencing reading and hearing parts read, and seeing the visuals (photos or drawings in their text) make students more likely to remember the particulars of the plot and theme and connect the actions in the plays with their own lives. These visual depictions also provide memory aids students may recall during written assessments and when they begin drafting their own plays.

Deciding to Show or Not to Show

You may decide to show video clips to supplement the study of the play. You could use clips of the same scenes from different productions—such as different versions of Shakespeare's *Romeo and Juliet*, or an English production and French version of *Cyrano de Bergerac*. In addition to using clips to give more insight into the setting, show a video clip of a conflict similar to one dealt with in the play you are reading. Afterwards, ask the students to compare the way each set of characters responds to the conflict. Showing video of the play you are studying may be a good time for an in-context talk about the grammar or structural rules of film. See chapter 10 for more extensive suggestions for incorporating media grammar in language arts instruction.

Comparing and Contrasting Film Versions of Plays

When you study *Cyrano de Bergerac*, for example, you could show video clips both from an English version of the play and also the French version of the play starring Gerard Depardieu.[3] The French version can be advantageous even if students don't speak that language; students can pay attention to the action that is implied by the dialogue they've been reading. The fact that this version is performed "in the field" and "on location" and not on stage provides an opportunity to discuss how stage and screen communicate differently—especially with camera angles, scene transitions, and background music. This lesson may give students ideas about lighting and sound instructions to include when they flesh out the scripts of their own plays.

Then ask students to discuss or write about the differences they note between the two media. Some students are disappointed because they have imagined the people, places, and scenes to be different from what is shown in the video. This gives an opening to talk about the power of language to create images in our minds and the pleasure of reading widely and independently. The key for you is to decide why the video clips are being shown and to determine whether they help or hurt students to reach the standards for reading, viewing, and critical thinking laid out for the course. Sometimes more is just too much.

KEEPING THE PEACE WHILE ENJOYING THE PLAY

As the students get further into the play, they become eager to read aloud and act out the scenes. And because they are adolescents who have a strong sense of fairness, it is important for you to be perceived as such. To be fair, arrange it so that each one who wishes to read a "good" part has the opportunity to do so; keep a chart of who reads which part each day. At the end of each class period, during those closing ten minutes, you can write on the board or project a list of characters they are to meet in the next assigned scene(s) and then ask for volunteers to prepare for the reading.

Those who have had small parts should have first choice for choosing the character they would like to read the next day. Those who are scheduled to read ought to understand that they are expected to practice reading their lines aloud at home so that they can read in character, without stumbling over unfamiliar words during class. Holding this casting session at the end of each class period is a subtle way of tantalizing them all to keep reading to find out what happens next and anticipating how well their classmates are going to interpret the upcoming scenes.

If practice at home is not realistic in your school setting, invite the readers to come before or after school and practice in your room. Young teens abhor embarrassment, so they take seriously their responsibility to bring alive the characters for their peers. And meetings like this can be a great opportunity for you to have one-on-one time or get to work with a smaller group of students.

Acting and Pantomiming Scenes

Allotting time to act out the scenes is particularly important to ensure that your teaching appeals to multiple learning types. To demonstrate the ways that dialogue demands certain action and activity, you could give the same scene to multiple groups and ask them to do a dramatic reading that includes some staging and movement. If your class tends to be noisy, with talkative young teens, how about assigning them to present scenes silently, with pantomime only! Then, after they present the scene, ask the group members to justify their choices for acting or reacting.

Creating tableaux of the later scenes in the play further extends student understanding of the relationships among characters. This time, raise the level of reflection and observation and ask students to pay attention to posture as well as position in relation to other characters. One may have a dominant character standing, a neutral one sitting, and a subservient one kneeling. Students may decide to have one character standing farther away from the audience and another nearer, depending on the mood of the scene. In a quiet scene, ask the students to decide what gestures would be appropriate during a particular speech. What would the nonspeaking characters be doing during that speech? Why?

You can maintain more consistent control in the classroom during acting scenes by planning backwards—clarify for yourself what you expect to accomplish when you schedule those lessons. First, consider the dynamics of each class: How have the students interacted in prior situations? Next, give clear directions before "letting them loose," and then circulate among them as they work. Finally, set your timer to signal about five minutes before the end of the period. That way, you can call the students back to order and conduct a short oral reflection on what they learned by acting out the scene. When students know what is expected, know what is allowed or not allowed, and know that you are nearby to help them behave themselves, they usually live up to your expectations. You can achieve your goals and retain your sense of humor.

Deepening Understanding of Literary Devices

By the second semester, your middle school students probably are at ease identifying, discussing, and writing about most of the literary devices except theme and irony. So when you plan lessons for drama study, design activities to help them develop greater confidence with these features of literature. You could quiz them with quotations from the play and ask students to identify the speaker, the situation, and the importance of that speech to characterization, plot advancement, or setting. These informal assessments measure their retention of this knowledge.

To understand and identify literary themes in plays, students must understand the plotline. They may find it useful first to refer to their one-paragraph summaries of the "five Ws and H" questions. Just as you taught during the short-story unit, ask the students to write thematic statements in which they identify the universal situation based on the conflict and the universal response to the situation based on the character's response to the conflict.

BOX 9.2: KRISTIN'S STATEMENTS ABOUT THEME IN *CYRANO DE BERGERAC*

- When people have a crush on someone, they show off for their crush. (In some neighborhoods "crush" is also slang for the object of one's affections.)
- When someone dies, their loved ones mourn for them.
- People respond to tense situations with brave action.
- People are willing to battle physically or emotionally to get what they want.
- People with physical flaws try to impress others to avoid rejection.
- People are attracted first to external features.

It may help them write these theme statements if you provide a sample formatted sentence with missing words:

When people _____ (the students fill in the situation), they _____ (the students fill in the response to the situation).

For one homework assignment, ask students to try writing some of these sentences in their reading journals or digital notebooks, and later they can convert the SWBST phrases (Somebody Wanted But So Then) into simple sentences that generalize the concept captured in their preliminary drafts. Students soon recognize the universal quality of plays in much the way they saw them in other literary works studied this school year.

WRITING PLAYS AND CROSS-CURRICULAR COLLABORATIONS

Middle school students learn well when they see a link to topics or subjects they are studying in other classes. Collaborating teachers who take time to create such lessons tend to have more success in getting their students to engage. One activity that lends itself well to cross-curricular collaboration is playwriting. For example, in many schools, eighth-graders study physical science, which includes units on geology, weather, and the planets. Many eighth-grade literature lists include legends and myths. What a wonderful opportunity to write plays based on those tales that attempt to explain early man's rationale for the way the earth is formed, what causes weather, how stars come to be arranged in particular patterns, and why the planets exist. The same kind of teaming could work with colleagues in the history or social studies department, when students write plays about historical people and events. Invite a teacher in the other departments like art and music to work with you to design a joint assignment for which your students write a play relating to that other class.

Then you can share the grading. Consider using the features of the familiar Six Traits rubric or one that teachers from both departments create together. For example, one of you could read the student-written plays for accuracy of facts and ideas, voice, and sentence fluency. The other could read for organization, word choice, and conventions of drama writing as well as for mechanics, usage, and grammar. Such sharing could halve the labor and double the pleasure of working together on a project that enhances authenticity of assessment in both areas of study.

You may also consider teaching playwriting after studying a group of short stories. Small groups could choose different stories and then create a script based on one that demonstrates the elements of drama they learn in this drama unit. The students may find it helpful to use such questions[4] as those that follow to self-check their progress in playwriting on the topic you assign or they choose.

Playwriting Checkup List

- *Who* are the two or three main characters in your play?
- *What* myth, short story, or incident is the basis for your play?
- *What* do you want the audience to think, feel, and know as a result of reading or seeing your play?
- *When* does your play take place?
- *Where* does your play take place?
- Simple set requirements?
- Simple lighting required?
  Why are the characters in conflict? (universal issue)
  - Parent-child disagreement
  - Sibling rivalry
  - Desire for power or glory
  - Peer pressure
  - Boy meets girl
  - Love triangle
- *How* well does your play follow the guidelines for an effective drama script? These are questions students could consider about peer drafts during read-around groups or in-class peer feedback as described in "Teacher Resource H" in the appendix.
  - Plot is focused on a single problem to be solved within brief period of time
  - Personality of characters is revealed primarily in dialogue; secondarily in action (In other words, would a blind person be able to follow the flow of the story?)

- ○ Dialogue introduces conflict early in the play
- ○ Dialogue sounds like real conversation—brief, overlapping speeches and some fragments
- ○ Play has an identifiable beginning, middle, and end
- ○ Rising action includes three increasingly more challenging obstacles in solving the problem
- ○ Climax is realistic but not given away too soon
- ○ Resolution makes sense based on the personality of characters
- Do you avoid the use of a narrator and let characters reveal themselves through dialogue?
- Do your minor characters serve as foils and help reveal personality of the protagonist?
- Do you include suggestions for lighting, sets, and props, but allow dialogue to guide the director in his or her choices?

Depending on the students you have, assign each student to author his or her own personal play or assign them to work as a group. By the second semester, when you may teach playwriting, you have a better feel for what works best for the classes you have any particular year. If possible, arrange for a final performance of the best two or three plays your students write. This may be a practiced reading performed for other classes or a full performance in your theater space for an invited audience of families and friends. If you begin planning early enough in the first semester, your drama teacher may have time to join forces with you and plan time for the drama classes in the second semester to perform selected dramas of your teen playwrights. You can imagine how gratifying it would be for these middle school authors to see their words come to life! And knowing their work is to be seen by their peers, families, and/or friends encourages the students to do a better job on the assignment. Win. Win. Win.

Grading during Playwriting

During the preliminary stages of playwriting, just give credit for completing each step, making note of participation instead of giving letters or percentages. It works better to keep the students focused on the process rather than the grades, so any student who completes the step in the assignment on time should receive full credit. For example, a project worth one hundred points could have subdivisions worth ten points for the plan, twenty points for first draft, twenty points for the first revision, and fifty points for the final script. Although students who do not complete a particular step receive no credit for that step, encourage them to participate fully in each group meeting and earn partial credit. Their contributions can enhance the final script, and they are likely to stay involved knowing they have not lost all by missing one assignment.

Observing Work Sessions—No-Stress Assessments

As the students work together, use the opportunity to add to your notes about student behavior and contributions. You may have photocopies of seating charts on which to record these comments. Or have student names printed on large address labels to remind you to make notes for each of the students by the time each of the group playwriting meetings is finished, keeping these notes to consult when needed. These labels then can be added to the file pages you may have for each student. If you do not maintain individual student record sheets, you still can keep these notes in a folder to consult when needed. Your documenting student learning with these anecdotal assessments helps you to plan subsequent lessons and to prepare reports to parents or administrators should the need arise.

At the end of such a group project, have students evaluate their own contribution to the task. It is not necessary to ask them to comment on what others have done. Everyone in the group already knows whether each has been supportive and cooperative, so you do not want to create situations for them to "tattle." You want to avoid creating schisms among classmates, ones that damage the fragile egos of adolescents, even those who hide them with bluster.

SUMMATIVE ASSESSMENTS

At the end of the unit, assess student learning by having students demonstrate their understanding of relationships among the characters or the author's use of literary devices and the newly taught elements of drama. You could include options for which they can choose to

- summarize their learning by writing a poem about the play;
- write an additional scene describing what happens next with characters who have survived;
- write a one-act play with the same conflict set in a contemporary time or place;
- take a test;
- write a paper;
- produce a video with live performers; or
- create an animated video to post on your class website.

CONCLUSION

The study of drama can be an enriching experience for students and teachers because it incorporates so many language arts skills: reading, writing, speaking, listening, representing, viewing, and using technology. And it offers a reason to practice cooperative learning. Moreover, while reading drama, students see how earlier learned literary concepts are used in another genre of literature. Finally, drama is just fun because it appeals to a wide range of students across the range of multiple intelligences, especially those who like to talk, watch, move, and act up. Who's left?

Yes, by the time you have completed a series of lessons with drama, you may find yourself quoting Cyrano's line that opens this chapter, "I order you to be silent!" With your careful planning, your students become so excited about playing their parts that you may need to "write down their names" and they each will want to be "at the top of the list." When you issue the challenge to "Step forward, young heroes!" even the shyer students volunteer to be a part of the fun and are ready to "break a leg."

NOTES

1. Edmond Rostand, *Cyrano de Bergerac,* trans. Lowell Blair, in *World Literature* (Lake Forest, IL: Glencoe/McGraw-Hill, 1991), 472.

2. *Common Core State Standards for English Language Arts & Literacy in History/Social Studies, Science, and Technical Subjects,* Common Core State Standards

Initiative, http://www.corestandards.org/assets/CCSSI_ELA%20Standards.pdf (accessed May 17, 2012).

3. *Cyrano de Bergerac* (with English subtitles), starring Gérard Depardieu and Anne Brochet, directed by Jean-Paul Rappeneau (1990; MGM/UA, 2000).

4. You may wish to see the website accompanying this book to see my *California English* article "An Audience of One's Peers," which describes in more detail writing a myth play, and then decide what kind of play would be best to assign to your class. An extended assignment handout also is there. The play in the article was written in response to a workshop presented by Playwrights Project, a nonprofit arts education organization in San Diego, about its approach to teaching playwriting in schools. Students and teachers at the Bishop's School worked with Playwrights Project for years (www.playwrightsproject.org). The organization's basic curriculum, written by founder Deborah Salzer, is available as *Stage Write*, published by Interact (www.catalog.socialstudies.com).

RECOMMENDED DRAMA

A Doll's House by Henrik Ibsen

The most well-known of Ibsen's realism plays, *A Doll's House* boldly addresses the issue of women's rights. Nora Helmer is a seemingly empty-headed wife, only around to be a pretty object in her husband, Torvald's, perfectly run house.

A Raisin in the Sun by Lorraine Hansberry

This Pulitzer Prize–winning drama is fully accessible to middle school students primarily because it tells a story with which many of them can identify—the struggle to improve the living conditions of a family.

Bull Run by Paul Fleischman

Northerners, Southerners, generals, couriers, dreaming boys, and worried sisters describe the glory, the horror, the thrill, and the disillusionment of the first battle of the Civil War.

The Mousetrap by Agatha Christie

The Mousetrap had the longest initial run of any play in the world. The play is a murder mystery, famous for its twist ending. The story is about a couple that starts up a new hotel and is soon snowed in with five guests.

The Diary of Anne Frank by Frances Goodrich and Albert Hackett

Set in Holland during World War II, this perennial favorite is a dramatization of a real young girl, based on a diary her father found at the end of the war.

The Monsters Are Due on Maple Street by Rod Serling

This dark tale begins innocently with what appears to be the passing of a meteor that causes a power outage. Very quickly, in an attempt to explain why the power to their gadgets ceases, the neighbors on Maple Street give in to mob psychology. One young boy, Tommy, says that he has read in his comic books about monsters that send a family ahead of their invasion to take over the town. Each one wonders who the monsters' emissary family could be. This television script of an episode from *The Twilight Zone* series includes camera cues and lots of stage directions.

These Shoes of Mine by Gary Soto

This short play is about Manuel, a young man who resents the too-large shoes his mother has bought for him at the thrift shop. Spanish dialogue is translated, making it accessible to all readers.

Trifles by Susan Glaspell

This short mystery play explores gender differences in a way that amuses middle school students and leads to lively discussion. Interested students could easily put together a performance of this simple play.

Witness by Karen Hesse

In this play, a series of poems expresses the views of various people in a small Vermont town, including a young black girl and a young Jewish girl, during the early 1920s when the Ku Klux Klan is trying to infiltrate the town.

10

SPEAKING OF GRAMMARS, MEDIA ARTS, AND PUBLIC SPEAKING

The mark of an effective speaker is "the ability to adapt to a variety of audiences and settings and to perform appropriately in diverse social situations."

—Clella Jaffe[1]

A dear friend of mine is an accomplished welder and a talented musician and can skillfully navigate a luxury tour bus through dense urban traffic and parallel park it with only inches to spare. And, except in casual conversation, she is pathological about talking in public. She believes people judge her intellect by her speech; given her accented regional dialect and limited experience reading and writing Standard English, she doesn't want to appear ignorant, so she self-muzzles. She seldom writes anything formal and only writes an informal note in an emergency. She owns a computer but seldom uses it. She believes people generally judge her intelligence by her writing. So she corrals her speaking and writing, keeping her thinking to herself.

True, my friend left school early, married young, and soon became the sole wage earner for her family of three children. Even though she is gifted mentally and manually, she still feels hampered, unable to advance on any of her career paths primarily because she lacks proficiency communicating in Standard English. So sad. So frustrating.

This story of my friend illustrates just one of the reasons for this chapter. How one speaks, how one writes, and how one uses technology matter. The ideas that follow can help you fulfill the charge, meet the obligation, and ensure that the middle school students you teach do not have to live like this, stifling their thoughts because they are ashamed of their oral and written skills or their inability to navigate in the digital world as receivers or senders.

Teachers have to help students realize that their future success may be thwarted if they do not know Standard English grammar, continually resist lessons to improve their speaking and writing, and avoid learning the grammar of the media. Share your own stories with the young teens you teach and inspire them to take full advantage of the opportunities provided in school for them to read, to hear, and to speak Standard English, to write in a style or version of English appropriate for the setting, and to use current technology for researching, writing, and communicating in a range of situations. Working toward these Common Core Anchor Standards for Language[2] will help guide you and your students to achieving the goal of skillful communication.

WHY TEACH STANDARD ENGLISH

It is important, in the middle school, to teach students the rules of Standard English and to hold them accountable for following the rules when doing so is beneficial to them. They should know that in the national and international communities, English is the language of commerce, technology, and diplomacy. You can substantiate these claims by showing them "An English Speaking World," part of the video series *The Story of English*, narrated by journalist Robert McNeil.[3] Hearing from others in a resource such as this one not only helps your students understand the history and development of the English language but also can convince them of the value of knowing how to write and speak English well.

Your young teenagers, like most humans, yearn to be understood and respected for their mental acumen, and you can build on this basic desire by designing classroom activities to review and teach the basics of English grammar, planning writing workshops in which students hear comments on the effectiveness of their writing, and structuring guided discussions in which students receive feedback on their oral presentations. These lessons raise their awareness, demonstrate the impact of their choices, and help your students see that using nonstandard grammar can obscure their own written and oral communication, while using Standard English grammar clarifies both. The challenge for you is to honor their home language and, at the same time, give them the knowledge to be able to code switch or blend dialects when a situation deems it appropriate.

INSTRUCTING IN OR OUT OF CONTEXT—FORMAL OR INFORMAL GRAMMAR LESSONS

By the end of middle school, teachers expect students to be familiar with parts of speech, parts of a sentence, and the concept of verbals: infinitives and participles. They also expect students to write using consistent agreement between subject and verb and between pronouns and their antecedents. Most curricula for the later grades include lessons on a range of sentence structures, various sentence starters, and appropriate punctuation for these more complex sentences. Sometimes formal grammar lessons are taught and students take tests on identifying grammatical structures and correcting errors in sentences or paragraphs. Other times grammar is taught entirely through student writing. In either setting, when a problem arises, teach the rule and give students exercises to practice the rule.

In fact, both approaches to teaching grammar via writing and grammar separate from writing eventually work, but lasting learning seems to occur when you hold students responsible for correct grammar in their own, everyday writing and allot time for revision before grading for grammar. When they see grammar merely as a game of memorization or identification, students soon lose interest, and they seldom apply grammar rules beyond the classroom. Hold your students accountable and encourage them to become better speakers and writers.

After a concept is taught or reviewed, add the correct use of that concept to the evaluation standards on subsequent graded writing assignments. One by one, hold students accountable for agreement of subject and verb, pronoun and antecedent, and consistent verb tense within a paragraph. Consider adapting rubrics from your text or those found online, like the Six Traits rubric published by the Northwest Regional Educational Laboratory.[4] Most published rubrics include grammar as one criterion for evaluating speaking and writing in formal and informal settings.

SKETCHING TO CLARIFY THE FUNCTION OF PARTS OF SPEECH

Even though many students study some grammar in elementary school, you still can start this direct instruction lesson by showing students the function of "parts" of speech in everyday conversations. This first example is to demonstrate that grammar is not just about rules but about effective communication. You can show students what this looks like by using visual symbols to represent the shared understanding of ideas and images. If you were to visit a classroom to "see" and "hear" what this lesson would look and sound like on the opening day of direct instruction of formal grammar, like the paragraphs that follow, your notes may have recorded what happened in that particular teacher's classroom.

Draw a stick figure to represent the speaker, and then draw a second stick figure to represent the listener, and add thought balloons by the heads of each figure. Try to draw, as exactly as possible, the same image, say, of a bird flying over a bush, in both the speaker or writer's balloon and the listener or reader's balloon. The images are not precisely identical; but neither are shared messages. Explain that clear and effective communication occurs when you can transmit your ideas effectively to your listener or reader. Now sketch on the board another stick figure with a very large cartoon balloon that represents verbal communication—either written or spoken. Next, divide that balloon into eight segments to represent the eight common parts of speech. See Figure 10:1.

Of course, there is no need to use the exact words you hear when you visit this imaginary classroom, but you may find this to be an effective way to review these basic parts of speech with your middle school students who may not have thought about grammar in this way. Write or draw while explaining why languages have different parts of speech. So here goes . . .

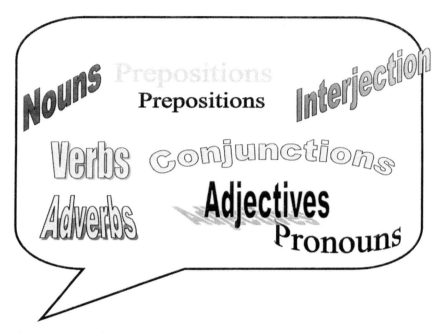

Figure 10.1.   Each Part of Speech Has a Function

When we want to name people, places, things, events, and activities, we use nouns. A noun is one part of speech. Nouns name. When we want to talk about what those nouns do, we use verbs. They are another part of speech. Verbs can express action as well as indicate when the action takes place. There are other functions of verbs we'll talk about later.

Now occasionally, we want to clarify what the listener or reader imagines by modifying the mental image of a noun. Adjectives modify or limit nouns.

Showing How Modifiers Function

Continue in this fashion and give examples of ways that adjectives limit or modify nouns. One incident you could relate is: "When I was eight years old, I got a ball for my birthday. On the opening page of the grammar section of your journal, draw the ball I received." Invariably, different students draw different types and sizes of balls. Now, add adjectives that limit the image of the noun by telling what kind (rubber), what size (little), and what color (purple with red diamonds around the circumference). By adding adjectives, thus creating a shared mental image, you communicate an image ever-closer to the ball received.

Reiterate this concept and use any noun that elicits a wide variety of images and enables you to limit the meaning of the noun simply by adding adjectives indicating kind, size, and color. Choose examples your students can imagine, like a dog, a horse, or a sweater. Begin by saying only "dog." Let the students draw the kind of dog they imagine. Then you add modifiers and ask how mental images come closer and closer to the dog you really received. Students begin to understand the value of linguistic precision.

Point back to the cartoon bubble depicting parts of speech, add the three you've described so far, and continue on to the next part of speech, the modifier for verbs. Remind students that speakers and writers often want to limit or modify others' mental image of an action. In this case, the writer would use another part of speech, an adverb. Adverbs modify verbs by telling when, where, how, and to what extent. If students bring up the fact that adverbs also are used to answer these questions about adjectives or other adverbs, acknowledge this fact and move on.

In the presentation, you may illustrate your explanation with the verb "to walk" and then ask the students to suggest adverbs that tell where the action could take place (outside, inside, around, out, etc.). Usually the students suggest prepositional phrases, too, such as "around the corner" or "in the mall." Go on to tell them they are correct, that sometimes phrases (or groups of words) can modify a noun or verb, and that you will talk about these kinds of modifiers later. You can expand your discussion about the verb *walk* by asking When (early, late)? How (quickly, slowly)?

Clarifying Conjunctions, Pronouns, and Interjections

The grammar lesson continues: "Sometimes speakers and writers want to combine words, phrases, or clauses, so they need another part of speech to do that—a conjunction. A conjunction joins words, phrases, and clauses." (Remember to include a simple definition of each of the parts of speech as you introduce the concept of "parts of speech." And have students add the definitions to their journals.)

Going on:

When speaking or writing, we sound monotonous or boring if we keep saying the same noun repeatedly to refer to the same person, place, thing, activity, or event. So we sometimes replace a noun with a pronoun. A pronoun replaces or stands for a noun. Pronouns change forms to indicate whether the noun being replaced is masculine, feminine, or neither, and to indicate whether we're talking about one noun or several.

By this time, as you have been adding the names of the part of speech to the balloon drawing, most of the students are getting the picture, and they can offer correct examples of the different forms of pronouns, showing that though they may not know the rules of grammar, many of them know how the language works grammatically. Some of your English language learners may perk up and comment that in their language the forms of nouns and pronouns change in much the same way. This is good because the next part of speech often throws them a curve—the preposition.

Continue with the lesson:

Sometimes speakers and writers want to show the relationship between a noun or pronoun and some other word in a sentence. They want to indicate the place or position of the other noun or pronoun. To communicate this, they use yet another part of speech—the preposition. A preposition shows the relationship between a noun or pronoun and another word in the sentence.

Look at this marker I'm using. Suppose I want to communicate to others that the marker is *in* my hand, or *on* my desk, or *under* the table. Notice that some of these words show the relationship or place of the noun, *the marker*, in relation to my hand, the desk, or the table. Those words are prepositions (notice the root, *position*). Suppose I put the marker here [hold the marker above the head]? What word tells the position or relationship of the marker to my head [*above* or *over*]? What word shows that relationship or position [*behind*]?

By now, students usually understand the concept or function of the preposition.

Now deal with the interjection.

This last common part of speech does not name, show action, modify or limit, join, replace, or show relationship or position. But because it serves an entirely different function in communicating; it is another part of speech. This eighth part of speech identifies those words that interrupt a flow of thought to express mild or strong emotions. This part of speech is called an interjection.

An *interjection* exclaims emotions and has no other grammatical connection in the sentence. The word *interjection* comes from a Latin prefix, *inter*, which means *between*, and a root word, *ject*, that means "to throw" (as in "project" to throw forward or "reject" to throw back). Speakers and writers sometimes "throw" in words to show emotion, like *wow*, *darn*, *ouch*, or *hey*!

For this eighth part of speech, invite students to suggest those words that speakers and writers throw into their communication between other ideas as interjections. Be prepared for them to get silly and try to throw in "no-no" words.

Pulling the Parts Together

Finally, a classroom dénouement: by this time, you have completed the drawing with names of the eight parts of speech all within the balloon, graphically illustrating that speech is made of different parts, each serving a specific purpose to communicate clearly exactly what we want to get across to our listeners or readers. And so, you conclude:

These, ladies and gentlemen, are the eight common parts of speech. Each has a different function in communicating what we speak or write. The more precisely you use parts of speech, the more likely the ideas you have are transferred clearly and accurately to your listeners and readers.

As you continue studying grammar, you'll learn ways that parts of speech are used in different ways in sentences. You'll soon learn that groups of words—phrases and clauses—can function as a unit in the same way that single-word parts of speech function.

The key for you is to remember the part that each of these single words or single units of words plays in communicating ideas. As you learn these functions and put them into practice in your own speaking and writing, each of you can become a better speaker and a better writer, getting across to the listener or reader the exact ideas you wish to communicate.

Then, smile big and bow with your arm across your waist.

Introducing or reviewing the parts of speech according to their function in the sentence prepares for an easy transition to teaching phrases, verbals, and clauses. When students see a prepositional phrase that modifies a noun answering the same kinds of questions that single-word adjectives answer, they can understand adjective phrases. For example, "Please bring me the box *in the closet*, not the one *under my bed*." Or when the students see a sentence in which a prepositional phrase answers questions about verbs in the same way that single-word adverbs do, the students get the idea of adverb phrases. For example, "Ahmad reached *into his pocket* to get his cell phone."

The same transfer of conceptual understanding seems to flow when students encounter verbals that name actions (gerunds). "*Walking* is good exercise, so my neighbor gets up early and walks three blocks just to get his first cup of coffee." Similarly, they can understand when they see verbs describing nouns (participles). "My grandmother still has the *carving* knife her mother received as a wedding gift." You get the point. Taking the time to teach parts of speech as functions of communication makes it easier for students to see the patterns in the language, even in more sophisticated settings.

ILLUSTRATING WHY SYNTAX MATTERS

In the middle grades, the curriculum usually moves beyond parts of both speech and sentences to phrases, verbals, clauses, and confusion-causing dangling modifiers. One of the ways to help students understand how much they use syntax (the order of words) to make sense of what they hear and read is to have them draw what they hear or see. Your grammar book probably includes a section on dangling modifiers, so you can ask the students to draw as precisely as possible just the sentences that you dictate or project one at a time. Or you may use the examples that follow:

1. A group of students was watching the movie in their cars on the gigantic outdoor screen.
2. The track star twisted his ankle (with the green sweatshirt).
3. I learned about the cat that was lost on the Internet.
4. Punctured by a nail, I had to repair my bike tire.

5. Or this famous quip from comedian Groucho Marx, "One morning I shot an elephant in my pajamas. How he got in my pajamas, I don't know."

You are right. Doing these drawings evokes snorts and sniggles. That is just fine. Your teens reflect on their own work and fear this may be the response others have to their speaking and writing. When you ask students first to enclose the dangling phrase in parentheses, as in number two above, and then to draw an arrow from the adjective phrase to the noun it modifies, students see the problem caused by misplaced or dangling modifiers. Thankfully, the activity illustrates emphatically that sentence syntax *does* influence communication. After the activity, your students become conscientious writers and work harder to avoid that confusion of imprecise language and sloppy grammar. For efficiency, you could ask half the students to draw the even-numbered sentences and the other half to draw the odd-numbered sentences. This way they read them all, draw half, and then see examples of all.

Patterning to Teach Syntax and Sentence Variety

Another way to make grammar come alive for students is to examine sentence patterns in the fiction and nonfiction writing of published authors. Sometimes, to demonstrate to the students that they can write similarly powerful sentence styles and grammatical patterns, ask them to model a piece of their own prose after a short passage from the literature they are studying.

Think about the evocative paragraphs students could write based on the Elie Wiesel's memoir, *Night*. Consider using the "Never shall I forget"[5] passage, which describes Wiesel's first night in the concentration camp. Similar remarkable writing occurs when students pattern the distinctive sentence structures from literary works by Cisneros or Dickens, Paulson, or Twain. Paying close attention to the way published writers organize their sentences helps students understand the power of word order and selection. You could alert them to different kinds of sentences: short, simple; balanced, compound; multilayered and complex—like this one from "My Name" by Sandra Cisneros:

It was my great-grandmother's name and now it is mine. She was a horse woman too, born like me in the Chinese year of the horse—which is supposed to be bad luck if you're born female—but I think this a Chinese lie because the Chinese, like the Mexicans, don't like their women strong.[6]

You could select specific sentences yourself and have all the students pattern the same sentences. Better yet, ask students to locate in a recent reading assignment two or three sentences they, themselves, find interesting. Next, ask them to pattern those on a topic of their choice and then to tell what makes the sentences appealing and ways that patterning them is a challenge.

Middle school students often have sophisticated ideas but may not easily write comparably complex grammatical structures to convey these thoughts. You can help them express themselves more fully and more adeptly. Design lessons such as patterning that cause these deep-thinking writers to slow down, pay attention, practice, and use the appropriate grammar as they attempt to write in precise prose. Patterning can help achieve this standard of communication.

One helpful book is Harry R. Noden's *Image Grammar: Using Grammatical Structures to Teach Writing.*[7] Noden offers students a variety of sentence starts, modifying strategies, and sentence endings to pattern. Activities from *Image Grammar* help your students vary their structure and create more interesting sentences as they write not only in your class but in classes across the content areas.

Mimicking Dialogue to Jump-Start English Language Learners

You likely have heard the admonition to students editing their papers to "just read it aloud." That works in some cases, but even if they are intellectually sharp and have fascinating ideas to share, your ELL students may not have developed "an ear" to recognize Standard English. Reading their writings aloud may not be enough to give students with an untrained ear the helpful clues they need for revision.

You can help them jump-start their English composition and avoid feeling hampered even with simple English language vocabulary or sentence structures they have already learned. How? By encouraging them to pattern sentences. They become more comfortable writing on their own if they are following the syntax of writing passages that you recommend. For some reason, paying close attention to the way that published authors structure sentences can speed the process and increase the confidence limited English speakers have in writing freely.

Another idea for ear training comes from Dr. Arlene Mulligan, who used drama to help her new English speakers improve their sentence syntax. She writes,

> Because second language learners, by necessity, must be acute listeners, they already have developed . . . ears sensitive to differences in diction, dialect, and speech patterns. Most of these young people are very bright and are attentive to the spoken word.[8]

Mulligan invites her new English speakers to write drama and to incorporate considerable dialogue in their writing, inspiring writers to attune their ears to the rhythms of spoken English and to imitate these patterns in their writing.

TEACHING GRAMMAR WITH RECORDED BOOKS

The oral language students hear in informal situations is not likely to be entirely Standard English. By encouraging them to attentively pattern the spoken word, we can help them train their ears for linguistic rhythms. This would be another reason to use audio books in your teaching. The more often all of your students tune into the rhythm and syntax of spoken English, the sooner they are likely to imitate it in both their own speaking and writing. So locate and create lists of appropriate audio-book resources, and recommend that your learners across the board listen regularly to good readers on recorded books on the Internet or downloaded onto student iPods or cell phones.

GRADING FOR GRAMMAR—NOT ALWAYS

After teaching a new concept, you could give a short writing assignment to see how well the students can apply that new concept. The National Writing Project calls this "primary trait"[9] grading. An alternative way to have students practice a newly taught or reviewed concept is to assign journal entries. At the beginning of the class period while you take attendance or collect homework, you could have students write a few sentences about a piece of text they are studying at the time. The twist in this situation is that you could require them to write using the newly taught grammar or syntax concept, such as using only active voice, or using three different kinds of sentences, or beginning each sentence with a different grammatical structure. Your grammar text has ideas and sample exercises to consider.

These five- or ten-minute writing assignments allow students to practice, to demonstrate the variety of forms one can use to communicate clearly, and to produce for discussion examples of problems that can arise when writers do not follow the rules. These kinds of writings should not be collected or graded. Instead, simply have the students exchange journals, read them, and comment to their partner about what does and does not fit the prompt. Encourage students to discuss what changes need to be made to make the sentences meet the assignment requirements. Then move on to the lesson of the day. Easy. Quick. Writing. Reading. Talking. Reviewing. Reinforcing.

ANALYZING THE GRAMMAR OF MEDIA

For decades English language arts educators have taught students the grammar rules for structuring writing. More recently the term *grammar* has evolved to encompass the structure of books and the layout of print and digital media in terms of words, color, and arrangement. So you may see "grammar of fiction" and "grammar of media" in pedagogical approaches to teach reading, viewing, and analyzing media.

Twenty-first-century students view other print and electronic media many more hours per day than they view or read traditional books. For this reason, you are beginning to see media literacy among the standards to which you are to teach and in the Common Core Standards for English Language Arts. The anchor standards require curricula to include assessment to determine how well students can "integrate and evaluate information presented in diverse media and formats, including visually, quantitatively, and orally."[10] You can design lessons to teach your students how to "read the media" found in magazines and film as well as on websites.

Lots of resources are on the Internet, at such sites as Edutopia.org and Media Literacy Clearinghouse, with interviews discussing the value of teaching the grammar of media literacy and a variety of video clips to use for classroom instruction. Or you can just use magazines or digital images. Some simple lessons introduce the students to the power of color and layout to create specific messages. Other, more in-depth lessons may involve learning the language of film—camera angles, use of lighting, timing of shots, and numbers of cuts—viewing samples and then, in groups, students creating short videos or web pages that illustrate the concepts you are teaching.

Deconstructing the Grammar of Media

Sometimes the most efficient way to build knowledge of the media is to deconstruct it. The Center for Media Literacy (CML) offers lessons like the ones that follow and encourages teachers to have students view print and digital media, consider five core concepts, and ask five key questions.[11]

Five Core Concepts
1. All media messages are constructed.
2. Media messages are constructed using a creative language with its own rules.
3. Different people experience the same media message differently.
4. Media have embedded values and points of view.
5. Most media messages are organized to gain profit and/or power.

Five Key Questions:
1. Who created this message?
2. What creative techniques are used to attract my attention?
3. How might different people understand this message differently?
4. What values, lifestyles, and points of view are represented in, or omitted from, this message?
5. Why is this message being sent?

You can give these same students assignments to practice communicating in these media, too. Instead of requiring each unit of study to include only writing to show what students know, offer options for them to represent graphically what they are learning. Assign PowerPoint or Prezi presentations, cartooning, photography, and video as ways to show what they understand about the literature they read, the writing they do, and the life they live and observe. With your students, create rubrics that refer to elements of layout, color, and design you teach about the media they view. Becoming critical viewers is just the first step in understanding the grammar of the media. Producing that media is the step that shows that learning is taking place.

Assessing News Grammar

This news-related assignment requires students to conduct research, practice citation and documentation, and think more critically about persuasive techniques. During the first two weeks of this month-long assignment, they are to select a topic reported in a print or digital medium and then bring in copies of three or four written articles or text transcriptions of television reports available on local and network websites. If your young folks have access to the Internet, they can follow the news easily. The purpose is to have them follow the news for a month and be prepared to assess ways the nonfiction writing is the same as and/or different from the text structure of fiction being studied in class.

It is efficient to incorporate lessons on media grammar into a unit in which students are reading fiction. After the students have read the exposition of the fictional text and have a solid sense of the personalities of the characters, ask students to write a brief rationale to explain why a particular literary character would be interested in some current event and what would be that character's response to those particular news stories the student has gathered. For example:

- Why would Jem in *To Kill a Mockingbird* by Harper Lee be interested in a particular trial reported in the news media? What would he say about the verdict?
- Why would Mercutio or Benvolio in *Romeo and Juliet* by William Shakespeare be interested in curfew laws that require teenagers to be at home before 10 p.m.? What would be their arguments for and against curfews?
- Why would Panchito from *The Circuit* by Franciso Jimenez or Esperanza from *Esperanza Rising* by Pam Muñoz Ryan be interested in

educational opportunities for undocumented immigrants? How would they advocate for more access?

- What social networking might the family members use to communicate about their trip in *The Watsons Go to Birmingham* by Christopher Paul Curtis?

As you and the class continue studying the text, the students can be gathering information to flesh out their persuasive essays or speeches.

This kind of multigenre and interdisciplinary assignment, looking at fiction and nonfiction concurrently in both print and electronic media, helps students make text-to-world connections, seeing that times change and people don't—a universal quality of good literature. Since a portion of the assignment requires the students to justify their reasons for choosing the particular kinds of news articles and relating them to fictional characters, this assignment requires your teen readers to consider the ways their fiction authors reveal the personalities and motivations of characters in the novels. Finally, incorporating a speech based on real news articles in the same instructional unit as the study of a piece of fiction gives students a chance to detect the different text structures used in fiction and nonfiction, a critical-thinking skill most schools expect middle school students to acquire.

Rather than link the writing to a piece of literature, you could have your students write a speech in your class linked to a topic they are studying in history, science, music, art, or math. Depending on your school setting and the access your students have to resources, you may need to allot in-class time for research as well as for practicing the speeches once they are written. This speech could be a demonstration speech, showing the class how to do or make something that can be completed in class. See chapter 6 for a review of persuasive writing strategies that can be applied to persuasive speech writing.

TELLING STORIES AND PRESENTING POETRY RECITATIONS

One way to help students gain confidence speaking before a live audience is to assign them to tell a story or to recite a poem. Invite students to prepare a two or three minute presentation of a story, fairy tale, or fable they recall from elementary school or have heard told in family gatherings. Invite your students to assume a persona and to imagine an audience of nursery school students. This approach tends to help shy ones relax and speak more dramatically.

Consider incorporating into your poetry unit an assignment for students to select, memorize, and recite a poem of their choice. This could be a published poem or an original one written by the students during the course. Invite the students to introduce the poem to set the stage for the recitation. See "Teacher Resources D" in the appendix for ideas.

You could even go a little further and have the students select the most dramatic presentation of stories and recitations from their class and have those students go on the road and tell their stories in whole-class meetings or as visiting storytellers at a nearby Head Start or nursery school.

GIVING AN ORAL REPORT OR PRESENTING A SPEECH

Are you one of the English teachers who bemoan the fact that you find it a challenge to teach students to give a "good" speech? Like other colleagues in your department, do you acknowledge that students do well on "oral reports," yet something still is lacking? Speech giving really is different from giving an oral report. But how?

Ask your students and the features become clear. Start your unit on public speaking by asking your savvy young adolescents what they notice about a good speaker. Surprisingly, they seldom comment on the content of the speech but instead point out aspects of delivery, such as giving verbal clues to organization pattern, making eye contact, using gestures, rate of speech, clear articulation, varied intonation, poise, and so on. Of course, middle school students probably do not use these terms, but what they mention shows clearly that how the report is delivered is the key feature that makes the speech an effective form of communicating.

Therefore, if you expect your students to become effective, competent, and confident speakers, it seems only right that you incorporate into your lesson planning opportunities for students to observe and critique good speaking and also the time to write and practice their own speeches. Ask them to watch television news reporters. Find and show them short video clips of politicians and businesspeople delivering speeches. Watch an inspirational speaker giving a talk. Websites such as TED Talks and online presentations on a range of topics by an even wider range of speakers make good examples for analysis. With careful screening, you will find video appropriate and inspiring for use in your middle school classroom.

Urge your students to watch their teachers. Encourage them to pay attention to the delivery styles of their imams, pastors, priests, and rabbis. After just a few observations, your teen monitors can assemble a list of those characteristics of content, structure, style, and vocal qualities that make oral presentations simple to follow and easy to remember. In all cases, encourage students to pattern effective deliveries that fit their personal style. See chapter 6 for further details on observing, preparing, practicing, and presenting written speeches.

Speaking for Different Purposes

There are four basic kinds of speeches, and during the course of a school year you can ask students to prepare and present one of each: to inform, to persuade, to entertain, and to commemorate. And you do not have to wait until the end of the school year to have a formal speech unit of two or three weeks, assignments for analysis of speeches, and the time for students to complete their presentation. While elements of preparation and practice both are keys to effective public presentations, having given oral presentations throughout the year, students will have personal experiences to reflect upon when you begin direct instruction about public speaking as a specific genre of writing and speaking.

The informative speech could be on what students learn about the author of an assigned book. A persuasive speech can be preparation for one of the service club speech contests, like those of the Rotary and Optimists Clubs, or can simply be presented to convince their classmates to read a particular book or change a belief or behavior about a current event on campus, in the community, or in the world.

To help students relax while giving the speech, you could give them the option to present the speech in the persona of a character from a piece of literature you read together as a class. In fact, the persuasive speech assign-

Figure 10.2.   Reading a Report and Giving a Speech Are Different

ment could be to persuade a character in one of the short stories to read the particular book the student has just finished! What book would students recommend to Rainsford in Richard Connell's "The Most Dangerous Game"? The speech to commemorate could be one honoring a special friend, family member, community leader, person in history, or literary character. These commemorative speeches such as those given at family birthday parties or school assemblies could be solemn and serious or entertaining and humorous, but always in good taste.

Picking a Topic and Planning a Speech

For older students, you may design a news-related speech assignment where students are expected to think critically about authentic purposes for persuasive speaking and then to conduct research, use correct citation and documentation, write, and present a speech on a current issue. In this case, they could write a speech to address a problem in the school or community. See "Teacher Resource G" for a sample handout for planning a problem-and-solution speech.

Constructing the Speech

Vital to your planning is allotting time for students to construct and practice the speech. Your future orators soon recognize that writing to speak is very different from simply writing an essay and reading it aloud. They realize that shorter, less complex sentences make for better speaking. They see that they need to state the goal or position, illustrate with example, explain it, and review it in much the way they used PIE patterns in class discussion and other writing assignments. As speakers, they are responsible for letting their audience know not only what the speech is about, by using some kind of verbalized signpost, but also for providing transitions to help the listeners process the information and stay on track.

Your particularly astute students may even recall and apply what they learned in the poetry unit about choosing and arranging words based on their sound and suggestive power. You can further reduce anxiety by sharing with your prospective orators these self-check questions about introducing their speeches as well as providing various kinds of explanation and supporting evidence that lead to more successful speeches.

Getting off to a Good Start and Using a Variety of Evidence

1. Does this speech open with an attention getter that will cause the audience want to listen?
2. Does the introduction include a *signpost* (like a thesis statement) that indicates the order of the arguments to follow?
3. Does this speech clearly show that this topic is important to me (personally or as the character)?
4. Does this speech clearly show why this topic is important to the members of my audience?

5. Do I provide adequate support for each main section of my speech? (Check the number of times you include each of these supporting materials in your speech).

_____ illustrations/examples		_____ explanations	
_____ definitions		_____ restatements	
_____ statistics/numbers		_____ humor	
_____ comparison/contrast		_____ opinions of experts	
_____ testimony		_____ quotations	

6. Does the speech include signal words (transitions) that show the relationship between and among ideas within the body and between sections of the speech?

Having the students write a script of their speech is a practical way to have them practice the grammar they have been learning, too. Their goal is to communicate clearly both in writing and speaking in an appropriate grammar, Standard English or otherwise. Their choice of grammar and vocabulary makes the difference in how well they get their ideas across to their audience, even if their purpose is to entertain peers in their class by commemorating a character in a story, a historical figure in history, a real friend, or a family member. For example, a speaker might make effective use of a sentence fragment that would seem merely incorrect in a written piece.

Practicing, Practicing, Practicing

Insist that your students get feedback on their speeches from a friend, family member, or classmate before presenting their speeches in class for evaluation. Practicing aloud is the only way for students to know for certain they are familiar enough with the content of their speech to deliver it with confidence, making eye contact, using gestures, pronouncing words correctly and clearly, varying the pace of the speaking, and maintaining their poise. See "Teacher Resource H" for a sample peer evaluation form that students can use during practice and adapt for in-class feedback, and that you can use for grading.

Students sometimes wonder what they should be paying attention to when they practice a speech, so provide a few guidelines to assure these soon-to-be speakers that they are on the right track. Strongly suggest that they time themselves as they give their speech at least three times standing in front of a mirror, holding their notes on the same index cards they plan to use when they give their speech in public. If they can look up at themselves and keep talking through their speech, they probably are prepared to look up and make more frequent eye contact with their audience. The index cards should have key words and few full sentences. Otherwise, the student speaker will be tempted to read rather than talk to the audience.

Encourage your students to wear an outfit that is especially neat, comfortable, and appropriate for their intended audience. Choosing what to wear reminds them that people in an audience are spectators, also influenced by the speaker's physical appearance and posture. When resources are available at home or at school, recommend that your students make an audio or video recording and listen and watch to hear and see what others are to hear and see when the students deliver their speeches.

It is obvious all the students in a class are not likely to be able to give their speeches on the same day. So once an assignment is given, invite students to sign up for a color team of five or six students to present on the day they prefer to deliver their speech. On the day they speak, students need not be expected to write feedback for classmates. On those other days, each team would be responsible for commenting on an assigned feature of oral presentations such as content, organization, vocal issues, and appearances.

Three benefits accrue from organizing presentations this way. Students are a little less nervous than they would be if all students were expected to be ready to speak on the same day, knowing all would not be able to do so. Students who know they have other family or school commitments can choose a day to speak that gives them a little more time to prepare. By the end of that round of speeches, each student will have focused on one speech issue per day and will have received written comments from the majority of the class. See the box in this chapter for a chart organizing speaking days and student feedback ideas.

Providing students with probing questions helps them evaluate their speech plans and encourages them to modify them before presenting to the public. For example, if you assign a speech to persuade, ask students to include arguments with a range of appeals.

Table 10.1. Speaking Feedback Chart

Each group is assigned to comment on one aspect of speech delivery each day except the day on which they are scheduled to give their speech.

DAY	RED	GREEN	PURPLE	ORANGE	BLUE
1	SPEAKING (NO FEEDBACK)	Comment on CONTENT (appropriate for audience, variety of support, appeals, quality of evidence and resources, sources cited, etc.)	Comment on ORGANIZATION (introduction with SIGNPOST [statement of purpose] TRANSITIONS [appropriate for kind of speech] CONCLUSION [summary, reflection, or projection without introducing new ideas])	Comment on VOCAL ISSUES (articulation, intonation, pace, pauses, volume, etc.)	Comment on APPEARANCE (appropriate gestures, use of physical space, visual aids, etc.)
2	APPEARANCE	SPEAKING	CONTENT	ORGANIZATION	VOCAL ISSUES
3	VOCAL ISSUES	APPEARANCE	SPEAKING	CONTENT	ORGANIZATION
4	ORGANIZATION	VOCAL ISSUES	APPEARANCE	SPEAKING	CONTENT
5	CONTENT	ORGANIZATION	VOCAL ISSUES	APPEARANCE	SPEAKING

- Does this speech make appeals to the head (definitions, statistics, explanations, and comparison/contrast)?
- Does this speech make appeals to the heart (humor, explanation, illustrations, quotations, testimony, or stories about real people)?
- Does this speech make appeals to the pocket (definitions, facts, statistics, and comparison/contrast related to money)?

Students who are asked to give a little more attention to observing, assigned to point out the qualities of a good speech, and given time to research, write, and practice become attuned to differences in effectiveness, and these young communicators no longer are content simply to give a report but endeavor to present a speech.

CONCLUSION

When students have personal reasons for "code switching" to communicate in the grammar of Standard English, they usually are amenable to learning how to do so. Whether they are writing for a specific purpose for a real audience, presenting a speech in class, or talking with their peers in middle school, students want to be seen as smart enough to use the right language for the situation. You can help them expand their knowledge and skills by incorporating regular opportunities to learn and use Standard English. Asking them to pay attention to effective writers and speakers raises teens' awareness about ways people judge others based on their skill in using appropriate language in specific settings as described in the personal story that opens this chapter.

Teaching middle school students to view the media with a critical eye helps them become defensive viewers and thoughtful creators in a variety of formats. Students become more sensitive to the impact that color, size, and design have on those with whom they wish to communicate.

If your middle school students know Standard English grammar, if they have had lots of practice delivering informal and formal speeches, they can access these skills when they want to be perceived positively by those they wish to impress with their improving education.

As your students increase their confidence and competence in selecting the appropriate grammars for a social situation and a particular audience, they are less tempted to muzzle their speech like my friend has done for so many years. They will be able to travel with ease across this country and abroad fairly certain they can adapt. As they mature and enter the world of work, students you teach are not likely to be passed up for a job promotion simply because they lack the writing, representing, and speaking skills called for in the Common Core State Standards for English Language Arts for College and Careers while in school and sought in twenty-first-century job markets.

NOTES

1. Clella Jaffe, "Introduction to Public Speaking and Culture," in *Public Speaking: Concepts and Skills for a Diverse Society*, 5th ed. (Belmont, CA: Wadsworth/ Thomson Learning, 2007), 6.

2. "English Language Arts Standards » Anchor Standards » College and Career Readiness Anchor Standards for Language," Common Core State Standards Initiative, http://www.corestandards.org/the-standards/english-language-arts-standards/anchor-standards-6-12/college-and-career-readiness-anchor-standards-for-language/ (accessed May 17, 2012).

3. Robert McCrum, William Cran, and Robert MacNeil, *The Story of English* (New York: Viking Penguin, 1986).

4. "Assessment," Northwest Regional Educational Laboratory, April 24, 2004, http://www.nwrel.org/assessment/department.asp?d=1.

5. Elie Wiesel, *Night* (New York: Bantam, 1960), 32.

6. Sandra Cisneros. "My Name," http://cmapspublic.ihmc.us/rid=1KR5FFQLY-1NXMX4T-4JQ/My_Name%20-%20Sandra%20Cisneros.pdf (accessed May 29, 2013).

7. Harry R. Noden, *Image Grammar: Using Grammatical Structures to Teach Writing* (Portsmouth, NH: Boynton/Cook Heinemann, 1999).

8. Arlene Mulligan, "Opening Doors: Drama with Second Language Learners," in *Promising Practices: Unbearably Good Teacher-Tested Ideas*, ed. Linda Scott (San Diego: Greater San Diego Council of Teachers of English,1996), 72.

9. Nada Ballator, Marisa Farnum, and Bruce Kaplan, "NAEP 1996 Trends in Writing: Fluency and Writing Conventions," *Education Statistics Quarterly* (1998): 11.

10. "English Language Arts Standards » Anchor Standards » College and Career Readiness Anchor Standards for Language," Common Core State Standards Initiative, http://www.corestandards.org/the-standards/english-language-arts-standards.

11. Fred Baker, "CML's Five Key Questions and Core Concepts of Media Literacy for Deconstruction," Center for Media Literacy, http://www.medialit.org/sites/default/files/14A_CCKQposter.pdf (accessed June 14, 2012).

CELEBRATING NAMES
A Unit about Community and Identity

We must wear our names within all the noise and confusion of the environment in which we find ourselves; make them the center of all our associations with the world, with man and with nature. We must charge them with all our emotions, our hopes, hates, loves, aspirations. They must become our masks and our shields, and the containers of all those values and traditions which we learn and/or imagine as being the meaning of our familial past.

—Ralph Ellison, "Hidden Name and Complex Fate"[1]

Names are important. They can distinguish one thing from another and link a person to families, cultures, and communities. For young adolescents, such as those in the middle grades, names can make them proud or embarrassed, one with others and separate from others. This paradox makes for an engaging unit in communication, community, and identity that incorporates lessons that also meet a range of English language arts standards in your school curriculum and those in the Common Core State Standards for English Language Arts that ask students to show and convey what they have experienced, imagined, thought, and felt.[2]

Depending on your school district, your eighth- or ninth-graders may be the oldest, youngest, or only students on campus. In any setting, they are in their early teens, eager to become independent of their parents or guardians, often straining against the ties that bind them. These adolescents are developing their own identities distinct from that of their families. For this reason, it is a good time to provide opportunities for these youngsters to rekindle fond relationships with their families, and talking about their names can do just that. These lessons require the students to consult their parents or other family members to complete some of the assignments for this unit of study. Family members may recall their own warm memories of choosing a name for their child, and for a few days, both the older and the younger ones can bask in that warmth.

This series of lessons based on names may become one of your favorites to teach early in the school year, mainly because it is a good way to learn a little more about the students through their writing. Whether the students in your classes have been together for several years or are just meeting one another for the first time, this assignment builds a more trusting learning community in a nonthreatening way. Perhaps it is because the students will be doing what so many teens like to do best—talking about themselves!

ALERTING YOU WITH WORDS OF CAUTION

This assignment could cause emotional difficulties for some students and their families. You must be sensitive to the fact that some students are unable get the information for this project for personally traumatic reasons. If you learn that any of your youngsters do not live with parents or do not communicate regularly with their parents or family members, it is wise to modify the assignment so that these young people can complete it without appearing uncooperative or inept.

Consider the ethnicities of your students. When children are in elementary school, their social studies assignments sometimes require students to trace their family history and create and display their family trees, a difficult or impossible task for many students. Because of the practice of chattel slavery in the United States, few African Americans know their family's genealogy; they cannot even talk without anguish about their ancestry.

Prior to the 1860s, the birth records of African Americans included few surnames and, when kept at all, the first names often were recorded among the cattle records. Even in the twenty-first century, few African Americans can trace their ancestry more than a few generations. Those families that can trace their history may already know that they carry the names of those slave owners. Most know that their families originated on the continent of Africa, but few have access to information that can verify the country or the tribe.

Discussing the issue of ancestry proves to be thorny for students from other ethnicities as well. This may be the case for current new-to-America students whose families may have come to escape unrest in their country of origin. If you teach in a community with a large number of immigrants from war-torn countries, you may discover that some families are able but unwilling to discuss their lineage. Ancestors may have changed their names to protect themselves from political repercussions. On the other hand, such families may appreciate the fact that you are interested in learning more about their cultures and are thrilled with the opportunity to share theirs.

Be similarly on the alert to situations with blended families in which parents and siblings have different last names and when students have blended or hyphenated names. And know that in some cultures, children have different names from those of their parents simply because it is part of their traditions. Clearly, you know to avoid any name-tracing assignments that may cause undue anxiety for students and families. The more diverse your school's community, the more careful you may need to be. You could redesign the project so that the final writings can be based on real or imagined incidents. You could have your students simply research names of characters in literature, articles, or films.

A teacher new to the school or community knows to confer with veterans at the school and then adapt the unit as needed to gain the benefits and avoid the pitfalls. You may be wondering, "With this many pitfalls, why bother?"

Here's why. Just reading literature about naming and living with names can be a rich intellectual experience revealing to your students how often naming is about both power and identity. Additionally, the accompanying assignments help meet several of the Common Core State Standards for English Language Arts in interesting and illuminating ways with lessons for

- reading, discussing, and analyzing literary works in a variety of genres;
- learning name-related vocabulary;

- conducting various kinds of historical research (online, library, and interview);
- writing essays, authoring vignettes, and drafting autobiographical sketches;
- composing short stories patterned after literary works read; and
- participating in peer-editing groups.

SELECTING LITERARY WORKS ABOUT NAMES

Begin with an overview of a unit you can call simply "What's in a Name?" One very popular name-related assignment is based on Sandra Cisneros's "My Name," a chapter from *The House on Mango Street*, her autobiographical vignette about growing up as a child of Mexican immigrants in Chicago.[3] Consider Santha Rama Rau's autographical sketch; "By Any Other Name," set in British colonial India; and "The Name," Aharon Megged's short story set in modern Israel and describing Jewish naming traditions. As you get to know your students and plan your unit, you can add or substitute other name-related narratives, especially stories and poems about various ethnic or cultural groups reflecting your school population and, each year, determined by the reading level of your particular students.

"Hidden Name and Complex Fate," a sophisticated essay by Ralph Ellison, an African American named by his father for Ralph Waldo Emerson, works incredibly well as a springboard for discussing issues of living with a name. Even if your students are not particularly strong readers, you still can begin with the Ellison essay. In that case, read it in class with considerable support to aid understanding. Remind your students that expository writing uses text structures they may have learned earlier. If necessary, do a mini-lesson reviewing these structures with your students. Ellison's essay inspired the questions you can use for the students' research and writing about their own names. See the Search It! box for an assignment.

You might also consider substituting or adding a chapter from Richard Kim's *Lost Names* about Korean families forced by the government of Japan to adopt Japanese names; *Not Even My Name*, an autobiographical work by Thea Halo about Pontic Greeks in Turkey; or *The Namesake*, a novel by Jhumpa Lahiri, about naming traditions of a family from India. Let your own

BOX 11.1: SEARCH IT! RESEARCHING YOUR NAMES

1. Use a dictionary and/or online resources to find out what each of your own names means.
2. Interview a family member to learn the sources of your name(s). If you have equipment, audio- or videotape the interview. Who named you, and why? Are you named for a friend or family member? Someone else?
3. Determine the kind of surname or last name you have. Is it a place name, like Al-Fassi, Hall, or Rivera; an occupation, like Chandler, Smith, or Taylor; a descriptive, like Braun or Strong; or a patronymic or version of a father's name, like Ben-Yehuda, McNeil, or Von Wilhelm?
4. Describe incidents you have experienced because of your name, including mispronunciations, misspellings, and misunderstandings.
5. Write about nicknames and related embarrassing or humorous experiences.
6. Identify challenges you feel because of the name(s) you carry.

interest and that of your students guide your selections each year. As always, select readings to fit your particular school setting, literature that serves as windows for seeing others and mirrors for seeing self.

READING, RESEARCHING, AND LEARNING VOCABULARY OF NAMES

During the first couple of weeks of this four-week unit, read and analyze the literature selections to discover their organizational pattern, diction, and sentence structure. Discuss the vocabulary of naming, including concepts such as

- surname
- given name

- nickname
- nom de plume
- pseudonym
- pen name
- alias
- anonymous

The assignment prompt that asks students to interview a family member provides enough information to get them started on learning how they acquired their names. You may need to review with young researchers the correct way to cite an interview in the text of the essay and the format for their bibliographies. The next step is discovering what their names mean.

With expanded resources available on the Internet, most students are able to find enough information to fulfill the basic purposes of the assignment—to consider their own names, to conduct research, and to write about traditions of naming they discover. If students have uncommon names or common names that are spelled uncommonly, they may need a bit of help identifying similar, researchable alternatives. Prepare them for research by showing them alternative spellings of the same name, such as mine—Anna, Ana, Anne, Ann, Annie, Anya, even Hannah, a name common among the English, Spanish, French, Russian, and Hebrew.

Students who have online access from home and some parental supervision of the project might benefit from using ancestry.com and similar websites to collect historical information about their family names. By all means, share your name story and write along with your students.

As students consider responses to these prompts, they reflect on who they are in their families, the school, the wider community, and perhaps even the world. Some of the students may learn family history never previously discussed. Other students awaken tender memories of relatives and family friends for whom they have been named. Some may just be embarrassed; others, pleasantly surprised. One such student developed a new appreciation for a stepfather and deepened her relationships with her biological parents. This student's first name is a combination of her biological parents' first names. Her stepfather later adopted her and she now carries his surname.

Discovering Fascinating Facts about Names

As students read about the name-related experiences during peer-response sessions, they discover surprising naming traditions observed in the families of their classmates. They might learn that in some villages in India all the girls in a family may have the same middle name, or that some Thai families carry extremely long, polysyllabic names, such as Prachyaratanawooti, for which each syllable represents a generation the family has lived in a particular region. Students might learn that in some families, it is the grandmother who chooses grandchildren's names; that the eldest son always is named for his father; or that the middle name for all the children is their mother's maiden name.

Your teens may notice interesting combinations of Anglo and Asian or Spanish names. Some students find out that their families' names have been Americanized to avoid discrimination based on ethnicity, religion, or nationality. A number of your students may have saint's day names or hyphenated last names that include both their mother's maiden name and their father's last name. Some learn that the spelling of their surname is simply the result of an error made when their ancestors entered the country through Ellis Island in New York or Angel Island in San Francisco. No one ever bothered to correct the mistake.

One of the assignments invites students to talk about the challenges of living with their names, as described in Ralph Ellison's essay, "Hidden Name and Complex Fate." Some student writing may reveal that carrying the name of a particularly famous or infamous relative causes them discomfort. One young man named for his father, a prominent businessman in the community, may acknowledge in his essay that he feels unworthy to be called Robert and insists that his peers call him Robbie, a diminutive version of the father's strong name. Cecilia, a talented singer, was depressed for a few days upon learning that the name she loves means "blind one" but then jubilant after discovering that St. Cecilia is the patron saint of music and musicians.

Other students may write about the embarrassment of having to correct the pronunciation of their name at the beginning of every school year and the frustration of having to spell their name everywhere they go. These examples of how sensitive students are about their names remind us to learn to pronounce and spell each student's name as early in the semester as possible. It is just another way of honoring each one as an individual with his or her own special name.

Springboarding to Writing

Distribute a copy of the vignette "My Name" by Sandra Cisneros, and prepare to conduct a "jump-in reading" activity to help students get a feel for the style and to think about what the writer may be "saying to them." But first, ask students to read silently, underlining words or phrases that catch their attention. Then you read the vignette out loud, asking students again to underline words or phrases they think are interesting or important. Finally, starting at the beginning again, invite one student to begin reading, stopping at the first mark of punctuation. Others jump in to read, without being called upon, and read to the next punctuation mark. If more than one student begins reading at the same time, urge each to listen to the other(s) and read as one voice. Between voices, let the silence resonate.

You may recall from doing this kind of reading of poetry that students are uncomfortable at first and might giggle a bit but soon catch on. The silence between and the sounds of different single voices and combinations of multiple voices leave indelible impressions and elicit powerful results in the next step of this assignment, writing.

To help the students comfortably share their stories, after reading "My Name" by Sandra Cisneros, ask them to do a "quick-write" based on a phrase or sentence that they select from the vignette. A "quick-write" is short, nonstop writing on an assigned topic; for a brief spurt of time—for example, three to seven minutes—students let their thoughts flow without censoring them. In this assignment, ask students to copy an underlined phrase or sentence from the reading. Then use that phrase or sentence as a jumping-off point to write rapidly about their own names for six or seven minutes. Write along with them. The following is a quick-write based on the Cisneros piece:

"My Name": A Quick-Write Inspired by Sandra Cisnero's Vignette of the Same Name

Anna Jamar Small Roseboro. Is this "me"? My name is a combination of my paternal grandmother's, Anna; my maternal grandmother's, Jamie; my dad's name, Small; and my husband's name, Roseboro. Everyone has had my name—made something of it, then passed it along to me. Anna means "gift of God." Is it I who am the gift or my grandmother who is a gift to me? Jamie is short for Jamar. My grandmother, whose full name is Jamar Elna, is named for her four aunts, Jane, Martha, Ellen and Nora—what a burden, what a privilege, to carry the names of so many relatives. Or is it a blessing? Am I standing on the shoulders of those who've come before me?

Small, my maiden name, always caused me trouble. "Small," they'd tease. "You're not small; you're tall!" I was always the tallest girl in my elementary school classes. In high school, however, I used the name to my advantage. I ran for a senior class office. My slogan was "Good things come in Small packages." Finally, success with that name.

Then I married Bill Roseboro during the years that Johnny Roseboro was a star catcher for the L.A. Dodgers. He'd been in the news because of a fight with Juan Marichal. Everywhere I went, "Are you related to Johnny Roseboro?"

"Yes, but what has that to do with me?"

Who am I really?

The extended writing assignment in this unit on names asks students to select an author's style they like and to pattern that style to write about their experience of living with their own names. Some of the students are comfortable with the familiar, formal essay style of Ellison; others enjoy the storytelling with strong sense of place in Rau's piece, "By Any Other Name," and others take on the challenge of using a series of symbols as in Megged's "The Name" and may choose one of these genres or blend the styles of one or two.

One ninth-grader, Alexis, of Jewish descent, was drawn to the Aharon Megged story "The Name" but preferred modeling Cisneros's poetic style with short phrases instead of consistently complete sentences. So Alexis modeled her essay after Cisneros's "My Name."

"So Much Like Me" by Alexis Rebecca DeSieno

My name is a strong name. In Greek it means "defender of mankind." It was the name of many rulers in the dynasty of Russia. Powerful and refined. It is energetic, strong, and beautiful, like a lion. It is not like other names like Kelly or Mary that end in a comma. It ends in an exclamation. Like a line, with a beginning and an end. It is like the number 1, or the beginning of the alphabet. The leader. The individual. It is like the finale number at the end of a piano concerto. Like Mozart or Beethoven, it leaves an impression. It has force. A car shares my name, though it is spelled differently, because it displays power and strength. It is durable, it will not disappear. Remembered. It is a name to be remembered. Alexis. My name. So much like me.

My great-grandmother should have been named Alexis because she was strong too. My mother and I are named after her in hope that we could carry on her strength. I wish I could have known her. She was a woman with a strong soul and a caring heart, so caring she had seven children which were all overly tended for. Ana. I think she must have been misnamed, for this names ends in a comma, as though it needs the help of another name, but she needing nothing to help her because she was strong. Alexis would have fit her better. That is why I am not named Ana as is the Askhenozic tradition. It is delicate like the petals of a blooming flower that need the help of the stem to grow. Both my mother's names and my name use the first letter of hers, which is the next closest traditional way, because she died before my mother was born, too. Allyn. Alexis. Names that continue to carry on her strength.

In Hebrew my middle names means to tie or bind. It was my other great-grandmother's name and now it is mine. It is a solid name, thought it was changed in America. Rifka. In Russia, that was her name. But now, it is Rebecca. It is not a common name, though it is known. It is like the color red. Energetic, and not easily defeated. It is bold. It is not plain or boring. It is like the flame of a candle, tame but with hidden strength that not many know about. It dulls the power of my first name. It is like me because I am not always what everyone thinks.

Of Sienna. In Italian that is what my last name means. It has Italian spice, like the peppers they put on their pizza. Solid and smooth. In Italy it is easily said while speaking with your hands. Like Boboli, or spaghetti. It is colorful like the Italian culture. Like the Italian wines. It bubbles. It is like a symphony of instrumental sounds, rhythmic and mixed. In America, it is always misspelled and mispronounced. Spoiled. As if the wine had turned to vinegar and makes you cringe. But in Italy, it is like the color blue. Like the blood of royalty. Free flowing and smooth.

My great-grandfather was the first DeSieno. He was the son of an Italian man of royal blood, and a less prominent maiden. They could not marry. It was against the aristorcracys rules. So he was given to a foster family at an early age, and was given a different surname from that of her father. He became a DeSieno, because he was born in Sienna, and he grew up with a different last name from his foster parents. I have inherited his name, but I am not alone like him.

When I was still playing with dolls, I used to want to change my name. I thought it was ugly. I wanted a pretty name like Samantha or Alexandra, just like the dolls I played with. To me, they were perfect. I used to dream that I was like them, and I lived in a Victorian furnished house in the early 1900's, rest next to central park.. But now I am content, and I look back at these memories and laugh. No other name could suit me. Not Alexandra or Samantha. They're just not me. Alexis. Yes, I am Alexis and could be nothing else.

To many, though, I am not Alexis. I am known as something else. I can become "Lexie Poo" or "Lex" or "X", "Xie" and "Lexus". But strangely, I am also "Betty Boop." I like my nicknames. Usually. People often tease me that Lexie Poo sounds like a name than an old lady calls her dog. But I think they are wrong, because Lexie Poo is me. It brings back so many memories, because my first grade teacher came up with that name. She had a nickname for everyone in the class. I was Lexie Poo. There was also Lindsey Tortolleni, Kelly Jelly Ben, and Jake the Snake. My friends created other nicknames. Most of them were "inside jokes." Sometimes, when I am angry with myself, I don't want to be Alexis. I can change my identity and put on m nickname mask. When I am Lexie Poo, I am an innocent first grader. When I am Lex, I am a best friend. When I am Lexus I am someone who is looked up too. My nicknames are not Alexis, but they are me too. They are each a different aspect of my personality.

Alexis Rebecca DeSieno. My full name. A powerful name with many memories. A name with hidden meanings, hidden like my grandmother's treasures in the attic. Though I am rarely called by my full name, without it I would not be me. It is like my personality. It fits me like a well worn shoe. Or an old pair of jeans. Alexis Rebecca DeSieno. Lexie Poo. Me. I could not have been named better.

On the final page of her essay, Alexis wrote each of her names in Greek and Hebrew. The assignment gave her an occasion to learn more about her family. But it also gave her classmates and me the opportunity to learn more about Alexis. Her essay demonstrated her pride in sharing what she learned and experienced living with her name. Alexis was in college when I contacted her about including this essay in the book, and I noticed that Alexis uses "Lexie Poo" in her e-mail address. As suggested by Ralph Ellison in the quotation opening this chapter, even nicknames sometimes remain and become a part of one's self-identity.

SETTING UP RAG SESSIONS FOR PEER RESPONSES

You probably know a number of ways to organize a class session during which students give and receive peer feedback. One that you may consider for this assignment is described by Jenee Gossard in Carol B. Olson's *Practical Ideas for Teaching Writing as a Process*.[4] In read-around group (RAG) sessions, students bring a completed early draft to class and sit in circles of five or six students. Review the rubric to remind the students of the criteria on which their writing is to be evaluated. It may be a rubric you create together, an adaptation of one in your textbook, or one you download from the Internet.[5]

The students write their names on the rubric and lay it on top of their drafts. One student from each group collects all the drafts and hands them to you. Now distribute the drafts to other groups so that none of the students in the group is reading the paper of anyone else in that group (group A gets group B papers, B gets C, etc.). This way a student is less likely to be distracted by watching how classmates respond to his or her paper. During the RAG, each student reads five or six papers but responds to only two.

Do not allow those without a draft to sit in on a RAG. Fairness suggests that paperless students sit out and use the time to work on their drafts. First, it is useful to give those who are behind on their own writing class time to catch up. Second, if a student in a group does not have a paper to be read each round, then someone else has to "sit" out because of too few papers.

No need to worry about students coming unprepared the next time. Most are ready for the next RAG because they want to see what others have written and also want to get peer feedback and suggestions for their own revisions. Curiosity is a great motivator.

Once the groups are formed and have their stack of papers, the group leader distributes the drafts to members in the group, and you set a timer for three minutes, which usually is enough time to read the two to four pages of these early drafts. Students read the first paper until the timer goes off and then pass the paper to the right and read the second paper, and finally the third paper and fourth, until the timer goes off again. After the fourth pass, set the timer for six minutes.

This time, the students read and comment on the content of the paper. On the fifth pass, again set the timer for six minutes, and the students read and comment on the structure and style. By this time, the students have learned a great deal about their classmates, about the ways their peers have responded to the prompts, about the problems that arise when one makes mechanical, usage, grammar, and spelling errors, and equally important, about the quality of the pool of writing in which their own papers are to be read.

While students are reading the first two or three drafts, you can walk around the classroom, rubber-stamp the written drafts, and record in your grade book a check for the students who have their drafts ready on this due date. If they are working on tablets, you can do something comparable to confirm that you have seen the draft. Afterwards, during the longer reading times, you have a few moments to confer with those who have come unprepared and can offer suggestions to get them back on track with their writing.

At the end of the RAG session, each leader collects the group's papers and hands them to you. Return them along with the completed rubrics to the students who wrote them. Spend ten minutes or so soliciting from the students what they noticed about the strengths of their papers and inviting their suggested strategies for improving them.

Use the remainder of the period for students to read the comments from their peers and write a plan to revise their papers. If time remains in the period, quickly scan and then stamp the plans the students have made to improve their papers. This simply creates a record that the student has received feedback and has outlined a plan for revising. If students are doing this assignment online, remind them to save their comments in the class folder. You can review them at a later time.

Assign the students to have their final drafts ready for you to read two or three days later. During the intervening days, schedule in-class writing time for students to work on their revisions. Then you can meet individually with students who are not sure what steps they should take to make their next draft better.

Do not feel frustrated if you find yourself adjusting the length of time needed for revision. Ask the students. If they feel confident and can quickly complete a revision they are eager to have you read, set a short deadline. If they are working diligently but believe they need more time, extend the deadline. Thankfully, the students become personally invested in these papers and want you to see their best work. Do both them and you a favor.

Create a schedule that is flexible enough to allow them to revise. Well-written papers are a pleasure to read and take less time to grade.

If you teach in a setting where it is unrealistic to expect students to word process the final drafts at home, allot additional class time for students to use school equipment. Especially in writing, it is more important that students complete a few assignments well than to rush through lots of assignments they cannot finish carefully and turn in with pride. This name assignment is one to which they are willing to devote time to do a good job on this writing. The subject, after all, is the students themselves.

On the due date, the students should submit for evaluation a packet that includes their stamped drafts, the rubric with their plan, and the final draft stapled to the top. This stack of papers substantiates that the process of writing is a lot of work. If they have worked totally online and have done online peer reviews instead of RAGs, then students should keep and submit all drafts in a file you can view online. See "Teacher Resource G" for an online peer-response lesson.

VALUING THE WRITING PROCESS AND THE ASSIGNMENT ABOUT NAMES

These steps in the process of drafting a paper are important for both writers and classmates. The writer has an opportunity to get feedback during the interim stages of the writing and to see how peers are addressing the assignment. For many students this is both a comfort and a challenge. When they see that they and their peers are having similar problems, they do not feel so odd or incompetent. On the other hand, when they see how well some of their peers are doing, individual students realize that the task is possible, and they are challenged to work a little harder to meet the assignment's standards.

Overall, this assignment is an important one whether given at the beginning, middle, or end of the school year because it allows students to write incorporating research that unifies both the personal and historical. During conferences, parents often express appreciation for being consulted as knowledgeable resources. What is more, this assignment creates a positive, supportive atmosphere in class. Young adults enjoy writing about themselves and reading about each other. Perhaps most important, "What's in a Name?" enables students to complete an assignment successfully anytime you give it. You and your students get to enjoy writing that is lively and interesting. Finally, even though students may model their prose after high-quality, published writing, they truly are developing their own authentic voices, one of the primary goals of the Common Core State Standards for English Language Arts.

CONCLUSION

People's names are important for identifying who they are, where they live, and what they might be like. This is especially true for learning about names in middle school language arts classes. Some of the oldest literature uses naming to identify characters and their relationships to one another. In fact, according to Hebrew scripture, the biblical Adam "named" the creatures in the garden. Most cultures have stories of rituals and naming ceremonies for infants and for those reaching a certain age, often when they enter their teens.

So even if you decide it is better just to read the literature about names, your students are sure to find pleasure thinking about their names as more than labels. Names reveal much about who and whose we are, where we have been and where we might want to be going. Generation to generation and place to place, names teach us about who we are as diverse communities. To be human is to name. To name is to be human. Naming is an art—a language art.

NOTES

1. Ralph Ellison, "Hidden Name and Complex Fate," in *Shadow and Act* (New York: Random House, 1964), 148.

2. *Common Core State Standards for English Language Arts & Literacy in History/Social Studies, Science, and Technical Subjects*, Common Core State Standards Initiative, http://www.corestandards.org/assets/CCSSI_ELA%20Standards.pdf (accessed May 17, 2012).

3. Brenda Borron offers a similar unit in "My Name, My Self: Using Name to Explore Identity," in *Reading, Thinking, and Writing about Multicultural Literature*, ed. Carol Booth Olson (Glenview, IL: Scott Foresman, 1996), 596.

4. Jenee Gossard, "Using Read-Around Groups to Establish Criteria for Good Writing," in *Practical Ideas for Teaching Writing as a Process*, ed. Carol B. Olson (Sacramento: California Department of Education, 1987), 148–50.

5. Six Traits rubric published by the Northwest Regional Education Laboratory and nwrel.org.

BON VOYAGE

Acknowledge the Challenge and
Maximize the Opportunity

*Ideal teachers are those who use themselves as bridges over which
they invite their students to cross, then having facilitated their
crossing, joyfully collapse, encouraging them to create bridges of
their own.*

—Nikos Kazantzakis[1]

Be honest. Are you planning to teach in middle school "just because" or
"until"? Over my years of experience, across the nation, I have noticed
that many teachers who are new to middle school accept a position not
because it is the fulfillment of a lifelong dream to teach preteenagers, but
simply to settle in middle school until an elementary or high school position
opens. Perhaps this is the case for many of your colleagues—they dreamed
of teaching in a suburban precollege high school and here they are, teaching seventh-grade urban middle school, or you anticipated teaching in the
parochial elementary school you attended as a child, but because of financial
reasons, you have accepted a position in a middle school thousands of miles
from home.

We've all been through this shift in goals, but with the right attitude, with
trust in yourself and your students, and (yes!) with this book, you will be a
successful educator wherever you are assigned. At this time, your reason

for accepting the middle-level position really doesn't matter. You have the skills, you have the ability—waste no time wishing you were in a different position. Instead, enjoy these challenging youngsters! Whether you are beginning your first, second, seventh, or seventeenth year of teaching middle school, you are set to embark on the trip of a lifetime. Each year of teaching can be different, unique, and surprisingly very much the same—an opportunity to learn and to inspire learning.

If you choose to remain as a language arts teacher in middle school, you will come to recognize that teaching young adolescents can be pure joy. You will realize that you are in the prime place at a pivotal time in the lives of your students, a time when they either develop a healthy respect for or a deep resentment of school. You will discover the satisfaction in helping the youngsters discover how they learn while they are acquiring skills and consuming information.

Language arts, you know, is the one course students take nearly every year they are in school. Those who teach them will come to appreciate the time and flexibility to adjust instruction in ways that enhance student learning across the curriculum and thus increase student enjoyment of schooling in general. Really?

The core components of the language arts curriculum—reading, writing, speaking, and listening—are skills that form the foundation for learning in all other academic courses. Now with the onset of the Common Core State Standards for College and Career Readiness, proficiency in these areas is expected when these youngsters enter their middle school social studies, science, and math classes. When such aptitude is missing or deficient, language arts teachers usually are called on the carpet to explain why they are not doing their job. How should you respond? What can you do to reduce the angst when accused of being an ineffective educator?

First, acknowledge the challenge of teaching young adolescents. Yes, most of them come to middle school in the throes of puberty, dealing with raging hormones and startling physical changes or lack thereof, on distressing emotional roller coasters, and stymied with uncertainty in figuring out what all these different teachers want from them! For the first time, some middle school students have multiple teachers daily, not just one teacher who knows what Gabrielle likes and dislikes and how she learns best; a teacher who makes allowances for Sydney when he's just moved from living with Dad for six months into the house with Mom, her current husband, and new baby; or one teacher who understands that Juanita freezes when asked to read out loud without having had time to practice. And these students may have to learn their way around a larger school building and even find a place to eat lunch with people they don't even know. How can they attend to class work?

All this may seem just too much for some of these early teens. Add to their challenge learning parts of speech and elements of fiction and how to research a contemporary topic or to write a persuasive essay on a controversial issue with correctly formatted endnotes and then to present the report out loud to the class with visual aids in a PowerPoint presentation! It is overwhelming to be expected to know which teachers will make Lailani work in small groups with Duong, the guy she has a crush on, and with Shakira, the girl she had a fight with during soccer practice. Anyway, Andrew's teacher last year didn't teach him how to use a wiki, and all the rest of the students in the class seem to know what the teacher's talking about. It's just too embarrassing, and why did Mom and Dad make Kwami come to this school anyway?

At the same time, the language arts educators have a curriculum to teach, a set of Common Core Standards for English Language Arts to see that each student reaches, and parents who expect the teachers to do what parents may not be able to do—keep Sally and Salvador happy. How can teachers of young adolescents be professionally effective and personally satisfied enough to feel successful in middle school?

Maximize the opportunity. Students in middle school want to learn, and they thrive with educators willing to learn how to teach such youngsters as individuals, not as receptacles of information. Research in the past twenty years has revealed what experienced teachers have suspected: their classes reflect multiple intelligences and students who learn in different ways; culture makes a difference; and males learn better in certain settings than females do, and vice versa. The researchers urge teachers to adapt instruction to boost all learning. No, this does not mean creating individualized educational plans for every student in your classes. It does mean designing lessons that teach the same lesson in a variety of ways and offering students choices in demonstrating what they know.

You are not alone on this journey, even within your classroom. Your students are there to help. They may know the school, the community, and neighborhood better than you, so let them teach you the ropes, but keep in mind that you are a professional. You are the adult hired to see that you all have safe passage through the sometimes tumultuous sea that is a year in the life of teenagers. Keep your eyes on the goal and, using your peripheral vision, keep your adolescents in view, too. They are who you are teaching. Yes, you are teaching kids, not just content. And with patience and persistence, you all can reach the shore safely, secure in the knowledge you have gained and the skills you have honed. How can you be assured that you can reach the shore intact?

- By carefully planning lessons based on what you know about the curriculum and what you learn about your students each school year
- By observing and documenting what goes on in your classes
- By varying the kind of performance and product assessments you assign
- By being willing to modify your lessons to meet the needs and interests of your students
- By being firm but fair in your interactions with students, colleagues, parents, and guardians
- By recognizing that help is available—right in this book and right in your classroom from your students, your fellow travelers on this journey
- By taking time each week to refresh yourself, spending time with family and friends or reading a good book
- By attending, every year, at least one conference, seminar, or workshop for professional and personal enrichment
- By believing that associating with excited, enthusiastic, and experienced educators is the best way to maintain your passion for the profession

Know that as you teach your young students to understand and use the language arts to receive knowledge and to express themselves, you are giving them the golden tickets to academic success and personal satisfaction. You, their language arts teacher, have the privilege of guiding, coaching, and accompanying young adolescents along the journey. You, who provide the balance between dependable discipline and appropriate play in a safe,

supportive environment, can help raise their self-esteem and increase their confidence and competence in communicating.

What does this approach to teaching look like in the real world? For some classes, it means incorporating more technology in your teaching, recognizing that students come to you with access to a range of technology and the skill to navigate within the cyber-world. It is your job to help them understand educational applications and encourage them to use what they know to learn what you teach. Many come to you comfortable in using a range of online platforms that can aid them in exploring sites from which they can expand their understanding of people, places, and concepts. Combining what they know with what you teach, your student travelers on the school year journey ultimately will be prepared for careers or colleges, wherever the next leg of their journey takes them.

So whether you are teaching middle school language arts because it is your dream job or until you get an assignment teaching in an elementary or high school, do what you can to make these crucial years for young adolescents ones during which they learn to love learning because you have recognized the challenge and are maximizing the opportunity to enjoy and teach each student as a unique individual.

Each time you design flexible lessons permeated with rich experiences for exploring fiction and nonfiction in the print and electronic media, you move your students further along the road to success. Each time you risk writing with them when you assign writing in a range of modes for a variety of authentic purposes, you demonstrate the importance of vulnerability in a learning community and honesty in writing. Each time you encourage their talking and listening to you, their peers, and those they encounter face to face and online and learning to critically view and use available technology, you are cultivating in them vital skills for growth. With diligence on your part and assiduousness on theirs, you all will complete a school year inspired by the success of the current year and eager to move on to the challenges of the next. So bon voyage! Enjoy the journey!

NOTES

1. Nikos Kazantzakis quotation from "Quotes by Nikos Kazantzakis," *Good Reads*, http://www.goodreads.com/quotes/show/301968 (accessed April 5, 2012).

APPENDIX

Teacher Resources

TEACHER RESOURCE A—COLLAGE ASSIGNMENT: *THE CIRCUIT* BY FRANCISCO JIMENEZ

Task

As an introduction to the study of literature this school year, you are to work with a group of your peers to present your impressions of ways Francisco Jimenez uses various elements of the narrative—point of view, setting, characterization, conflict, symbolism, and figurative language—to create a story that is engaging, meaningful, and stylistically unique and effective.

Using whatever poster board, cardboard, paper, fabric, and so on that your group chooses, create a collage that depicts the aspect of the story that your group has been assigned. The completed collages are to be no larger than eleven by fourteen inches. In addition to pictures and drawings, the collage should include words and quotations from the story. All group members must participate in a presentation of the collage to the class. Your group also may create a digital collage using a PowerPoint, Prezi, or Animoto program.

Preparation and Organization

With your group members, review the story and brainstorm about the people, places, events, and images that come to mind as you think about your group's focus. At home, hunt through magazines, newspapers, or online graphics and bring to class four or five pictures, words, and direct quotations from the story that can best illustrate your group's focus area. Bring your materials to class. As a group, decide which quotations, pictures, and so on can best illustrate the aspect of the novel your collage is to represent. Make the collage; then decide how your group can present the collage to the class. See "The Presentation" below.

Options: Review the options below in preparation for being assigned in class to a collage group.

- *Setting*: Choose five or six significant settings. Represent the settings in terms of the impact each has on Panchito; consider also the connection of the various settings with the title of the story. In your presentation to the class, be prepared to explain the reasons for your choices.
- *Characters*: Choose five or six important characters. Present or depict them in terms of their relationship with Panchito and the significance of their influence on him. In your presentation to the class, be prepared to explain the reasons for your choices.
- *Conflicts*: Choose five or six memorable conflicts in the story. Depict the characters involved in each conflict as well as the effect the conflict has on Panchito. (Note: He may have been an observer of the conflict and not necessarily directly involved.) In your presentation to the class, be prepared to explain the reasons for your choices.
- *Symbolism and Figurative Language*: Select examples of five or six particularly effective devices (symbols, images, metaphors, figures of speech) that Jimenez uses to illustrate character, conflict, or theme or to unify the story. In your presentation to the class, be prepared to explain the reasons for your choices.
- *Lessons Learned*: Put yourselves in Panchito's shoes. Identify three or four of the most important lessons that you think Panchito learns and, perhaps, benefits from in his experiences growing up in a migrant family. These lessons may be supported by any of the previous elements: setting, characterization, conflict, and use of symbolism and figurative

language. In your presentation to the class, be prepared to explain the reasons for your choices.

The Presentation

Plan a six- to seven-minute presentation during which you display and explain your collage. All group members should speak for about an equal time. Plan the order in which each member is to speak. Feel free to use notes, but please do not read them word for word. Decide where each group member should stand so that the whole class can see the collage as you make your presentation. Practice what you plan to say so that you can establish and maintain eye contact with members of the audience. If your group makes a digital collage, be sure to save and send a copy to the teacher the evening before your presentation day.

TEACHER RESOURCE B—TELLING TIME IN A POEM

Telling the TIME for (title) _____

T = Title, Thought, and Theme

- Who could be the speaker?
- Who could be the audience?
- What is the message in your opinion?

I = Imagery and Figurative Language

- What *kind(s)* of imagery are used?
- What words or lines from the poem support your answer?

M = Music and Sound

- If there is a rhythm pattern, mark the poem: use stressed "/" and unstressed "u" marks to show rhythm pattern.
- What kind of rhythm pattern is in this poem?

- On the poem, use "ABCs" to show rhyme scheme.
- What special kinds of words or techniques does the author use to create sound for effect in this poem?
- What words prove your answer?

E = Emotion (expressed/experienced)

- What emotion is expressed by the poet in this poem?
- What words or lines support your answer?
- What emotion do you experience as the reader of this poem?
- What words, phrases, or lines evoke this emotional response for you?
- How well does this poem reflect our definition of poetry? (See notebook for exact wording.)

TEACHER RESOURCE C—SHORT STORY EVALUATION AND PUBLICATION

You are to read, rate, and rank the manuscripts of the students in another class. Below is the chart with criteria to consider. To get in practice for using these guidelines, read and rate your own manuscript. Fold your evaluation and staple it to the back of the manuscript you turn in to be graded.

1. Manuscript requirements: two printed copies and one posted on our class website.
2. Printed copy 1: Do not put your name on the text of the story. Staple a title page on a separate sheet with your name, class, period, and date.
3. Printed copy 2: Have complete heading and title on the first page.
4. Website: Name your file—last name and period number, for example, Roseboro I or Roseboro III.

   Upload a copy of your story to our class website, and then submit your story for publication on at least three online magazines and to our school literary magazine. See class website for suggestions.
   - Read and rate independently, and then, as a group, rank the stories.
   - Rate the stories on a scale of one (low) to five (high).
   - Rank the stories A (first place) through D or E (fourth or fifth).

TEACHER RESOURCE D—BOOK REPORT 2: SHORT STORY COLLECTION

Due days one and two of next week.

Basic Requirements

1. Report on three different stories from the collection.
   a. Write one of the selections about a story that could complement the short stories in our world literature anthology. Indicate the title and author of the *World Literature* story and the reason for your choice—similar characters, conflict, theme, literary devices used, and so on.
   b. Write about another story that you would recommend to a character from *A Day No Pigs Would Die* OR from *A Christmas Carol* or any of the full-length books we've read. What is it about the story that the specific character would/should read? Similar personality, similar situation, a lesson to be learned, or something else? Explain the specific reason with details from the short story and information about the character from the novel you've chosen.
   c. Write about a third story that is the one you most enjoyed. Be specific about reasons for your choice.
2. For the body of the report, write three PIE paragraphs with topic sentences, specific references and/or quotations from the stories, appropriate transitions, and conclusion sentences.
3. Include in each paragraph the title and author, a one-sentence summary of the story that includes main character(s), setting, conflict, point of view, and other facts, and explanations for each specific story.

Task One—Plan Before You Write

1. Determine the kind of collection you've read. Write a sentence or two to explain this. Same author, genre, theme, or audience? Use this information in your introduction paragraph.
2. From your collection of short stories, select the three stories you plan to use. Save your favorite.

3. Reflect on the stories we've studied in the *World Literature* book. Choose one of these stories to write about. Which stories from your collection do you recommend to complement that world literature story? Remember to include titles and authors of both stories. Make notes.

4. Reflect on the characters from *A Day No Pigs Would Die* and *A Christmas Carol*. Which of your short stories would appeal to a character from ONE of these novels? Remember to include the titles and authors and explanations in the paragraph about this story. Make notes.

5. Now, make notes about your favorite story from this collection. What is appealing about the story? Characters, conflict, theme, writing style, identification?

Task Two—Draft Your Report

1. Write an interesting introduction that includes the title and author or editor of the short story collection and kind of collection or organization of the collection. Use two or three sentences.

2. Write each body paragraph, making certain to include required information. See notes from planning steps.

3. Revise each paragraph, paying attention to using appropriate transition words and phrases.

4. Edit your paragraphs. Check for spelling, punctuation, and verb tense (remember to use present-tense verbs to talk about incidents in the plot of fictional works). Have you used quotation marks around words you've quoted from the text? Have you used quotation marks around the titles of the short stories and underlined or used italics for the titles of the short-story collection and the title of the novel?

Task Three—Prepare Your Final Paper

1. Include an appropriate title for this assignment—something interesting and inviting.

2. Put the complete heading in the upper right-hand corner of the paper.

If time permits, add a computer graphic that highlights the stories you've read and written.

TEACHER RESOURCE E—PERUSING, PICKING, PRESENTING, AND PERFORMING POETRY

Spend some time reading poetry and deciding which poem you like well enough to share with the class. (Please select a new poem, one not done for previous assignments or projects.)

Steps to Selection

1. Select a collection of poems (a collection by the same or by different authors).
2. Start with the first poem in the book. Read the first four lines, and then decide whether you understand them.
3. If you also enjoy the poem you understand, stop, and go on to preparing your class presentation.
4. If not, read the next, continuing by reading the first four lines of each successive poem until you find one you understand and enjoy enough to share with the class.
5. Keep a record of the number of poems you read before selecting one to share in class.

Preparation for Presentation: Written and Visual

1. In your own words, tell what the poem seems to be saying.
2. Tell why you enjoyed the poem. What about the poem got your attention?
3. Copy out your favorite line from the poem, and tell why it is your favorite.
4. Tell what you noticed about the way the poet wrote the poem—the special way the poet used words, lines, stanzas, sounds, ideas, and comparisons. If you can use the language of poetry analysis, do so.

5. Pattern this poem by writing one of your own, using some strategies used by your poet.
6. Photocopy or word-process the poems or write them in calligraphy or other attractive print.
7. Mount and illustrate or select an appropriate border for them.
8. Bring to class the day you are to present your poem. We plan to make an anthology of favorite poems.
9. Memorize the original poem.

Presentation Day

1. Recite the memorized poem dramatically. You can recite it twice. Once at the beginning of your presentation, and again at the end.
2. Your presentation should be about three minutes. During this sharing time, state the title and author of your poem, relate some of the information from your writing about the poem, and perhaps play some music in the background. (Let me know ahead of time so that I'll have equipment in the classroom to play your music.)
3. Let me know if you wish to bring "neat to eat treats" on presentation day.
4. Turn in your illustrated poem and your writing about the poem.

ENJOY!

TEACHER RESOURCE F—OUTLINE FOR PROBLEM-SOLVING SPEECH

Topic:
Purpose: to inform my audience that they should listen to me about . . .
Introduction technique:
Body organization plan—Describe *problem* with details from research.
Who is affected, concerned, involved?
A.
B.
C.

What is the nature and significance of the problem?

When did it become a problem? How long? Into the future?

A.

B.

C.

Where is the problem experienced? Where are solutions planned?

A.

B.

C.

Why should the audience be concerned?

A.

B.

C.

How is the problem solved (or how can it be solved)? Says who?

A.

B.

C.

Conclusion technique: (What are some reasons the audience should believe you are worthy of their consideration?)

TEACHER RESOURCE G—PEER EVALUATION OF TEXT FOR PROBLEM-SOLVING SPEECH

"Optimism Is the Right Stuff"

Speechwriter: _____ Period: _____

Topic: _____

Use a scale of one to five (low to high) to indicate how close the speech writer has come to meeting the goal of writing a speech that is an interesting, effective, believable, and winning speech?

Introduction: Opening grabs and holds attention by using

_____ Startling statistics?

_____ Heartwarming, heart-wrenching story?

_____ Amusing anecdote (story that illustrates problem)?

Manuscript #_____		1	2	3	4	5
Criteria						
Characters	flat, round, dynamic					
Conflict	unclear, typical, compelling					
Rising Action	single or multiple attempts to solve					
Resolution	anticipated, believable, surprising, but logical					
Setting	sight, sound, taste, touch, smell					
Dialogue	stiff, believable, realistic					
Mechanics, Usage, Grammar	not, somewhat, very distracting					
Vocabulary	flat, adequate, vivid					
	Overall Rating (1-5)					

Figure A-1.   Short Story Evaluation Chart

Body organization plan—describes *problem* with details from research and answers the following questions:

_____ Who is affected, concerned, involved?

_____ What is the nature and significance of the problem?

_____ When did it become a problem? How long? Into the future?

_____ Where is the problem experienced? Where are solutions planned?

_____ Why should the audience be concerned?

_____ How is the problem solved (or how can it be solved)? Says who?

_____ Each paragraph develops/explains the main idea.

Conclusion technique: Shows how optimism has helped cope with the problem or gives reasons for optimism?

Grammar:

_____ Fewer than three spelling errors

_____ Fewer than three punctuation errors

_____ Fewer than three grammar errors

_____ Long quotations are indented

Bibliography:

_____ Includes at least three different sources

_____ Conforms to format in middle school grammar handbook

Overall style shows:

_____ Acknowledgment of borrowed information within text
_____ Colorful words that sound impressive
_____ Minimum repetition of key ideas
_____ A memorable quotation or expression
_____ Transition devices to help audience follow main points or arguments
_____ Clear picture of way(s) that "Optimism Is the Right Stuff" when considering the problem talked about (topic)

Speech evaluator: _____

TEACHER RESOURCE H—IN-CLASS PEER FEEDBACK

It is effective use of time to have students respond in class to the writing of their peers. Here's a structure that works well for a fifty- to sixty-minute class meeting. Keep in mind that it may take three tries doing it before students feel comfortable with the process.

Seven Values for This Use of Class Time

Value 1: Students get feedback on their drafts from at least three peers. Each reader focuses on one feature of the draft.

- Classmate A—*Content* sufficient to meet requirements of assignment
- Classmate B—*Structure* of essay, of paragraphs, of sentences
- Classmate C—*Language, quality of resources or evidence, MUGS* (mechanics, usage, grammar, spelling), and so on

Sometimes it would be better to use a version of the *Six Traits writing* rubric and organize responses where students respond to

- Classmate A—traits 1 and 4
- Classmate B—traits 2 and 5
- Classmate C—traits 3 and 6

Value 2: Students get to read ways their classmates respond to the assignment and have a sense of the pool in which their paper will be graded. They can see how strong or weak their writing may seem when read before or after that of their classmates.

Value 3: Students get to see what works and what doesn't work in the writing and maybe even see ways to improve their own work as they use the same rubric or grading guidelines as the teacher will use to evaluate their writing.

Value 4: Students receive feedback from three different readers who will have given specific commendations and recommendations the writers can take into consideration during revision stage.

Value 5: Teacher does not have to spend hours reading and responding to drafts when he or she can teach students to do the work.

Value 6: Teachers can scan the drafts and responses posted online and be prepared to tailor lessons for the next class meeting that include commendations on what already is well written and recommendations to help students during the revision step.

Value 7: Teachers receive empathy from students who see how long it could take to read and respond succinctly to a whole set of papers. Students may be a little more patient when it takes a teacher longer than twenty-four hours to return graded assignments.

BIBLIOGRAPHY

Asian Pacific Economic Cooperation. "21st Century Competencies." http://hrd.apecwiki.org/index.php/21st_Century_Competencies (accessed March 16, 2012).

Assembly on Literature for Adolescents. "ALAN Online: The Official Site of the Assembly on Literature for Adolescents." http://www.ncte.org/adlit (accessed March 16, 2012).

Bacon, Francis. "Essays of Francis Bacon—Of Studies." Authorama Public Domain Books. http://www.authorama.com/essays-of-francis-bacon-50.html (accessed March 8, 2012).

Baines, Lawrence. "Cool Books for Tough Guys: 50 Books Out of the Mainstream of Adolescent Literature That Will Appeal to Males Who Do Not Enjoy Reading." *Alan Review* 22, no. 1 (1994).

Baker, Fred. "CML's Five Key Questions and Core Concepts of Media Literacy for Deconstruction." Center for Media Literacy, 2011. http://www.medialit.org/sites/default/files/14A_CCKQposter.pdf (accessed June 14, 2012).

——. Media Awareness Network. 2010. http://www.media-awareness.ca/english/teachers/media_literacy/key_concept.cfm (accessed March 27, 2012).

Ballator, Nada, Marisa Farnum, and Bruce Kaplan. "NAEP 1996 Trends in Writing: Fluency and Writing Conventions" (report, United States Department of Education Office of Educational Research and Improvement, 1999).

Beers, Kylene, Robert E. Probst, and Linda Reif. *Adolescent Literacy: Turning Promise into Practice*. Portsmouth, NH: Heinemann, 2007.

Blair, Walter, and John Gerber, eds. *Better Reading Two: Literature*. 3rd ed. Chicago: Scott Foresman, 1959.

Blau, Sheridan D. *The Literature Workshop: Teaching Texts and Their Readers*. Portsmouth, NH: Heinemann, 2003.

Borron, Brenda. "My Name, My Self: Using Name to Explore Identity." In *Reading, Thinking, and Writing about Multicultural Literature*, edited by Carol B. Olson. Glenview, IL: Scott Foresman, 1996.

Bransford, John D., Ann L. Brown, and Rodney R. Cocking. "How Children Learn." In *How People Learn: Brain, Mind, Experience, and School*. Washington, DC: National Academy Press, 2000.

Burke, Jim. "Teaching English Language Arts in a Flat World." In *Adolescent Literacy: Turning Promise into Practice*, edited by K. Beers, R. Probst, and L Reif. Portsmouth, NH: Heinemann, 2007.

———. *The English Teacher's Companion: A Complete Guide to Classroom, Curriculum, and the Profession*. Portsmouth, NH: Heinemann, 2007.

Busching, Beverly, and Betty Ann Slesinger. *"It's Our World Too": Socially Responsive Learners In Middle School Language Arts*. Urbana, IL: National Council of Teachers of English, 2002.

Carrasquillo, Angela. *Beyond the Beginnings: Literacy Interventions for Upper Elementary English Language Learners*. Clevedon, UK: Multilingual Matters, 2004.

Carter, James B. *Building Literacy Connections with Graphic Novels: Page by Page, Panel by Panel*. Urbana, IL: National Council of Teachers of English, 2007.

Carter, Myron, and Christie L. Ebert. "Arts Education and 21st Century Skills." http://community.learnnc.org/dpi/music/AECoordinators.Sept08.CLErevisions.ppt.

Chabris, Christopher F. "How to Wake up Slumbering Minds." Catholic Education Resource Center. http://www.catholiceducation.org/articles/education/ed0371.htm (accessed May 22, 2013).

Cisneros, Sandra. "My Name." http://cmapspublic.ihmc.us/rid=1KR5FFQLY-1NXMX4T-4JQ/My_Name%20-%20Sandra%20Cisneros.pdf (accessed May 29, 2013).

Claggett, Fran, and Joan Brown. *Drawing Your Own Conclusions: Graphic Strategies for Reading, Writing, and Thinking*. Portsmouth, NH: Heinemann, 1992.

Claggett, Fran, Louann Reid, and Ruth Vinz. *Daybook of Critical Reading and Writing: World Literature*. Wilmington, DE: Great Source Education Group, 2008.

———. *Daybook of Critical Reading and Writing*. Wilmington, MA: Great Source Education Group, 1998.

Coffey, Heather. "Code-Switching." UNC School of Education. http://www.learnnc.org/lp/pages/4558 (accessed March 16, 2012).

Cornell University, University of Rochester, and the NYS Center for School Safety. "Adolsecent Brain Development." ACT for Youth Upstate Center of Excellence, May 2002. http://www.actforyouth.net/resources/rf/rf_brain_0502.pdf (accessed July 12, 2012).

Daniels, Harvey, and Steven Zememan. "Conferences: the Core of the Workshop." In *Teaching the Best Practice Way: Methods That Matter, K–12*, edited by Harvey Daniels and Marilyn Bazaar. Portland, ME: Stenhouse Press, 2005.

"Education: The What, Why, and How of 21st Century Teaching & Learning." http://www.pearltrees.com/#/N-p=34752422&N-play=1&N-u=1_494424&N-fa=4099999&N-s=1_4100175&N-f=1_4100175 (accessed July 16, 2013).

Ellison, Ralph. "Hidden Name and Complex Fate." In *Shadow and Act*. New York: Random House, 1964.

"English Language Arts Standards » Anchor Standards » College and Career Readiness Anchor Standards for Language." Common Core State Standards Initiative, 2011. http://www.corestandards.org/the-standards/english-language-arts-standards/anchor-standards-6-12/college-and-career-readiness-anchor-standards-for-language/ (accessed March 15, 2012).

Epstein, Joseph. "The Personal Essay: A Form of Discovery." In *The Norton Book of Personal Essays*, edited by Joseph Epstein. New York: Norton, 1997.

Gossard, Jenee. "Using Read-Around Groups to Establish Criteria for Good Writing." In *Practical Ideas for Teaching Writing As a Process*, edited by Carol B. Olson. Sacramento: California Department of Education, 1987.

Gregory, Gayle H., and Lin Kuzmich. *Differentiated Literacy Strategies: For Student Growth and Achievement in Grades 7–12*. Thousand Oaks, CA: Corwin Press, 2005.

Gutièrrez, Kris. "Teaching and Learning in the 21st Century." *English Education* 32, no. 4 (2000): 290–98. http://centerk.gseis.ucla.edu/teaching_in_the_21st_century.pdf (accessed March 16, 2012).

Hansen, Heather. "Speak English Clearly and Grammatically, and Boost your Success!" Articles Base, August 8, 2007. http://www.articlesbase.com/communication-articles/speak-english-clearly-and-grammatically-and-boost-your-success-195745.html.(accessed March 16, 2012).

Hazell, Ed. "21st Century Teaching." *Access Learning* (March 2005): 8–9.

Hubble, Jeremy. "'Here We Are Now, Entertain Us': Poe's Contributions to the Short Story." Jeremy Hubble, April 7, 1996. http://geocities.jeremyhubble.com/poe.html (accessed April 16, 2013).

Jackson, Anthony, Gayle A. Davis, Maud Abeel, and Anne A. Bordonero. *Turning Points 2000: Educating Adolescents in the 21st Century.* New York: Teachers College Press, 2000.

Jaffe, Clella. "Introduction to Public Speaking and Culture." In *Public Speaking: Concepts and Skills for a Diverse Society.* 5th ed. Boston: Wadsworth, 2007.

Jefferson County Schools. *Academic Vocabulary Project.* http://jc-schools.net/tutorials/vocab/TN.html (accessed March 16, 2012).

Jolls, Tessa, and Elizabeth Thoman. *Literacy for the 21st Century: An Overview & Orientation Guide to Media Literacy Education.* 2nd ed. Center for Media Literacy, 2008. http://www.medialit.org/reading-room/literacy-21st-century-overview-orientation-guide-media-literacy-education (accessed May 23, 2013).

Jones, David K. *Online Teen Dangers: The Five Greatest Internet Dangers Teenagers Face and What You Can Do to Protect Them.* Scotts Valley, CA: CreateSpace, 2008.

Jones, Raymond C. "Can You Tell What It Means." Reading Quest. August 26, 2012. http://www.readingquest.org/premises.html (accessed August 21, 2013).

Keene, Edmond O. "The Essence of Understanding." In *Adolescent Literacy: Turning Promise into Practice*, edited by Kylene Beers and Robert Probst. Portsmouth, NH: Heinemann, 2007.

Literature for All Students: A Sourcebook for Teachers. Sacramento: California State Department of Education, 1985.

Mackenzie, Jock. *Essay Writing: Teaching the Basics from the Ground Up.* Markham, Ontario: Pembroke Publishers, 2007.

"Mathematics, Grade 8, Introduction." Common Core State Standards Initiative, 2012. http://www.corestandards.org/Math/Content/8/introduction (accessed April 16, 2013).

Maxlow, James, with Shannon Panko and Nicole Sneddon. "Digital Language Arts: A 21st Century Approach to Instruction." Paper presented at the Florida Educational Technology Conference, Orlando, FL, January 2009.

Miller, Jane, and Toni McGill. "Using Writing to Improve Learning in the Classroom." Chula Vista, CA: Sweetwater Union High School District, 1989.

Mission, Ray, and Wendy Morgan. *Critical Literacy and the Aesthetic: Transforming the English Classroom.* Urbana, IL: National Council of Teachers of English, 2006.

Moberg, Goran. *Critical Literacy and the Aesthetic: Transforming the English Classroom.* New York: Writing Consultant, 1984.

Mulligan, Arlene. "Opening Doors: Drama with Second Language Learners." In *Promising Practices: Unbearably Good, Teacher Tested Ideas*, edited by Linda Scott. San Diego: Greater San Diego Council of Teachers of English, 1996.

National Council of Teachers of English, International Reading Association. *Standards for English Language Arts*. Urbana, IL: National Council of Teachers of English, 1996.

National Governors Association Center for Best Practices and Council of Chief State School Officers. *Common Core State Standards for English Language Arts and Literacy in History/Social Studies, Science, and Technical Subjects*. Washington, DC: Common Core State Standards Initiative, 2010.

"The NCTE Definition of 21st Century Literacies." National Council of Teachers of English. http://www.ncte.org/positions/statements/21stcentdefinition (accessed May 13, 2013).

Noden, Harry R. *Image Grammar: Using Grammatical Structures to Teach Writing*. Portsmouth, NH: Heinemann, 1999.

Northwest Regional Educational Laboratory. "Six Traits Rubric Writing Scoring Continuum." http://www.thetraits.org/pdfRubrics/6plus1traits.PDF (accessed March 16, 2012).

O'Hanlon, Leslie Harris. "Teaching Students Better Online Research Skills." *Education Week*, May 23, 2013. http://www.edweek.org/ew/articles/2013/05/22/32el-studentresearch.h32.html?tkn=QWCCgXpStXBSdGy%2BRabLBT9BSWvJPFfQ47w2&cmp=clp-sb-ascd (accessed May 23, 2013).

Peacock, Molly, Elise Paschen, and Neil Neches. *Poetry in Motion: 100 Poems from Subways and Buses*. New York: Norton, 1996.

Plato. *The Republic*, II, III, and X. Internet Classics Archive. http://classics.mit.edu/Plato/republic.html (accessed March 16, 2012).

Professional Development for 21st Century Education. "English Language Arts (ages 11 to 15) Literacy to Learn Standards for Students and Teachers." United Star Distance Learning Consortium. http://www.usdlc-l2l.org/ela_mid.pdf (accessed March 16, 2012).

Reutzel, D. Ray, and Robert B. Cooter. *Strategies for Reading Assessment and Instruction: Helping Every Child Succeed*. Upper Saddle River, NJ: Merrill Prentice Hall, 2003.

Richardson, W. *Blogs, Wikis, Podcasts, and Other Powerful Web Tools for Classrooms*. Thousand Oaks, CA: Corwin Press, 2009.

Roseboro, Anna J. Small. "Professional and Personal Lives." *California English* 16, no.1 (September 2010): 8–9.

——. "Writing and Learning Groups in Math." Unpublished master's thesis, University of California, San Diego, 1989.

Rostand, Edmond. *Cyrano de Bergerac*. Translated by Lowell Blair. In *World Literature*. Lake Forest, IL: Glencoe MacMillan/McGraw Hill, 1992.

"Royce Sadler: Conversations about the Learning Record." The Learning Record. http://www.learningrecord.org/sadler.html (accessed March 16, 2012).

Rubistar. "RubiStar: Create Websites for Your Project Based Learning Activities." http://rubistar.4teachers.org/index.php (accessed March 16, 2012).

Sandel, L. "Review of *Literature for the 21st Century: A Balanced Approach*, by Gail E. Tompkins." *Childhood Education* 75, no. 2 (Winter 1998).

Shafer, Gregory. "Standard English and the Migrant Community." *English Journal* 90, no. 4 (2001): 37–43. http://www.ncte.org/library/NCTEFiles/Resources/Journals/EJ/0904-march01/EJ0904Standard.pdf (accessed March 16, 2012).

Smith, David I., and Barbara M. Carvill. *The Gift of the Stranger: Faith, Hospitality, and Foreign Language Learning*. Grand Rapids, MI: Eerdmans, 2000.

Stevenson, Chris. "Curriculum That Is Challenging, Integrative, and Exploratory." In *This We Believe—and Now We Must Act*, edited by Thomas O. Erb. Westerville, OH: National Middle School Association, 2001.

Stone, Linda. "Continuous Partial Attention." Linda Stone. http://www.lindastone.net (accessed March 16, 2012).

The Story of English. DVD. USA Home Video, 2001.

Tapscott, Don. *Growing Up Digital: The Rise of the Net Generation*. New York: McGraw-Hill, 1998.

"Top 15 Educational Tools/Sites for Middle School Language Arts." Hartman Instructional Technology Consultant (blog), January 3, 2008. http://theitclassroom.blogspot.com/2008/01/top-15-educational-toolssites-for.html (accessed March 16, 2012).

Tuckman, Bruce W. "Developmental Sequence in Small Groups." University of Florida. http://aneesha.ceit.uq.edu.au/drupal/sites/default/files/Tuckman%201965.pdf (accessed March 16, 2012).

Twain, Mark. *The Adventures of Huckleberry Finn*. Los Angeles. University of California Press, 125th edition, 2003.

"21st Century Skills." Thinkfinity. http://www.thinkfinity.org/21st-century-skills (accessed March 16, 2012).

"21st Century Skills Map: English." Partnership for 21st Century Skills. http://www.p21.org/storage/documents/21st_century_skills_english_map.pdf (accessed March 16, 2012).

Urquhart, Vicki. "Using Writing in Math to Deepen Student Learning." McREL, 2009. http://www.mcrel.org/~/media/Files/McREL/Homepage/Products/01_99/prod19_Writing_in_math.ashx (accessed April 17, 2013).

Vincent, Tony. Learning in Hand (blog). http://learninginhand.com/blog/ (accessed March 16, 2012).

Wiesel, Elie. *Night*. New York: Bantam, 1982.

Williams, Raymond. *Keywords: A Vocabulary of Culture and Society*. New York: Oxford University Press, 1976.

Williams, Terry, and Jenny Williams. "Image, Word, Poem: Visual Literacy and the Writing Process." Workshop for the National Council of Teachers of English, Detroit, MI, 1997.

Woessner, Patrick. "21st Century Literacy: Basic Literacy." Technology in the Middle (blog). http://pwoessner.com/2008/11/29/21st-century-literacy-basic-literacy/ (accessed March 16, 2012).

Wordle. http://www.wordle.net/ (accessed March 16, 2012).

WordNet Search. http://wordnetweb.princeton.edu/perl/webwn?s=renaissance (accessed March 16, 2012).

Zenkel, Suzanne S, ed. *For My Teacher*. White Plains, NY: Peter Pauper, 1994.

INDEX

ABOUT THE AUTHOR

Anna J. Roseboro is widely known for her work with groups like the National Council of Teachers of English (NCTE), the Conference on English Leadership, the California Association of Teachers of English, the Michigan Council of Teachers of English, and the California Association of Independent Schools. With forty years of experience in public and private schools, she is a National Board Certified Teacher vetted by the National Board of Professional Teaching Standards.

A sought-after convention speaker, Ms. Roseboro earned a BA in speech communications from Wayne State University and an MA in curriculum design from the University of California, San Diego. Her articles have appeared in journals such as *English Journal, English Leadership Quarterly, Fine Lines: A National Quarterly, Creative Writing Journal, California English, Utah Journal of Teachers of English, San Diego Museum of Contemporary Art Journal,* and the *CAIS Quarterly.* Additional publications include *Black Boy, Autobiographical Guide* (1995) and "Multicultural Literature: A Challenge and an Opportunity," in *Multicultural Voices Teacher's Resource Book* (1994). Recent publications include "Geometric Characters and Of Mice and Men," a chapter in *Engaging American Novels* (NCTE, 2011) and "Literacy Is More Than Books and Pens," in *English Journal* (September 2012).

Ms. Roseboro has consulted with and read manuscripts for textbook publishers and represented Rotary International in a group-study exchange with educators in Africa. She taught at Rochester Theological Institute, Grand Valley State University, and Calvin College. From 1989 to 2005 she directed summer sessions at The Bishop's School, La Jolla, California—a program for grades 5–12. She was English Department chair at Bishop's from 1999 to 2005. She has served as a faculty leader at the NCTE Affiliates Conference, working with ten national finalists who submitted proposals for education leadership projects in their local districts. In 2009 she was honored with the California Association of Teachers of English 2009 Distinguished Service Award. From 2008 to 2011 she mentored early-career educators as part of the National Council of Teachers of English Leadership Institute, and for 2012–2013 she was a mentor for the Conference on English Leadership's Emerging Leaders Fellowship.